Willie Nelson

WITH Bud Shrake

SIMON AND SCHUSTER
New York   London   Toronto   Sydney   Tokyo

WILLIE

AN AUTOBIOGRAPHY

Simon and Schuster
Simon & Schuster Building
Rockefeller Center
1230 Avenue of the Americas
New York, New York 10020

SIMON AND SCHUSTER and colophon are registered
trademarks of Simon & Schuster Inc.

Designed by Helen L. Granger/Levavi & Levavi
Manufactured in the United States of America

10   9   8   7   6   5   4   3   2   1

Library of Congress Cataloging in Publication Data

Nelson, Willie, 1933–
   Willie

   Includes index.
   1. Nelson, Willie, 1933–   .   2. Country musicians—
United States—Biography.   I. Shrake, Edwin.   II. Title.
III. Title: Willie
ML420.N4A3   1988   784.5'2'00924 [B]   88-18449
ISBN 0-671-64265-0

This book is dedicated
to my mother, Myrle,
who went on the road
long before I did.

I could never have put
all these memories together
without the loving aid
of my daughter, Lana.

I wish to thank
Cheryl McCall, Fred Burger,
Townsend Miller, Bobby Arnold,
Jody Fischer, and Jo Ellen Gent
for their help in preparing
this book.

CONTENTS

WILLIE

"I didn't come here,
and I ain't leavin'."
—WILLIE NELSON

PROLOGUE

A long time ago when I walked onto a stage to do a show, I would search the room with my eyes. I was looking for somebody who was looking at me, who appeared interested in learning what I was doing in front of the microphone with a guitar in my hands. Once I found that friendly face, I would sing to that person all night long. I would zero in and make heavy contact with their spirit. And it would grow. The flash of energy between me and the one friendly face would reflect into others, and it would keep growing—these bolts of energy ping-ponging from one table to the next, or from one pair of dancers to the couple dancing nearby—and before long I would have the whole crowd caught up in my music and me.

But it all had to start with one friendly face.

It's like now when I hug some girl in the front row. I'll reach over and put my arm around her, and some other girl will give me a flower and I'll kiss her, and the rushes of excitement will wash out through the crowd like the waves of the ocean, touching everyone. I don't want any security guards between me and the front row, roughing up the crowd or preventing anyone from trying to touch me. I want to hug these people and let them feel how much I love them and are thrilled they are here with me.

But it don't always happen just like that nowadays. There are many nights when I walk onstage in some enormous dark venue and I can't see a friendly face in the audience unless I took a Boy Scout flashlight and walked among them.

I do a number of big concerts at night in arenas or at outdoor picnics—by big I mean crowds of 100,000—and I have to work those shows by feel. I can see nothing but a wide deep-purple canyon blinking with the fire of thousands of cigarettes.

Even before I step onstage I can tell how hot the crowd is. If they're hot they're screaming or they're rumbling with pent-up emotions. Sometimes there is so much noise from the crowd that I never hear a note I am playing or a word I am singing. My sound guys are the greatest at getting monitor music back to the band, but some nights it is impossible. I went to a couple of Beatles concerts in the sixties and I couldn't hear their music for the screaming crowd.

I can't say I never dreamed such a thing would happen to me. I knew it would.

The biggest crowd I ever played to—the biggest live and in-person crowd, as opposed to the worldwide audience that saw *We Are the World* on satellite TV—was at the US Festival in Los Angeles a few years ago. The Apple Computer guy—Steve Wozniak—had a lot of money he wanted to spend so he built a huge concert stadium around L.A. somewhere and hired a bunch of bands and paid us all way too much money. There was a constant stream of helicopters and limos arriving and departing backstage. Wozniak said there were a zillion people in the audience and how can I argue with a computer guy? The newspapers said there were more than 500,000.

I walked out onstage and saw more people than I ever imagined seeing all at once, only they were speckled and flashed and hidden by the darkness and the theatrical lights. It was exciting, like standing in a spotlight at the fifty-yard line with five Rose Bowl crowds screaming and cheering from the darkness.

I got a sense of people waving at me, and I waved back. Every now and then, thousands lit up like the exploding bridge scene from *Apocalypse Now*, sparking and booming like a fireworks display amid that immensity, that forest of people.

They were hot. But I thought, well, if they're this hot now, I better work a little harder and make them a little hotter.

The way to do that if you can't look them in the eye is to play music—one song after another, driving at them with the music—and that's what we did. I felt electricity like my tennis shoes were wired to a generator. The screaming as we finished our set reached the pitch of jet engines. I was so high from the experience I wanted it never to end. There was so much noise and backstage confusion that I had to ask myself, "Self, did you arouse them tonight?" And self said, "Son, you lifted them up."

Really it's the same thing I used to do on the road in the early days when I was looking for one friendly face. Many of those old shows the audience was hung over from the night before and not feeling that great to begin with, but you've got to get them to jump up on their feet and start dancing.

What I do for a living is get people to feeling good.

It's not a power that I feel I have in and of myself. It is a power that is exchanged between me and my audience. By the fact that we musicians are out there with a bunch of big amplifiers and we know we can be heard by 100,000 people—or in high-tech terminology a zillion people—we know there is a tremendous lot of energy leaving the bandstand, and we can tell from the feeling coming back whether we're having a big time or not.

My band and stage crew and my sound and lighting guys have been with me so long now and know me so well that we communicate by instinct on the nights the crowd is so loud we can't hear each other onstage. Paul English on drums and Bee Spears on bass can read me like a diary. By the gestures I make or the mood I'm in, Paul and Bee always know what I'm getting ready to do. To me it seems like I just go ahead from one song to another as they pop into mind. It's a great help to have old friends onstage and at the control boards who anticipate what I'm about to do before I've even consciously decided.

The whole experience is very electric. It's the utmost high. Crowds come to see us and pay ten to twenty dollars apiece to stand up and scream for two hours. It's probably very therapeutic. Psychiatrists encourage people to scream, holler, and laugh. Music raises their spirits, which is why they go to concerts. Music is a motivator. Music will make you leap up off your ass and move. It will make you dance, it will make you do jumping jacks. It's no wonder music has been incorporated into exercise videocassettes that sell way up in the millions.

Of course, our band is onstage to have a good time, too. If we don't have a good time, chances are the audience won't enjoy it so much either. Musicians who grow tired and cynical and begin playing just for the money instead of for the love of the music and for the crowds find their audiences start slipping away. You can't fool a crowd for long, whether it's a concert for 100,000 or a honky-tonk with 300 in it. People will pick up sour vibrations and take their business elsewhere. When you open your heart to an audience, you share your deepest feelings with them. They want to find love in your heart. They don't want to see that it is nothing but a bank vault.

When I say we have fun onstage, I don't mean we're not taking our music seriously and working as hard as we can. But we can still laugh at ourselves and get downright giddy up there. A few years ago we were playing to a packed house at Caesar's Palace in Las Vegas. I started singing "Angel Flying Too Close to the Ground." The crowd started laughing. "Angel Flying Too Close to the Ground" is one of the best songs I ever wrote, but there is nothing funny about it.

I couldn't figure out what the hell was wrong. I wondered if my jeans were unzipped or maybe I had my hat on backwards. Then I noticed the guys in the band were laughing, too. This was during my guitar chorus, and I didn't think it was all that great to have my whole band laughing behind my back.

So I turned around to check it out, and just then Bee Spears came flying right over my head wearing ballet tights and one of those puffy skirts.

Bee was flying back and forth across the stage, playing his guitar, and the room was rocking with laughter. What had happened was they had been performing the musical *Peter Pan* on that stage and had left the wires in place that made Peter Pan fly. Bee had found a costume and hooked himself to the wires, and he was having a terrific time swooping and sailing and doing his impression of an angel flying too close to the ground. It was the funniest thing I ever saw onstage, not counting certain heavy metal rockers who are funny but don't seem to know it.

We're not like a lot of bands who demand the promoters to cart them around in limos and stuff their dressing rooms with champagne and caviar and wall-to-wall blonds. Some of the guys in the band who smoke want cigarettes in the dressing room. But we don't even ask for beer backstage. The truth is, I don't want beer backstage. We used to have beer available all the time, and it got where there was such a mob of freeloaders around the beer cooler that I could hardly make my way to the exit. Then one day Paul English and I got a look at our beer bill for the past month. It was $85,000. We put an immediate stop to having beer or any stronger drink backstage, and you know what? There's hardly anybody backstage now who doesn't belong there.

When I walk off the stage after a hot show, I'm so wired on a natural high that for the next two or three hours my feet barely touch the floor. It used to be, when the regular show was over and everybody was roaring, we'd go to a bar or somebody's house and the band would keep playing until we could see the sunlight through the windows and hear the birds singing outside. Now we get into our caravan of buses and leave town as soon as the show is over. There's plenty of time to come down when you're rolling all night on the highway, and you ain't someplace where you're liable to hurt somebody or get thrown in jail.

But there are times when so much energy has built up over a long road trip and the glands are pumping so much juice that even a 2,000-mile ride on my bus, *Honeysuckle Rose*, won't bring me back to earth.

When I feel this happening, I know I must go home—either to my cabin at my golf course in the hills west of Austin or else to my house in Abbott, the town where I was born.

For really allowing myself to rest and relax, there is no place quite like Abbott. That is where my dreams began, and I go back there to begin dreaming again, like a child . . .

PART ONE

Let Me
Be
a Man

Let Me Be a Man

Explain to me again, Lord, why I'm here;
I don't know, I don't know.
The setting for the stage is still not clear;
Where's the show? Where's the show?
Let it begin, let it begin.
I am born. Can you use me?

What would you have me do, Lord?
Shall I sing them a song?
I could tell them all about you, Lord;
I could sing of the loves I have known.

I'll work in their cotton and corn field;
I promise I'll do all I can;
I'll laugh and I'll cry, I'll live and I'll die.

Please, Lord, let me be a man,
And I'll give it all that I can.
If I'm needed in this distant land,
Please, Lord, let me hold to your hand.

Dear Lord, let me be a man
And I'll give it all that I can.
If I'm needed in this distant land,
Please, Lord, let me be a man.

CHAPTER ONE

A jab of pain in my back, above my right hipbone, meant morning had come for me, no matter that I could see stars in the plum summer sky through the window. I rolled over on my pallet on the floor of the upstairs room, trying to settle into a position for a few more minutes' sleep. I could hear the electric fan humming on the floor and felt a wash of cool air across my naked body. In hours it would be a typical Texas midsummer afternoon, 1987, my fifteenth Fourth of July Picnic—the sun so hot and the sky so bright that you couldn't stand to look at them—but for now there was a nice, wet breeze and I could gaze out the window and lie and bathe in starlight, the stuff that makes us all.

The pain hit again. I rolled over onto my knees, straightened up slowly, and walked to the window. Abbott, in the middle of Texas, is a smaller town than it was fifty-four years ago when I was born a hundred yards from where I was now standing. The sky is still clear in Abbott, and the stars look close to the earth, like they did when I was a kid.

With my arms raised at the window, I could smell grass and trees on the breeze, and the sharp odor of fresh paint. Old Bill Russell was painting the house for me and had worked late. I saw his ladder and buckets down in the yard below the second-floor window, throwing shadows toward the barn. With both hands I combed back my hair and felt it fall free against the bare skin of my shoulders. Listening to the hypnotic vibrations of the electric fan, I inhaled deeply, swallowing air into my diaphragm like my grandmother had taught me. I held my breath until I was almost dizzy—as kids we'd hold our breath for fun until we passed out—and let it all out slowly and thoroughly, relaxing my neck and shoulders, letting my arms hang limp.

I did twenty-five deep breaths standing naked in the starlight. I felt strong and clean. Deep breathing at an open window is a wonderful thing unless you live in Los Angeles or down the block from an asbestos plant. Everybody knows that filling your lungs with oxygen is good, but not many people do it. It's like most of the choices you have in life. You know inside what is right. Whether you do it is up to you.

A lot of people think I sing nasal. It's not true. It may sound nasal to some ears, but actually it's the sound that comes from deep down in the diaphragm. That's where you get the most strength. It's the result of controlling your breathing, which is the secret to many things, including peace of mind. Indians, for example, concentrate on listening to themselves breathe. As they listen to their breath coming in and going out, they are hearing the sound of God. Breathing is a way for all of us to meditate and get close to the spirit. It's a key to mental and spiritual health. We've all heard the advice to take ten deep breaths when we're excited or agitated. Ten breaths will slow your mind, your metabolism, your heart rate, so you can get control and avoid making a dumb move or saying something stupid. Deep breathing gives you energy and makes you high.

You can bring divine energy into your lungs by breathing. Feel the beat of your heart. It is holy light. When you become conscious of the Master in your heart, your whole life changes. Your aura goes out and influences everything around you. You have free will to recognize it or to blind yourself to it. Be quiet and ask your heart. I mean, really shut up and listen to your inner voice. It will tell you this is the truth.

I looked at my watch. It was 4 A.M. We had come back from preproduction meetings at the Picnic site at Carl's Corner about midnight on the *Honeysuckle Rose*. I must have slept three hours. Not bad. Three or four hours is a good night's sleep for me.

Stepping away from the window, I started my stretching exercises. Putting one foot on a chair and bending toward it to pull the hamstrings. Standing on one foot, grasping the other behind me with my hand and lifting my head toward the roof. I took my time, not racing against time but forgetting about it, as I went through a stretching nonroutine—some of it yoga, some of it chiropractor, some of it Hawaiian Kahuna medicine, and the rest of it me.

The thought crossed my mind that my wife, Connie, wouldn't be at the Picnic today. In the fifteen years since I had begun these annual concerts, Connie had been backstage at nearly all of them. That first crazy but important Picnic in Dripping Springs in 1973, she was eight months pregnant with our youngest daughter, Amy. It made me sad to think of Connie not being around anymore. But we had recently separated again. Even though I've been married for what seems like my whole life—ten years to Martha, ten years to Shirley, and now eighteen years to Connie—I ain't really cut out to be a good husband and a perfect father. This time I had stomped out of the house Connie had bought in Westlake Hills on the shore of Lake Austin and said I wasn't coming back. It was after yet another argument about the same old subjects—I didn't spend enough time with Connie and our daughters, and I smoked too much weed. For me, the choice came down to staying in the Westlake Hills house with Connie all the time when I came off the road—which meant giving up all my pals who I hung around with on the golf course or in my recording studio in Texas—or never going back to the West-lake Hills house again.

Apparently, my third marriage was headed toward the divorce court, just like my first two, and for the same reason.

It's not easy to be married to somebody like me and be a wife and stay home and take care of the family while I'm out here traveling around and acting like a big star. I mean, it rubs. It's hard to find a woman who would put up with that. Now Connie put up with it for a long, long time and it's just too much strain. So whatever happens to my and her relationship, it has nothing to do with anything she did wrong. It was just one of those things. If I had to make a list of all the things that Connie did right, and all the things that she did wrong, there wouldn't be anything on the wrong side, zero. Because she did what she instinctively thought was the right thing to do and you can't blame a person for that.

I am as simple as I look, hard as that may be to understand. I am an itinerant singer and guitar picker. I am what they used to call a troubadour. I would love to be married, I love having a home, but my calling is not compatible with staying put. Sorry to say, I felt the time had come when I had to move on down the road again into the next phase of my life.

Whatever the next stage is, I don't believe it will include another wife.

Groping in a pile of clothes on the floor, I found a T-shirt and put it on. It read WHEN IN DOUBT KNOCK EM OUT. I pulled on a pair of shorts that looked like the Lone Star flag of Texas, stuffed my feet into running shoes, and crept down the stairs, trying not to wake my daughter Lana and her four kids who were sleeping on their pallets in what will be the living room when we finish restoring the house like it was when Dr. Sims owned it. Dr. Sims and his wife lived in this house in 1933, and on an April night of that year Doc was fetched by my cousin Mildred to tromp across the field to the little frame house where my mother, Myrle, was laboring to present the world with a new old soul—me.

I had bought Dr. Sims's house early this year for $18,000 and started fixing it up to look as pretty as it did in 1933. I would have bought the house I was born in, but it had been torn down. Only our old bedroom was saved, and it has been moved to the other side of the highway and added to the house of a black family.

One of the first things I did after buying Dr. Sims's house was set about removing the big signboard outside of Abbott that says HOME OF WILLIE NELSON. Me and Zeke Varnon got drunk and tried to burn down the sign with a gasoline fire, but five gallons only singed those old creosote posts and blackened my name so it looked even worse. At least, I showed I was serious. I got them to change the sign to HOME OF THE ABBOTT FIGHTING PANTHERS, my old high school team.

I heard Lana and the grandkids sleeping. The sound of children sleeping entrances me: their slow, peaceful breaths, their little snorts and yips, the occasional words spoken aloud in their sleep, all coming from a soul that is living in sleep in realms that, not knowing how else to put it, we say dreams are made of.

Stepping over paint buckets in the kitchen, I let the screen door close quietly and slipped into the warm, purple morning and began to run.

I set a slow pace down the road by the house of my old childhood friend Jimmy Bruce, who still lives in the same house and is now the town postmaster. I ran past the old tabernacle—the scene, in my youth, of singing and preaching and playing knuckles-down marbles —and on past the Baptist church a few blocks away, and past the Methodist church across the street, where I sang every Sunday even though I thought I was doomed to hell, and way deep into the fields of Abbott, home of my heart.

When I was young in Abbott, on summer nights and early mornings like this you could look up and see the Milky Way and it was awesome. Kids in urban areas today have no idea how the Milky Way looked forty or fifty years ago. It was like Bill Russell had taken his brush and painted a wide white swath across the sky. We knew this white celestial highway was made of countless stars and constellations inconceivable distances away, yet the Milky Way looked like a solid white path near enough that you thought you could hit it with a cannon. And somehow you knew that the starlight reached you from glory, that you drew all your strength from the starlight, that eternity was immense and your knowledge was small. There are countless planets full of life out there among the stars. How do I know? I've been there. So have you.

Beholding the Milky Way in the night sky in Abbott when I was a kid would reveal me to myself—in a mystical sense—so strong that I could only reconcile my vision with real life in a broke farm town during the Great Depression by picking fights and showing off.

I ran towards Willie Nelson Road, a stretch of county road between Abbott and West, the town where I first played in a band when I was about eight or nine years old. It was funny to think about this road being named for me. If they'd named it for me fifty years ago, when I walked down this road to go pick cotton, they might have called it Booger Red Boll-evard. Booger Red is what they called me back then.

Running along the road, at home in my thoughts, I was aware that grass and trees and crops and animals are among the essence of life, and I am a part of them and need continual support from them. The Indians—which means me and my brothers and sisters of like mind —say only the spirits and the earth endure. When I see the destruction wrought upon our small planet by human beings who forget the supreme good of caring for our natural world that mothers us, I wonder if our species will last long enough to wake up to the truth that we must obey the old laws of cause and effect and treat the earth as our mother instead of as our gravel pit and garbage dump. The trash that washes ashore on Texas beaches—bleach bottles, syringes, plastic bags, ice chests—comes from Venezuela, France, Brazil, and Greece, among other places. West Germans and Saudi Arabians own half the buildings in downtown Houston. It is a small world, indeed.

The constant struggle between good and evil is approaching another great climax in our lifetime. By good I mean your inner voice that comes from God—maybe you call it conscience—and by evil I mean negative thinking, materialistic, greedy attitudes that you know are wrong but can be reduced into acting as if you believe they are right. This is the Devil—to be overwhelmed by desire for things of the material world, to be swept under by negative thinking, to be selfish and petty, to use power and wealth to dominate others: this is hell and we make it for ourselves.

Running alone in the dawn, this is the sort of thing I think about. It's nothing mysterious. People may think I'm mysterious, but I don't plan it that way. It all seems clear enough to me.

The sunrise began to glow at my right shoulder, clods of earth and brown shoots taking shape in the growing light. I felt a real *déjà vu*. This is how it had looked when I had walked these same fields during the Great Depression with my grandmother and my sister Bobbie, filling our burlap bags with cotton. I turned and ran back toward the house with the sunrise over my left shoulder.

On a soft spring afternoon a few months earlier, the kind of day when I open the moon roof of my car and lower the windows and thank God for putting me in Texas, I was cruising along the back roads of Hill County in my silver Mercedes 560 SEL—I've always loved to drive a good car whether I could afford it or not—with my old buddy Zeke Varnon, who could have been the world domino champion if he'd been willing to leave home.

Zeke was drinking a beer and scratching the stubble on his chin. We had been up most of the night playing dominoes and passing the tequila bottle back and forth in Zeke's trailer house outside of Hillsboro. I've been close friends with Zeke since our teens, when we'd decided we were both insane, by the standards of the time. We loved being insane. We thought of ourselves as true rebels, living strictly by our own rules. Of course, when we had a sick hangover and a nagging piece of memory about some outrageous act we'd pulled the night before, it helped a little to think of ourselves as rebels instead of just nuts.

"Willie, there's a guy you ought to meet," Zeke said after we had been driving a while.

I had been looking out the window at fields where forty years ago I had picked cotton and baled hay. I was remembering when cars first got air conditioners after World War II. I would look up, sweating like a pig in the field, and see cars zooming down the highway in the middle of the summer with their windows shut. That, for me, was what it meant to be rich—to drive down the highway in the middle of the summer with your windows shut.

"Who?" I said.

Zeke began to tell me about Carl Cornelius.

Talk about crazy. Listening to Zeke, I knew Carl Cornelius was some kind of brother. Actually, he was living one of my biggest fantasies: he owned his own town. I've *always* wanted to own my own town. We'd built me a town once in the hills outside Austin—an authentic, one-street Old West town like Texas in the 1880s—for our movie *Red Headed Stranger* and for the *Pancho and Lefty* album video I did with Merle Haggard and Townes Van Zandt. But when the cameras quit turning the citizens of my town went away, leaving the paint to fade and the brush to blow across the dirt road, except on Sunday afternoons when Lana gathers a group at the little church for nondenominational services. Somebody will play the piano and we'll sing hymns standing in our old-fashioned pews, and maybe somebody in the crowd that always includes lots of kids will want to tell a story. Or we'll get out a portable machine and play a tape of a lecture by Father A. A. Taliaffero of St. Alcuin's Church in Dallas. Father Taliaffero is a wise man. I listen to him as I would listen to a great teacher. I must have fifty of his taped lectures in a cabinet on my bus. It sort of surprises strangers who expect to hear music always blaring from the speakers on *Honeysuckle Rose* to hear a man telling them instead there is no such thing as death, and that creative imagination rules the universe.

But the rest of the week my town doesn't even have a sheriff in it. When I first built the town I wanted to hire a sheriff who would dress like Wyatt Earp with two big six-guns, and rock back in his cane chair on the porch in front of the jail with his spurred boots propped up on the hitching rail.

My fantasy was I would amble up to my sheriff and offer him a hit off my Austin Torpedo and the sheriff would squint at me and drawl, "Well, no thanks, Willie, I'm on duty. But you ain't harming a soul or tearing up nothing, so you go right ahead and smoke all the weed you want. Can't nobody bother you here, Willie—not in your own town with your own sheriff on duty."

Carl Cornelius, however, owned a real town and his own gang of law officers who dressed like state troopers.

Until eighteen months ago, Carl's Corner had been just a big truckstop and cafe. But Carl dreams big. He took the circus-size, ten-foot polyurethane musical frogs down from the roof of a fancy Dallas disco and put them on the top of his truckstop. He erected a drive-in movie and a sauna and a swimming pool and surrounded them on three sides with a bunch of mobile homes—"changing rooms," Carl said.

Carl found some backing in Dallas and bought a couple of thousand acres of the flat farmland around his truckstop. He made it easy for 180 people to move onto the land in mobile homes and stay until they qualified under state law as local voters. At that point they called an election and voted themselves an official town called Carl's Corner with Carl as the mayor. Carl owned the liquor sale permit and the water well and held notes on the land. The only other business was Paula's Pet Boutique.

Approaching the town of Carl's Corner in my Mercedes, I saw a thirty-foot advertising billboard rising up from the highway—a huge painted cutout of three figures standing arm in arm and peering out at the landscape. The figures were Carl, Zeke, and me.

"Ah . . . there's something I ain't told you yet," Zeke said.

I parked my Mercedes in the lot crowded with trucks. Zeke led me though the back door.

Inside the truckstop I could smell chili, an aroma of cuminos that watered my sinuses. There, in front of a big projection TV screen, were a dozen truckers eating chicken fried steaks and cheeseburgers, watching soap operas.

A burly fellow with a big open country face approached me, his cheeks blooming with whiskey flush, a straw cowboy hat pushed to the back of his head, his belly hanging over his big silver belt buckle on crumpled jeans over lizard-skin boots. He had a wide, yellow-tooth grin and eyes that looked like they had just been through a sandstorm.

Carl is not bashful. He cut straight to the meat of the matter.

"Hi, Willie," Carl said. "Let's have your 1987 Picnic right here in my town this Fourth of July. Carl's Corner is ideal. There is not a single tree to block the view of the stage."

I wasn't real sure I wanted to have a Picnic this year. I say that every year, and I always mean it.

"Why don't we start off with a beer and a bowl of chili?" I said.

Carl served Great Depression chili, the greasy red ambrosia that used to cost a dime a bowl with all the soda crackers you wanted. Dish of pinto beans on the side. Jar of jalapeño peppers on the table next to a bowl of chopped white onions. Not a trace of tomatoes or celery or other foreign objects that over the years have drifted into what people who don't know better call chili. Chili was invented in South Texas as a dish to make tough stringy beef taste good, and sold by vendors on the streets on San Antonio before the Battle of the Alamo in 1836. Chili is a serious matter to any native-born Texan old enough to remember when a ten-cent bowl of red would keep you feeling feisty all day.

After our chili and a couple of beers, Carl drove me and Zeke to the Picnic site he had picked out—177 acres of grassland at Interstate 35E and FM2959 four miles north of Hillsboro. Like Carl had said, there was nothing to block the view—or to block the sun and wind. But the site was within easy driving range of maybe four million people, counting Dallas, Fort Worth, Waco, and Austin. We went back to the truckstop and played dominoes in Carl's office where he kept glancing at his empire on ten television monitors

Carl is a good domino player. I am better than good. Zeke is better than me. We all drank from the ample supplies of beer and tequila. At some point during the night Zeke and I were about to win the truckstop and the town from Carl.

I got up to go to the bathroom and took another look around the truckstop. There was lots for sale: sacks of cookies, cans of motor oil, glass unicorns, bronze western statues, a rackful of books by Louis L'Amour, stacks of trucker logbooks. Coffee mugs and T-shirts with Carl's face on them. There was a jar of peanut butter on every table. Carl had been telling me his plans to open a trucker chapel for prayers and weddings soon, and then a trucker museum and a trucker bank. "Your Picnic," he'd told me, "will put this place on the map."

"Okay," I said. I admire dreamers, being one myself.

I woke up the next morning on the couch at Zeke's house. Zeke was standing at the refrigerator making breakfast, which means, for him, popping the top on a can of beer.

"Do I remember telling Carl he could have the Picnic at Carl's Corner?"

"Yep. She's all done sealed, pardner," Zeke said. "We're dedicating it to truckers."

"We didn't win the town, did we?"

"Naw, the game sort of fell apart. We'll pick it up later."

Carl announced the Picnic in newspapers and on TV. Crews showed up to dig ditches and lay pipe for water. Surveyors were sighting out the parking area. My old Austin Opera House pardner, Tim O'Connor, took over as the producer and built a stage, cleared the ground, chose the spots for concession stands and portable toilets. The Hard Rock Cafe jumped in as official Picnic restaurant. Tim started selling tickets. The Picnic at Carl's Corner was rolling with its own momentum.

I climbed onto *Honeysuckle Rose* and rode a long way out of town to a series of shows, which I had learned was the best place for me to be while the Picnic was being put together. I had, after all, fifteen years experience with Willie Nelson Fourth of July Picnics. They usually ended with me slipping into a plane in the middle of the night and flying off to Hawaii to hide for a week while the damages were assessed. Over the years I realized it could be an advantage to be unfindable before the Picnic, as well. The Picnic grows beyond control, and I try never to worry about what is out of my control—just to give it my strongest positive thoughts and trust for it to turn out well.

Now I loped back to Dr. Simms's old house in the early Abbott morning—daydreaming, several voices inside me talking all at once, as they usually do, telling me tales, offering advice; they are my guardian angels mixed in with some malicious spirits. I listen to the voices argue all the time but my inner Mediator makes the decisions unless my ego jumps in front and screws it all up.

Honeysuckle Rose's generators were humming in the yard as Gator Moore, my driver, got the bus ready to roll. Gator is a tall, well-built guy with long hair and a beard and healthy biceps. He's a good companion on the road and a conscientious driver who always gets me to the show on time, or the movie set or the recording studio or the motel. I depend on Gator.

I stopped in the kitchen to eat two plums and a bowl of plain yogurt with walnuts and sliced bananas and strawberries on top. I washed down a couple of painkillers with a slug of grapefruit juice, hugged Lana, and talked to my grandkids.

I climbed onto *Honeysuckle Rose* with a random group of friends. Gator drove us along the streets I ran that morning and headed up the highway until we came upon an enormous Texas flag—I mean it looked like it was ten stories high—and turned down a side road into the backstage area. I climbed out and walked up onto the stage to gaze at what we had brought forth.

Beyond the stage the ground fanned out in a field that could hold the 80,000 capacity crowd Carl and Zeke had been predicting in the papers. It was already getting hot. I found myself sweating on stage, and not only because of the heat. I had begun to realize that a crowd of 80,000 was a crazy prediction for a blazing 100-plus-degree day out here on this shadeless prairie at Carl's Corner. You would have to be a lunatic to fight the traffic of the predicted mob to Carl's Corner on such a blistering day, no matter that we had loaded the show with Kris Kristofferson, Roger Miller, Ray Benson and Asleep at the Wheel, Billy Joe Shaver, Don Cherry, Stevie Ray Vaughn and the Fabulous Thunderbirds, Rattlesnake Annie, Bruce Hornsby, Jackie King, Joe Ely, Joe Walsh, Eric Johnson, and had a hell of a show scheduled.

I heard a mellow, husky voice crooning behind me. The voice was singing gibberish—"the old church . . . the bells . . . the yellow house on the corner . . . oh I am fucked . . ."

Don Cherry was pacing back and forth at the rear of the stage, rubbing his hands together. Besides being a good, stylish singer, Don is a scratch golfer who used to play on the pro tour—two qualities that I admire above most others.

"What's the matter?" I said.

Don stared at me with blue eyes that showed intense concern, like maybe a contact lens had gone crooked.

"Oh, shit, Will," he said.

"What's wrong?"

"Do you know the lyrics to 'Green Green Grass of Home'?"

I thought about it for a moment. I could hear the melody in my head, but the words didn't come.

"No," I said.

"I've been driving up and down the highway for two hours trying to remember that fucking song. I must have sung it five thousand times in nightclubs. I could walk on stage in Vegas right now, and 'Green Green Grass of Home' would burst out of my throat, I couldn't stop it. But now it's gone. I can't remember the fucking words."

"Sing something else," I said.

"Are you crazy? That's what I open with."

I left Don huddling onstage with Bee Spears, Mickey Raphael, Grady Martin, and Poodie Locke—stalwarts of my band and crew— all of them singing at the same time, working on the words to "Green Green Grass of Home."

At 10 A.M. my band and I kicked off the show to a couple of hundred folks camped below the stage with folding chairs, umbrellas, and coolers. I recognized many of them, people I had seen at my outdoor shows in Texas for twenty years, aging hippies like me with earrings and tattoos and hair under the women's armpits. They danced and waved their hands. A big Viking woman in a green undershirt pulled out two breasts the size of volleyballs and bounced them in her palms while her biker old man screamed with toothless joy.

I introduced Don Cherry at 10:30 in the morning. Looking cool, loaded with big-time nightclub aplomb, Don snapped his fingers and swung into "Green Green Grass of Home." He sang that song as good as anybody could sing it, like he was headlining the song to a sellout crowd at a star hotel on the Strip in Las Vegas.

The aging hippies listened with a sort of bemused curiosity. When Don gave it his show-biz finish, they sat and looked at him like he was a Hottentot. The crowd—if you could call it that—clapped politely and began to yell "Let's boogie!"

Instead Don sang them a patriotic song about what this country means to him and every true American within hearing. This time the people cheered and whistled when he finished with his arms outlifted and his head held high. Pro that he is, Don bowed and fled the stage while they were still whistling—we call it getting out of Dodge.

"Fuck it," he said as he passed me on the steps. "Which way is the airport?"

By the middle of the afternoon the temperature was 103. The wind had started blowing hard enough to flap the banners on the stage so they sounded like horsewhips cracking—it was some relief from the heat. The crowd had grown to about 4,000. It was clear the prediction of 80,000 had been nuts.

Darkness fell. My old pals Kris Kristofferson and Roger Miller showed up. Kris was, as usual, in an uproar. In the newspaper that morning had been a story that accused Kris of throwing away a plaque some Vietnam vets had given him after he played a benefit for them up East the night before.

"How could they say such shit?" Kris yelled. "In all the confusion backstage, I didn't know the plaque got left behind. For God's sake, I'm on these guys' side, I'm busting ass for these guys, I'm not gonna do anything stupid and humiliating like throw away their plaque!"

Kris would be happy if this was coffeehouse time again, like the fifties and early sixties, where he could sit on a stool with his guitar and sing his songs to a packed house of beatniks. Kris is, of course, one of the best songwriters of all time. He shows more soul when he blows his nose than the ordinary person does at his honeymoon dance. But commercial is a word Kris refuses to hear. He has written a lot of hits and some standards, but he writes what he wants and sings what he wants—even if the record labels drop him—and for my Picnic he was going to do his new songs about the Sandanistas in Nicaragua and about Jesse Jackson. By now the night wind had dropped the temperature into the 80s, and the crowd had grown to an estimated 8,000.

My manager, lawyer, and accountant arrived, counted the house, looked at the bills, and slunk around with subdued and mournful expressions. The Picnic stood to take a $600,000 bath.

Zeke was a pardner for profits but not for losses. That was understood from the start. I would never put Zeke in a loser. The money to pay the losses would have to come from Tim, Carl, and me.

Carl got drunk as soon as he saw the size of the afternoon crowd, had slept it off and was back aboard *Honeysuckle Rose* telling me with all the certainty a forty-seven-year-old guy born in Kleburg County in South Texas, father of seven children including a two-year-old, could muster that in another hour we'd have a crowd of 50,000. He hit the tequila again.

"Want to play some dominoes?" Carl asked.

"Mix 'em up," I said.

"What'll we play for?" Carl said.

"Your town."

"Shit, you own it already. Let's play for cash," Carl said.

I went onstage with my band to play the last set at 2 A.M. I couldn't tell how many people were listening down there in the dark. I knew I was going into the tank financially on this Picnic. We had made some major miscalculations. But none of that mattered when we struck up "Whiskey River" to open the final set. That was only money —this was music. The excitement I felt at that moment was too powerful to carry a price tag.

Standing in the spotlights, with the old stars above me in the Abbott sky, I saw the satellite TV truck sending our picture and our music all over the cosmos. And from that stage at Carl's Corner I could see, too, the dark blanket of the fields where little Booger Red had picked cotton and busted his back baling hay so many, many years ago.

Regardless of what this 1987 Picnic may have cost me, in the end we wound up with a good permanent concert site not ten miles from the barbershop where I used to give a shoe shine and a song for fifty cents. How's that for using the creative imagination?

The Chorus

MILDRED WILCOX

It was about sundown when Myrle's waters broke. I remember the period of day because Mama Nelson and I were doing the evening milking of our cow, and Myrle had wandered out to watch and talk with us. She was too pregnant to work, but maybe she could sense it was near and wanted company. Anyhow, Myrle's waters broke while Mama Nelson was milking the cow. Mama Nelson sent me running to fetch Dr. Simms, who lived only three houses away. But there was a lot of land between houses in Abbott in 1933.

I ran as fast as I could. A couple of years earlier, when I was thirteen, Myrle had given birth to Bobbie Lee, and it had scared me to death. Bobbie Lee was born on the first hour of the first week of the first month of the first year—1 A.M., January 1, 1931. They had made me go upstairs and told me to go to sleep. Myrle was only sixteen herself, and I was frightened and curious what was happening to her.

Myrle used to iron for Dr. Simms. She ironed his white shirts. Mrs. Simms wouldn't let her iron anything but the collar and the sleeves, because that's all that showed when he put on his vest. Myrle would

---

Mildred Wilcox, Willie's cousin, helped raise him and his sister Bobbie. Mildred was at Willie's birth—and named him Willie.

starch and iron his collars and cuffs one day a week. I don't know what she got paid, but it was a little bit of money.

Dr. Simms came to the house to handle the birth. Mama and Daddy Nelson were there. Myrle's husband, Ira, must have been at work. He could have been off playing music someplace—Ira was always playing music—but he wasn't at the house.

Because I had enjoyed Bobbie Lee so much, had babysat with her all the time instead of working, Myrle had told me, "You've loved my first baby dearly, so when my next one is born, whatever it is, you can name it."

I gave the new baby my daddy's name, Hugh. Then to go with Hugh I chose the name Willie. It sounded kind of musical—Willie Hugh Nelson. I wasn't old enough to realize that Willie wouldn't be a mature, grown-up man's name someday, that he might be more proud to have a name like Granddaddy Nelson's—William—stuck on a marriage license. But he was never William. He was always Willie.

Willie's granddaddy and grandmother—our grandparents—used to teach singing in Arkansas before the family moved to Abbott, Texas, in 1929. They would take over some country schoolhouse for ten days or so and teach music to the families—men, women, children, everybody loved singing. My goodness, up in the Arkansas mountains no shows came through. When you weren't working, you were either in church singing or you were at a party singing or a schoolhouse singing. I was only eight or ten years old, but I was the pump organ player. Granddaddy Nelson would have me learning new songs constantly. He was the song leader. Whatever he wanted to sing, that's what I learned to play. I would help chalk music on the blackboard at the singing schools. Everybody would learn to read music, read the lines and spaces. And they would sing by notes. *DO, RE, ME.* I played by shape notes, and that's why it was so hard, because *DO* remains the same shape but it changes lines every time you change keys.

We would ride horseback to the schoolhouse for the singing schools and spend nights with the people who came to study. Everybody brought food and gathered to study music for maybe two weeks at a stretch. We mostly sang gospel hymns. We would sing all six verses of every hymn.

Granddaddy sang bass. At night he would hold little Willie on his lap and sing him to sleep with his beautiful bass voice—songs like "Polly Wolly Doodle All the Day" and "Show Me the Way to Go Home," "She'll be Comin' Round the Mountain," and "Where Have You Gone Billy Boy."

Willie's father, Ira, was always wanting to go off and play in a band somewhere, and Myrle would go with him, so I would take little Willie, just a few months old, to our house and he would sleep in the curve of my arm. Bobbie would sleep with Mama Nelson.

When Willie was about two, some of us bought him a little Christmas gift. It was a mandolin made out of tin with real strings on it, so he could strum the chords. That was his first musical instrument. Willie kept it a long time. He and Bobbie weren't destructive, they kept their toys. Of course, they didn't get a lot of toys like kids do now. They had to take care of their things because they weren't going to get something new every time somebody went to town. People didn't go to town every day, either.

Myrle and Ira got divorced and went their separate ways, leaving Bobbie and Willie with Ira's folks, Dad and Mom Nelson. Times were hard in the Great Depression. Our granddaddy was a blacksmith. Sometimes people would have work done and then not pay him. Some were well-to-do farmers around Abbott, but they wouldn't pay and never did pay even after Granddaddy Nelson died and left Mama Nelson with Bobbie Lee and Willie to take care of. Bobbie Lee and Willie had to wear clothes somebody handed down to them, or gave them, but they didn't mind. If Bobbie and Willie only had one good dress and suit to wear to church, it was always nice and clean.

It was such a blow to us all when Dad Nelson, our grandfather, suddenly died at age fifty-six. He was a powerful man, not tall but real strong, but he had a bad heart. He caught pneumonia and tried to take some kind of sulfa drug that went against his heart. He took sick one day and died two weeks later.

I spent all the time I could with Bobbie Lee and Willie. We played games—hide-and-seek, Annie Over, follow the leader, little games that groups could join in and play. Sometimes we'd play paper dolls with the girls and little Willie would help us cut dolls out of the mail-order catalogues.

Before I got married and left home, I helped look after Bobbie Lee and Willie. Mama Nelson would never let me spank them. I used to tell her, "If you just let me take a broom weed, just a broom weed, and spank their little old naked legs when they get out of line . . ." But Mama Nelson said no.

After I moved a mile down the road with my husband and couldn't see Bobbie Lee and Willie so much anymore, Mama Nelson had to stake little Willie in the yard, like a cow. She used a twenty-five-foot rope, which gave him plenty of grazing room. I would walk over to the Nelson house to visit the children. When I had to leave, Bobbie

Lee and Willie would follow me as far as they were allowed to go away from the house, up to the next street. Then they would lay down in the grass and cry until I was out of sight.

I couldn't stand that. Finally one day I stopped and went back and said, "Let me have a little talk with y'all. If you keep doing this, I can't come back. I'll just stay home and not come see you. So you promise not to follow me up the road and cry."

They cried some more and promised.

There was never anything said about the children being raised by their grandparents and not having a momma and daddy all the time like other children did. Bobbie Lee and Willie never seemed to mind the fact that they didn't have something other children had. Of course, it was depression time, when nobody had a whole lot. But Bobbie Lee and Willie were happy, well-adjusted kids.

They made good grades in school. Bobbie always played the piano for the school, and Willie would play the guitar and entertain the kids. Every fall the Abbott school would hold a carnival to raise money, and each class would pick a boy and a girl to be the king and queen of the class. Whatever grade they were in, Bobbie Lee and Willie were nearly always chosen.

Myrle and I used to try to write songs together when Bobbie Lee and Willie were babies. After school we would sit and try to put words together so they would rhyme. I'd say, "Did you think of anything that rhymes real good today?" We'd sit down and work some more. We weren't worrying with music, just trying to put words together to make a song. We never did get anything written. What made us want to make a song, I don't know. But we worked frantically at it.

BOBBIE LEE NELSON

Our grandmother would wake Willie and me up in the morning by throwing ice water on us. Mama might call our names once or twice, but if our feet didn't immediately hit the floor, here would come this flood of ice water. Usually I would jump out of bed before the water struck—because I knew it was on its way and I didn't like it—but some mornings she needed a whole pitcher of water to get Willie up. Willie says he would have grown up to be a pretty even-tempered guy if it hadn't been for the way he was woke up as a kid.

Bobbie is Willie's sister and plays piano in his band.

Mama Nelson just didn't have time to fool with coaxing us out of bed. There were chores to be done. The cows had to be brought to the barn and milked, the hog had to be fed, and the chickens. Willie would go out and ride the milk cow into the barn—his first experience as a real cowboy.

Mama would fix breakfast for our granddaddy and Willie and me before we went off to work—Daddy Nelson to his blacksmith shop and the rest of us in the cotton- or cornfields. Later Mama got a job as a cook in the school lunch room, but still we had to be up and moving while the stars were in the sky.

My earliest memory, I was three years old playing outside our little house in Abbott, under the cottonwood and cedar trees, and our mother Myrle and our daddy Ira—not our grandparents but our real parents—were standing by the car having a loud disagreement. Oh, it was so unpleasant, such an awful thing to hear. I started crying and ran to our bedroom at the back of the house and hid. Willie was just a little baby in his crib. I didn't know what was happening, but I knew somebody was leaving.

It was our mother Myrle who was leaving. She and Ira were breaking up their marriage. Pretty soon Ira would hit the road, too, leaving his parents—Mama and Daddy Nelson—to bring up Willie and me.

Thinking back on it now, the only time I can remember Myrle and Ira together is the day they split.

But after our mother and daddy left, Willie and I felt just as warm and secure with our grandparents, maybe even more secure because we didn't have to hear Myrle and Ira fighting. It was a real neat deal to go into the fields with Mama Nelson. You felt like you were helping the family. We had a happy family. We were poor, but we didn't know it because everybody we knew was poor.

Before I got my first real piano, Mama and Daddy Nelson made me a toy piano out of a pasteboard box. We colored it with Crayolas and drew the keyboard. I put it under the peach tree in the backyard and played concerts for hours.

Willie would be listening to me and eating mud. We weren't starving or anything. We just ate a lot of mud. Willie would bake mud pies and mud cookies on our little toy stove and then let them cook in the hot sun. When they were ready, he'd serve them like he was the dessert chef at a fancy restaurant.

"These is especially great today. You'll love my cookies and pies," he would say. "Taste this, Bobbie. Ain't it great?"

Willie was always very convincing. I would eat the mud pies, some of the other kids would eat them, Willie would eat them. Willie ate so much dirt as a kid that I'm sure he really must have liked it.

After our dessert of mud pies and mud cookies, we would have a smoke like the grown-ups did. We smoked cedarbark, corn silk, and grapevines that we called our Camels, Chesterfields, and Lucky Strikes. We'd inhale and get dizzy and stagger around.

Willie was trying to fly in those old days. He would put on his Superman cape and jump off the roof and knock himself out cold.

We had a friend named Moody who would hang out and help us in the fields, cutting the corn tops and all. Moody and Willie were big boxing fans. In the evenings they'd pull off their shirts and box. Moody was bigger than Willie and I think took it kind of easy, but hour after hour they would slug it out, Willie swinging as hard as he could and Moody punching hard enough so Willie would know for sure he'd been hit. Then they'd go to the well and bring up a bucket of clear cold water and duck their swollen, sweaty heads in it. They would shake hands and then fight for another hour. I've never seen Willie back down from a fight in his whole life, but I saw him start plenty of them.

When it got too dark to fight, we would play hide-and-seek or kick the can or Annie Over—we had a lot of fun.

After I got a real piano, Mama taught me to play it. I caught on quickly. I could read music just as clear as I could read English. Willie would sit on the bench beside me while I practiced. I'd tell him what chord I was hitting, what key I was in. Later when he got a guitar, he would try to find the chords and play along with me.

We had a houseful of music books. I'll never understand how Mama and Daddy Nelson could afford so many music books. Any music Willie and I asked for, they'd order it by mail.

Right from the time we were five or six years old, Mama and Daddy Nelson had us performing. They sat us up onstage and said, "Our kids do things." They'd look at us and say, "Now start doing." And we did.

At first it was mostly gospel songs. Maybe Willie would sing "When Irish Eyes Are Smiling" or "Tumbling Tumbleweed" or something, but we were strong church folks, Methodists. We went to church and Sunday school and Wednesday night prayer meetings. We could hear the Baptists singing across the street. Most of the Bohemian farmers around there were Catholics, and we could hear them singing, too. But the best singers were the Church of Christ. The Church of Christ didn't allow musical instruments, so their choirs and congregations really learned how to sing beautiful harmonies.

When I was sixteen I met Bud Fletcher and my life took a radical turn. Bud was six years older than me, quite an older guy in my eyes.

He was good-looking, smooth, had the gift of gab, a real charmer. Bud invited me to go to a place named Shadow Land to dance. That place was so big and dark and mysterious—kind of dangerous, it seemed, with people drinking and carrying on in ways I hadn't seen. I didn't know how to dance. But Bud was such a great dancer that he taught me in no time.

I met Bud in March and married him in April.

Well, Mama Nelson was dismayed. Daddy Nelson had been dead for seven years, and I was Mama's responsibility.

"That boy is too rough for you. He's too old for you," she said. "Tell him he has to go ask your father."

So Bud went and asked Ira, who was then working as an auto mechanic in Fort Worth, if he could marry me.

Ira said, "Sure. I'm all for it."

Bud organized a band called Bud Fletcher and the Texans. I was on piano, Willie played guitar and did vocals, Ira would sit in with us. Bud couldn't play an instrument, so he stuck a broom handle down into a bucket of sand and whacked it like a bass. Bud fronted the band, told jokes, inspired people to get up and dance.

Bud was so slick he got us booked into places we'd never dreamed of. Sometimes we only played a joint once, but we got in the door— which is a big thing when you're starting out. We played Friday nights, Saturday nights, Sunday afternoons. Willie was thirteen years old, and Bud paid him $8 a show. In today's terms that would be like a thirteen-year-old kid making $75 or $100 a show.

We would go home and give our money to Mama Nelson to buy whatever we needed—clothes, food, school supplies. The $40 or $50 a week we took Mama, between us, was a fortune.

Willie would hock his guitar every Monday for about $20. He said he hocked it so often the pawnbroker could play it better than Willie could. On Friday, Bud would get Willie's guitar out of hock and the Texans would hit another weekend of beer joints. That's sort of the story of our life ever since.

After my sons Randy and Freddy were born, Bud got killed in a car wreck. I remarried, divorced, went to live near Willie in Tennessee, played cocktail lounge piano in Austin, remarried again—and finally joined my brother's band nearly twenty years ago to keep on doing what Willie and I have been doing since we were children. Playing music together.

You know, it's funny. When we were kids, he was my little brother. Now that we're grown, I think of him as my big brother.

PART TWO

Family Bible

Family Bible

There's a Family Bible on the table
Its pages worn and hard to read,
But the Family Bible on the table
Will ever be my key to memories.

At the end of the day when work was over
And when the evening meal was done,
Dad would read to us from the Family Bible
And we'd count our many blessings one by one.

I can see us sitting 'round the table
When from the Family bible Dad would read,
And I can hear my mother softly singing
Rock of Ages, Rock of Ages, cleft for me.

Now this old world of ours is filled with trouble.
This old world would oh so better be
If we found more Bibles on the table
And mothers singing Rock of Ages, cleft for me.

I can see us sitting 'round the table
When from the Family Bible Dad would read,
And I can hear my mother softly singing
Rock of Ages, Rock of Ages, cleft for me.

CHAPTER TWO

Y ou can grow up side by side with a blood relative, be bound to that person heart and soul through love—and yet no two human beings remember the same experiences in the exact same way.

Some people call it Old-Timer's Disease. That's when you think everybody you know is losing their memory.

But even two people as close as me and my sister Bobbie Lee, who were never apart from the day I was born until she ran off and married Bud Fletcher at the age of sixteen, look back on our childhood in Abbott and recall the same events with wildly different emotions and impressions.

She remembers it was fun to pick cotton when we were little barefoot kids, before we ever started to school. Mama Nelson, our grandmother, would let Bobbie ride on her cotton sack and pull her between the rows. Bobbie wore a bonnet to protect her beautiful skin from the sun—look at her today, not a wrinkle on her face—and when she got tired of picking, she took a nap in the shade.

It wasn't fun from my point of view. When I was three or four Mama would pull me along on her sack, too, and I'd sneak off and sleep if I got tired. But by the time I was seven or eight, I worked the rows beside Mama Nelson, and it was serious business. You got paid by the amount of cotton you put in your sack. The nice bosses would let the little kids like me pick whatever we could, but the nasty bosses would chase little kids out of the rows as a nuisance even though the kids needed work as bad as anybody. I saw grown men and women—whites and blacks and Mexicans—stooping to pick cotton in the most forlorn time this country has known since the Civil War. Mama Nelson, Bobbie, and I weren't in the fields for exercise. We desperately needed the few dollars we could earn in a day. I saw the bigger boys who could pick more than me were getting higher pay. I knew that, eventually, I would have to outpick them, fight them, or outwit them. But mostly I just wanted to get out of those fields.

I already knew, while Bobby and I were toiling in the fields for a living and beginning to learn music, that we weren't going to spend our lives hauling sacks of cotton. Though I have total respect and admiration for people who labor with their hands—farmers like my folks, blacksmiths like my grandfather, mechanics like my dad Ira, hod carriers, carpenters, and other physical jobs that fill me with awe —my desire to escape from manual labor started in the cottonfields of my childhood and cannot be overstated.

Four years before I was born my daddy, Ira, then sixteen years old, married my mother, Myrle, fifteen, and they packed up with Grand-dad and Grandmother Nelson and moved from the ridges and valleys of Searcy County, Arkansas, to Abbott, Texas, in search of a better life. They were tired of picking shoetop cotton on the slopes of the Ozarks for pennies and trusted that the fields of Central Texas would treat them better. It was the year of the stock market crash, called Black Tuesday, when Union Cigar stock dropped from $113 to $4 in only three hours and the company president took a header out of a hotel window. The stock market crash was big news in New York, but I doubt if my folks paid much attention to it. The big story of 1929 to most Americans was Admiral Byrd flying to the South Pole.

The Great Depression didn't really hit until 1931, a few months after Bobbie was born. By the time I came along in 1933, there were bread lines and soup kitchens in the cities. Franklin D. Roosevelt took office as president and started the New Deal six weeks before my opening act in Abbott, which was a loud yell at Dr. Simms. Prohibition was repealed, which opened up my future in beer joints. Adolf Hitler became chancellor of Germany, Chicago opened its World's Fair, Walt Disney introduced a cartoon movie short of the Three Little Pigs singing "Who's Afraid of the Big Bad Wolf?" and the top song of the year was "Stormy Weather."

Not that I knew any of this at the time, of course.

But I did know, even as a baby, that I had been born into a world of music.

All of my people on both sides of my family were musical people as far back as I know. I am including my Indian blood—which I got from my mother—as being musical. If you ever spent the night dancing and chanting in a huge circle with 15,000 Indians, like I did when they made me Indian of the year in the spring of 1987 in Anadarko, Oklahoma, you would understand how powerfully musical Indians are.

My mother's family was the Greenhaws of Arkansas and Tennessee. They were talented bootleggers and moonshiners as well as musicians. My mother told me that her folks used to run hideouts in the mountains where outlaws could come and find safety. When I was little, I would daydream about Billy the Kid hiding out with my mother's family. My mother was a very strong woman, a beautiful woman. She had long hair and an Indian profile like Bobbie's and mine. Sometimes, if it was necessary for their survival, the Indians in the Greenhaw family would claim to be Mexicans. Whether they were Indians or Mexicans makes no difference to me—I would be just as proud either way—but if you've ever seen an Indian head nickel you've got a pretty good idea of what I look like side-on with my hair down.

The other side of the family—my daddy Ira's side—was totally different than the Greenhaws, but they were even more musical. My granddaddy on Ira's side was William Alfred Nelson. He'd made it through the second grade before he had to quit school to work in the fields. He married Nancy Elizabeth Smothers in the year 1900. The Ozarks in those times were full of English and Irish who were moving west in large numbers now that the Indians had been thrown off their land by the U.S. Army. These English and Irish immigrants like the Nelsons brought their folk music with them from the old country. They had a tradition as storytellers and singers and dancers and fiddle players. I believe in reincarnation and the laws of Karma. If I could have chosen as a soul about to be reborn, I would have chosen to come into the family that produced me. It wasn't an easy life I was reborn into, but it was the right one for me.

I never had any problem understanding why my parents split up. Myrle hit the road to get out of Abbott when I was six months old. Ira took off for Fort Worth a couple of years later. But they would come back to visit us and it was easy, even for a child, to see why they couldn't live together. Myrle was smart, flashy, full of energy, sharp-tongued, and beautiful. She was a dancer and a card dealer and a waitress, and she loved the road and one honky-tonk after another. Ira was a handsome guitar picker, so naturally he attracted the ladies. But Ira wasn't much for long-distance travel. He loved his life playing music in the beer joints, but he had another aptitude that has totally escaped being passed on to me. Ira was a master mechanic, like his daddy. Ira became the top mechanic at the Frank Kent Ford Company in Fort Worth. My mother could never have stuck it out as the wife of a Fort Worth mechanic who played music on weekends. Myrle had to be moving on. A child could see it.

Dad and Mom Nelson filled our house with music. They studied music by kerosene lantern. Granddad would put me in his lap and teach me to sing "Polly Wolly Doodle All the Day" when I was barely out of diapers. They pushed Bobbie and me into music and into performing.

I really don't believe that our grandparents expected us to do anything but play music. Our dad, Ira, felt at some point in my life that I should give up a lot of that music bullshit and go find a job to support my family. Ira didn't think I was a good enough musician to go on, and that's not to say anything against him. It was his own personal opinion, and there were plenty of people who agreed with him. One problem my dad had was he couldn't learn to pick guitar behind me. My style was nothing like his. He was on the beat, and to him it sounded like I was playing all over the place.

Bobbie and I developed perfect pitch. All this means is our grandparents trained us to reproduce the memory of how many vibrations were passing through the tunnels between our ears. Music is vibrations. A housefly, for example, hums in the F key in the middle octave of your piano. Hit that key and hear it for yourself. The sense of pitch changes with the number of vibrations. A B-flat is 400 cycles of vibrating molecules, G is something else. You might hit a Bach note at 415 or hear the Austin Symphony playing at 440. Perfect pitch is when you can remember these vibrations and go back to them any time.

The most powerful influence in my early life was Granddaddy Nelson. Along with teaching us music, he and Mama Nelson tried to raise us to be solid Methodists and obedient kids. They taught us if we ever took a drink of booze or smoked a cigarette or went dancing we were doomed to hellfire. This never did make sense to me, but a little kid was supposed to believe that his grandparents and the Methodist Church knew all about heaven and hell. I can't tell you how many Sundays I would be singing in the choir in front of all those nice, churchgoing folks, and my heart would be sad because I was thinking I was going to fry in hell because I had already drunk beer and smoked grapevine, cedarbark, and coffee grounds. It didn't seem right or fair, but how could a little kid disagree with the whole Methodist Church?

One day when I was five, I ran off from Daddy Nelson's blacksmith shop and went home without telling him. He was upset and worried about me. When he found me at home, he took his razor strap and hit me on the butt six or seven times. It hurt and it popped real loud and scared the daylights out of me. I never ran off from Daddy Nelson again.

At the age of six, I got my first real guitar. Daddy Nelson put it in my hands. It was a Stella they bought out of a Sears catalogue. The strings were about an inch off the neck. My fingers would bleed from playing it. He gave me a chord book that had the basic simple major and minor guitar chords in it. I would watch Daddy Nelson make a D chord, and then I would take the guitar and he would put my fingers on the same notes, the same frets. I learned the D, A, and G chords—the three chords you have to know to play country music— from Daddy Nelson. I picked up the C and F chords later as I progressed. If I was teaching a child to play the guitar today, I would do it exactly like Daddy Nelson did. Once the kid learns these and can hit them nice and clear any time he wants to, then he can play almost any song you can think of.

I hated music lessons when they interfered with me going outside and playing games. I wouldn't sit there and learn to read music and learn theory like Bobbie did. I wish I had, so I would know more about what I'm doing these days, but Bobbie learned it all. She is a very accomplished musician.

After a while we didn't need to be pushed to perform. You only had to hold still a minute and the Nelson kids would play you a concert. But at first we were both real shy about getting up in front of people. Bobbie and I are still shy deep down, but not when it comes to performing music.

The only time in my life I ever had stage fright, I was four years old.

I couldn't play an instrument then, but I suppose our grandparents knew stage fright was something we would have to conquer, the sooner the better. They gave us elocution lessons and taught me a poem to recite in front of a crowd. I'll never forget the scene or the poem. Nothing that bad has ever happened to me since.

It was an all-day gospel-singing picnic where I made my public debut. I had on a little white sailor suit trimmed in red, with short pants. I loved that sailor suit. But while I was waiting for my performance to begin, I was very nervous and started picking my nose. I got a forefinger up in my nostril, and stuck a thumb up there, got to picking my nose real thoroughly, concentrating on it—and first thing I knew my nose was pouring blood.

I heard a voice saying, "And now here's little Willie Nelson." Blood ran down my chin and dripped down the front of my white suit. It wouldn't stop. I was scared and embarrassed.

I stepped up in front of the crowd and recited:

> *What are you looking at me for?*
> *I ain't got nothing to say.*
> *If you don't like the looks of me,*
> *You can look the other way.*

It was hilarious to everybody but me. I wanted more than anything to get out of there. I had learned an important show-biz lesson—when you finish your act, get out of Dodge.

Anyhow, I have never been scared performing on the stage since that day. What could possibly be more horrible than a four-year-old reciting a poem with blood gushing out of his nose onto his sailor suit?

I've performed during barroom brawls, stabbings, and shootings. I've performed for presidents and royalty, for packed houses in Las Vegas and Reno, for crowds of 100,000 in outdoor stadiums. Sometimes I've been too drunk or too high to know what I was doing up there, but, since that day, I've never been scared of guitar picking or singing.

Daddy Nelson came down sick when I was going on seven years old. They said at first he had a cold, and then it became the flu, and then they were whispering he had pneumonia. But I wasn't worried. Daddy Nelson was a giant in my eyes. Nothing could hurt this noble, powerful man. All of a sudden he was gone. It was the first time Bobbie and I ever encountered what they call death.

I didn't know what to make of it. I think I was sad because the whole family naturally was weeping and moaning, everybody crying. It was an almost unbearable situation. It's not that I don't think you should grieve for loved ones who die. I just knew, even then, that there were things more terrible than death, that death is not necessarily bad.

Maybe I knew at that early age that death is just an illusion. Maybe I believed in reincarnation. But I think it was even more basic than that. I had learned in Sunday school about heaven and hell. If you were a good person, when you died you went to heaven, which is a beautiful place. From the way my grandfather treated me and everybody around him, I knew he was a very good man. If heaven was the greatest place imaginable, with streets of gold, I couldn't see the necessity of getting so upset. My mother and my dad had divorced way before that point, and I hadn't even had time to grieve for the loss of a mother and a daddy, much less my grandfather.

Our separation from Mother and Daddy seemed worse than a death because they were still out there in the world but they weren't with me and Bobbie where they were supposed to be.

After Daddy Nelson died I started writing cheating songs. I was writing songs about infidelity and betrayal, at the age of seven, long before you could sing such songs in Texas. There was heartbreak in all my early songs—a lot of you-left-me-but-I-want-you-back-again.

CHAPTER THREE

I t was 1939 when Daddy Nelson passed on. Superman and Batman were my comic book heroes. *Gone with the Wind* and *The Wizard of Oz* were playing the movie houses in Dallas. There was a World's Fair in New York. The *Fort Worth Star-Telegram* said Hitler invaded Poland, whatever that meant.

But the most important thing to Bobbie and me was we got our first radio.

It's impossible today to understand what a big event that was. The radio opened up the world to us. A godlike presence came into our home and our lives.

We heard Bob Wills singing "San Antonio Rose" on the Philco. It was a number-one hit. Little Orphan Annie was giving away decoder badges on the radio. You could turn the dial and hear songs like "Over the Rainbow" and "Deep Purple." We listened to Kay Kyser's Kollege of Musical Knowledge and laughed at his comic, Ish Kabibble.

Grandmother and Bobbie listened to soap operas like *Stella Dallas* and *Gal Named Sunday* and *Ma Perkins*. On sick days when I stayed home from school with mumps or measles or whooping cough, I listened to all the soaps. It was great when I wasn't real sick, just sick enough to get Mama Nelson to take my temperature and give me some ice cream. When everybody got sick of me being sick, they'd leave the house and I'd crank up the volume on the radio and twist the dial and the radio would put wings on my imagination and fly me to places I had never dreamed of.

I'm not sure why we didn't have a radio while Daddy Nelson was alive. Maybe he didn't believe in it.

After he was gone, our grandmother couldn't afford to keep us in the two-story house Bobbie and I were born in, so we moved to a smaller place that today I guess people would call a shack. But I didn't know it was a shack. Like most other families in Abbott, we had an outhouse and a water well. We never had a telephone all the years I was growing up there. You could see the bare earth through the floor planks. We pasted *Fort Worth Star-Telegram* newspapers on the walls to keep the wind from blowing through. In some places we had a layer of *Star-Telegrams*, covered by a layer of wallpaper, covered by another layer of *Star-Telegrams*. If there was nothing else to do, I could read the walls.

I would lie in my bed and look through the cracks in the roof and watch the stars. When it rained we put buckets down to catch the rainwater and used it for washing our hair. Everybody knew rainwater was the best for washing hair.

There had been a serious family conference after Daddy Nelson's funeral about who we should live with. Bobbie and I didn't want to leave Mama Nelson. We did not want to be anywhere else and we refused to be split up. We'd been with our grandmother all our lives. She lived and breathed for us, worked for us, gave us her undivided attention. We were allowed to stay in our own little home with her, and we were happy.

By the time I reached the first grade I was a confirmed believer in the customs of Abbott boyhood, codes as definite as those of *Ivanhoe*'s knights. You showed respect to women and were halfway afraid of girls. If any boy insulted your sister or stood in your way in a challenging fashion, it was your duty to kick his ass. If you didn't, he would definitely kick yours.

Soon as I knew how to lick a stamp, I started sending off for all these books on self-defense that were advertised in *Batman* and *Superman*. Since I had to fight a lot—and I liked it—I wanted to be good at it. I got all the books on jujitsu and judo, which were the main martial arts of the time. I've always been interested in martial arts. Twenty-five years later I took kung fu classes where I learned how to let things slide instead of trying to act macho. Kung fu taught me about patience. I learned I didn't need to jump to get in fights.

All the great teachers have said we can't handle power unless we learn to love. But this concept was considered pure chickenshit when I was a boy in Abbott. No matter what size you were in Abbott, if you let anything at all slide, you were a sissy. A sissy could not possibly avoid a fight.

If somebody said, "Hey, Booger Red, I hear you said my ears are too big. Maybe you'd like to pull 'em off?" and I said, "No, indeed, I never mentioned your ears and in fact consider them pretty normal-looking," I wouldn't get any credit for patience.

If he says, "My ears ain't as big as your sister's boobies" and I say, "You're right," I don't get credit for truthfulness.

When he'd come back with "Your feet stink so bad it makes my uncle sick across the road, you yellow turdknocker," and I'd say, "Kiss my ass," by the time he'd say, "It looks too much like your face," I would have had to turn into the Incredible Hulk to regain my status in the pecking order.

So instead of going through all that, I'd just land the first lick. I rushed at chances to fight. I had a real hot temper. At morning recess you might challenge a kid to meet you after school. The news would be all over the school in ten minutes: Booger Red and Johnny are going to fight after the bell. Sometimes the teachers would hear about it and put boxing gloves on me and Johnny and let us fight in front of everybody.

But usually I'd meet my opponent in a vacant lot with a crowd around, and after the first punch or two we would go to wrestling. Maybe I had stung the kid with the first blow, and then I got a headlock on him. I pushed his face down in the dirt and said, "You take it back?" Usually he didn't until I choked him some more. When he finally took it back, I said, "You give?" When he gave up to my satisfaction, I would rise and dust off my clothes, hoping I hadn't torn my shirt—which could mean a *real* ass whipping—and stand proud as my opponent walked off, crying. Not only had I won approval, I also had one less kid I'd have to fight.

Every time a new kid came to town, you had to try him before he tried you. The score had to be settled constantly. The way to go straight to the top of the pecking order and avoid dozens of fights at lower levels was to call out the toughest guy in school and whip his butt.

Naturally, romance goes along with fighting. The first girl I fell in love with was Ramona Stafford in the first grade. She was beautiful. She had long hair, and she was tall and thin. I tried to talk to her but I was pretty bashful. She knew I liked her, though, and she liked me.

Ramona and I went to the Texas State Fair in Dallas where I took her through the Tunnel of Love. I put my arm around her. Was I nervous! You drape your arm on the seat in back of her, not daring to touch her, and then slowly you reach over and kind of brush her coat with your arm and look over to see if she's getting ready to slug you.

We went through the Tunnel of Horrors, where we screamed and —yes!—*hugged* each other! Lord, it felt like an electric charge to hug Ramona Stafford.

I used to hate to ask girls to dance because I'd been told no a couple of times, and I didn't like that at all. So I was pretty shy with girls until I started playing the guitar. When I was up on stage, I didn't have to talk to the girls. I could watch the whole evening progress in front of me and see who was left at the end of the dance. A few years later, the girls would be drunk when the evening was over, so it was easier to talk to them after the show.

Life's not so much different now from when I started playing the guitar for girls at age seven. It's the same line, just different phases.

The old tabernacle stood between Mama Nelson's house and the intersection that separated the Baptist and Methodist churches.

The tabernacle had a wood frame with vines growing on it—morning glory and sweet-smelling honeysuckle—and people sat on benches on the dirt to hear the music and the preaching. Us kids would move the benches out on the grass to play marbles between services. Those were great nights at the tabernacle, listening to the singing. The nights were always full of lightning bugs, winking in the sky like thousands of tiny flashlights. I'd get so sleepy and so comfortable I would doze off before the preaching was over. Then when I heard the singing I would wake up and join in.

I was sprinkled in the Methodist Church when I was real small. The Baptists used to say they waited until kids got old enough to make up their own minds about the Church before they got submerged in the baptismal tank. But the Methodists sprinkled sacred water on your head and saved your soul as early as possible. I was one of those kids who kept going down front when the preacher called for converts at the end of each sermon. I'd see somebody next to me start to the front, and, well, there I'd go again. I joined the Methodist Church at least thirty times when I was a kid. Every time I'd do something bad, I'd go join the Church again. I'd walk down to the front and renounce my sins and ask Jesus Christ to come into my heart and make a date for another sprinkling, and all of a sudden

I had a new slate in the eyes of the Church. Then I'd slip off and smoke a long strip of cedarbark rolled up in a newspaper—and suddenly I was back facing the fiery furnace again.

Each time I went to the front and rededicated my life, I wanted to leave my sins with God and walk away clean. Scot-free. Except I never felt scot-free. I felt like, *wait a minute, that wasn't enough payment for all my sins.* I felt I shouldn't have got off so easy. I mean, the Church had let me off, but I hadn't let myself off.

That was the real problem—learning to let myself off.

From the first moment I heard voices on the radio, I was practically hypnotized.

Working in the cottonfields I heard migrant pickers singing—the blacks would be singing in one field, the Mexicans singing nearby, us local hands singing our own stuff. It was an awesome sound, all those voices blending, and it sure taught me the blues.

But the radio was my real education.

Much as I love jazz and am knocked out by a good jazz player who knows what he's doing, like Django Reinhardt or Jackie King—I confess a lot of "modern jazz" sounds like rehearsal noise to me—the radio taught me I was born to country music. My fingers continually turned the dial, bringing in big band dance music from the Aragon Ball Room in Chicago and Tin Pan Alley music, Hoagy Carmichael and Johnny Mercer, Bing Crosby, jazz from the powerful station in New Orleans that covered the whole country.

My fingers, though, stopped the dial at country music.

The Grand Ole Opry was a necessity on Saturday night. In the daytime I'd listen to the Light Crust Doughboys from the Baker Hotel in Mineral Wells. "We are the Light Crust Doughboys from Burrus Mills," they would sing. Hank Thompson had a show on WACO there in Waco at noon, and I listened to it every day. I loved Lefty Frizzell, Bob Wills, Floyd Tillman, Leon Payne, Hank Williams, Bill Boyd and the Cowboy Ramblers.

A skinny kid named Frank Sinatra started on *Your Hit Parade* when I was ten years old. Sinatra's style caught my attention at once. I listened to his phrasing and admired his breath control. Somebody had taught him how to breathe.

But the same year Sinatra joined *Your Hit Parade,* 1943, a fellow called Ernest Tubb landed on the Grand Ole Opry, and the search was all over for me—I had found my first singing hero. They called him "The Texas Troubadour." He had a song called "Jimmy Dale," about his son who died, and it was one of the saddest songs I ever heard. Then there was "Walkin' the Floor Over You," which I loved and learned to play from the radio.

I could compare Ernest Tubb to Frank Sinatra, in that they both had distinctive styles that you wouldn't confuse with anybody else. I'd put Floyd Tillman in there with them. Floyd has an individual phrasing, a western swing-type jazz way of doing things.

Roy Acuff had his own style, too. I'll never forget his recording of "Great Speckled Bird," a truly mystical song that Mama Nelson used to sing to us. I think style is why a singer is either real popular or not. If you have your own style, it doesn't really matter whether you are technically a great singer. Hoagy Carmichael, Johnny Mercer—those guys were not great singers, but they were capable of singing a song and getting their message across a lot better than a lot of good singers.

Ernest Tubb says the two most important things for a singer are clarity of thought and individual style. He says there are thousands of people who can sing on the beat but not many with a clarity of message. If you don't say your words plain, like Ernest always did—you could understand every word he sang—then you damn sure can't sell them a song.

All my songs have been very simply stated, right from the beginning. How much cleaner can you get than "Hello Walls"?

While I was getting involved with the radio and with learning to perform, my daddy Ira was getting himself married again and starting a new family.

Ira had picked up a couple of girls hitchhiking to Fort Worth, and by the time they arrived he had decided he would marry one of them, Lorraine Moon.

I had the normal stepmother resentment toward Lorraine. She wasn't my real mother, so I had to get over seeing her living with my real father. But Lorraine liked me and was always good to me. As a matter of fact, I felt like I was her favorite, even of her own kids. She treated me like I hung the moon.

Come to think of it, women have always loved me and I've always loved them and gotten along real well with them—until I married them.

When I was in the sixth grade, I got my first professional gig.

It was with the John Raycheck Band there in Abbott. The whole Raycheck family—all fifteen of them—played in the band. They played polkas, shoddishes, waltzes—really fun songs to play—and they would have had more use for Harpo Marx on a classical harp than they had for me on guitar. I played a non-electric guitar in a band with fifteen horn players and drummers. There is no way the audience could have heard a single note from me. But I think the Raychecks thought I looked good sitting over there banging away.

Mama Nelson was horrified that I was playing music in a beer joint. She said, "Willie, I don't want you going on the road with your music. The road is full of temptations and pitfalls."

To her it was "going on the road" for me to ride six miles with the Raychecks from Abbott to West, where we played on weekends.

The Raychecks' Polka Band played in the SPJST Halls, the VFW Halls, all the Bohemian dance halls around West, Waco, and Ross. The Bohemians would drink beer and have a hell of a time. The old men would be back in another room playing dominoes, and the kids and the women would be out there dancing. Many of our songs sounded like a Mexican Hat Dance—*da da, da da, da da, da da da da da da da*. All them drunk Bohemians pounding the floor with their feet, and me on the stage whacking away at my guitar.

Grandmother Nelson started to relent about my career when she discovered I could pick up $8 or $10 a night playing the guitar. It would take me all week to make that much money working in the fields. So Mama Nelson reluctantly let me do it because we needed the money.

For my part, since I had already fucked up more ways than God would let me get by with and wasn't even ten years old yet, I had in mind that the sky was the limit. You couldn't go to hell more than once, could you?

My mother Myrle had been on the West Coast, working her way through the Pacific Northwest. She had married another husband and divorced him, too. He couldn't keep up with her.

My mother and I are just alike.

I never saw my mother when she wasn't having a good time, laughing, telling jokes. She loved to cook. After I got my own band and went on the road, Mother loved for me to bring the whole band to her house in Yakima, Washington, where she finally settled down. The Northwest meant something strong to my mother. It was about as far as she could go from Searcy County, Arkansas, without jumping in the ocean.

In later years, we'd play Yakima, Spokane, Seattle, and we'd always go to Mother's house and have dinner. Bring everybody, was my mother's outlook. Take all the buses and line them up out there, and everybody get off. It didn't matter whether it was me or Kris or whoever it was—she always loved Ray Price above nearly everybody —Mother would stay up all night and cook and drink and carry on.

When she married her third and last husband, Ken—they came to see Bobbie and Mama and me in Abbott when I was about ten to tell us the news—Mother found something that made her happy and at peace with her wanderlust.

I guess I was in my twenties or thirties when I got this letter from my mother:

Dear Willie,

I fully realize that no wealth or position can endure, unless built upon truth and justice. Therefore I will engage in no transaction which does not benefit all whom it affects.

I will succeed by attracting to myself the forces I wish to use and the cooperation of other people. I will induce others to serve me, because of my willingness to serve others.

I will eliminate hatred, envy, jealousy, selfishness and cynicism by developing love for all humanity because I know that a negative attitude toward others can never bring me success. I will cause others to believe in me because I will believe in them and in my self.

I will sign my name to this formula, commit it to memory, repeat it aloud once a day with full faith that it will gradually influence my thoughts and actions so that I will become a self reliant and successful person.

> Myrle M. Harvey
> Rt. 8 Box 291 D
> Yakima, Washington 98908

And, God love her, that's the person she was.

Funny How Time Slips Away

Well, hello there, my it's been a long, long time.
"How'm I doin'?" Oh, I guess that I'm doin fine.
It's been so long now and it seems that it was only yesterday
Gee, ain't it funny how time slips away.

How's your new love, I hope that he's doin' fine.
Heard you told him that you'd love him till the end of time.
Now, that's the same thing that you told me, seems like just
   the other day.
Gee, ain't it funny how time slips away.

Gotta go now, guess I'll see you around,
Don't know when tho', never know when I'll be back in town.
But remember what I tell you, that in time you're gonna pay,
And it's surprising how time slips away.

CHAPTER FOUR

I started writing poems when I was five years old. I called them poems because I hadn't yet learned to communicate the melodies I was hearing inside of me. My poems were songs without melodies.

After I learned to play the guitar, at the age of six, I thought of the songs I composed as poems with melodies. I'm not sure whether I'm a poet or a songwriter. But I do think the first poems I wrote would have turned out to be songs had I known how to set down their melodies.

I was a serious songwriter by the age of eight. One day when I was about eleven, already a veteran of the Bohemian polka band circuit, I was thumbing through a stack of songbooks when the idea struck me that I should have a songbook of my own. Jimmie Rodgers had a songbook. Hank Williams had a songbook. Johnny Mercer and Hoagy Carmichael had songbooks. Roy Acuff had a songbook. Obviously there should be a Willie Nelson songbook. This, I decided, would be my brochure. I would hand it out to show people what I had written.

I chose the straighforward title *Songs by Willie Nelson*, which I artfully printed on the front cover. For the back side of the songbook, I drew a lariat intertwined with the words "Howdy, Pard." Then I drew eight little cowboy hats on the cardboard and bound the book together with string. Once it was finished, I realized this was not meant for the public. I just wanted to keep it on the table with the songbooks by Jimmie Rodgers and the others I admired.

I haven't seen the songbook but a couple of times in forty years and yet I remember every lyric to every song in it as if I had written them yesterday. Ain't it funny how time slips away?

Looking at the songbook now, I see that at the age of eleven I was already a show-business kind of guy, a kid from Abbott claiming to be from the big town—Waco.

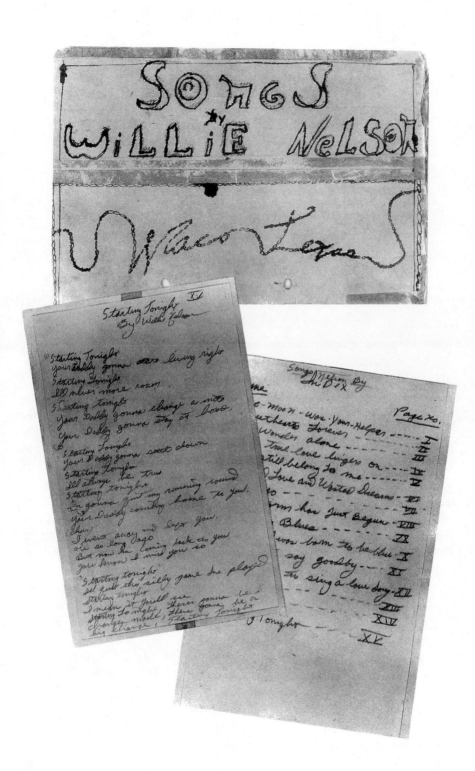

CHAPTER FIVE

A few years ago Waylon Jennings was pissed off at me over something or other. Flying down to Austin one day, Waylon wrote a song that went "It don't matter who lives in Austin, hoss, Bob Wills is still the king." Waylon sang it in public for the first time at the Austin Opera House before a crowd that had jammed in there shoulder to shoulder so tight that even the fire marshal couldn't get out. The crowd screamed with surprise when they heard it because they assumed Waylon was putting me down on my own turf. But the truth is, it was just a little jab because Waylon knew I agreed. Bob Wills *is* still the king.

Back in Abbott when I was thirteen years old, playing in the band that Bobbie's husband Bud Fletcher had put together, I actually went in pardners with Bud to book the great Bob Wills for a gig at the Oak Lodge, a beer joint with a dance floor over on Lake Whitney. It was the biggest thrill of my life to that point.

Bob Wills was such a big star that he looked like he was made out of wax. He was almost like an animation. Watching him move around, I thought: This guy ain't real. He had a presence about him. He had an aura so strong it just stunned people. I doubt very seriously if Bob was aware how much that had to do with his popularity. Everyone knows he wasn't a great fiddle player and he wasn't a great singer. But he did command respect, no argument about that. It was because of his charisma, his natural ability to take control. When he pointed at you, you *played*. Bob Wills was more than his music is what I'm saying. Elvis was the same. You had to see him in person to understand his magnetic pull. John the Baptist had the same pull. John the Baptist could sit in one spot for seven days and attract thousands of people.

The main thing is to attract people. I do it. I always thought that's what a musician was supposed to do—try to draw a crowd to hear you play. I started out thinking I want to draw attention to myself, and it was inevitable that it happened because of the power of my creative imagination.

Bob Wills taught me how to be a bandleader and how to be a star. He would hit the bandstand at 8 P.M. and stay for four hours without a break. One song would end, he'd count four and hit another one. There was no time wasted between songs. I learned from him to keep the people moving and dancing. That way, you don't lose their attention, plus your amplifiers drown out whatever the drunks might yell. The more you keep the music going, the smoother the evening will be.

Another thing he taught me was people came and paid their money to hear what they wanted to hear. Even if Bob had a mediocre band that night, the people knew his records and his radio shows and they heard what they *thought* Bob Wills sounded like. Whether he had a good night or a bad night, every night was a good night.

Western swing was just about the only kind of country music you could hear in the state of Texas until Hank Williams came along. Western swing was jazz, any way you want to look at it. It was jazz riffs inside a country lyric with a 4/4 beat behind it. That was the Bob Wills beat that made everybody get up off their ass and dance all night long.

There were probably a dozen road bands in Texas playing western swing when I was a kid. They all played Bob Wills songs. There was Adolph Hoffner, Easy Adams, Texas Tophand, Dewey Groom, Hoyle Nicks, Spade Cooley—he was California western swing—Olie Rasmussen and the Nebraska Cornhuskers with Teddy Wiles on feature vocals. They all copied Bob Wills. The bandleaders used the same structure as Bob Wills and the Texas Playboys. If Bob was carrying two fiddles, everybody else got two fiddles. If he had three, they'd go hire another fiddle player.

Bob sometimes carried a girl singer with him—like Ramona Reed or Laura Lee McBride—who could sing upbeat songs, not ballads, and yodel. He hired only female yodelers. Every musician's eye was on him because when he pointed his fiddle bow at you, you'd better be ready to jump in and do something. Bob allowed his musicians to take individual breaks and do their stuff. He tried to make stars out of everybody on the bandstand. He mentioned their names on records—like "Take it away, Leon," which made Leon McAuliffe famous. Bob didn't do many lead vocals. He'd stand there and smoke his cigar and wear his big white hat while Tommy Duncan sang, but everybody knew Bob was directing the band.

When you learned a Bob Wills song, you also learned the exact arrangements because they were so good. They were head arrangements of jazz riffs which the musicians would put together and add three- and four-part harmonies. The arrangements didn't change. They were group things that maybe Elton Shamblin or Tiny Moore or Johnny Gimble had as much to do with as Bob. He knew he wasn't the best musician, but he knew he was the best bandleader and could turn out the best sound. I tried to steal all the licks I could from his good musicians. I still do Bob's "Bubbles in My Beer" and "Stay a Little Longer."

There are a lot of old guys doing Bob's tunes nowadays. But young guys do them, too. Like Ray Benson and Asleep at the Wheel. They do Bob Wills songs exactly like Bob did. It's like going back forty years in time for me to hear Asleep at the Wheel.

When Bob went on the Grand Ole Opry he was already a huge star in Texas but not so much in Nashville. Nashville musicians in those days were mostly bluegrass. The Opry told Bob he couldn't use his drums, so he refused to appear. Finally they said he could use his drums. Then Bob went onstage with his cigar in his mouth. They told him not to smoke on the stage, and he walked off again. So far as I know, that was his one and only appearance on the Opry.

How western swing started was men like Milton Brown using jazz and blues musicians to play the songs they had written. It came out western swing. Before Bob Wills became popular, the big men were Lightnin' Hopkins, Jack Teagarden, Duke Ellington. White people used to go hear the black blues. Whites were the only ones who could afford to go to the clubs where the black blues musicians worked—and of course most of the clubs were segregated, anyhow. A white could go to a black club if he had the guts to buy a ticket, but a black couldn't go to a white club unless he wanted his head busted.

Poor Bob wasn't any better at business than I am. He had several managers and agents and bookers and thieves hanging around. He was too good-hearted ever to accumulate much. When you're the leader of a ten- or twelve-piece band, you have a lot of families to support. If Bob didn't work, a whole bunch of people didn't eat. There was always someone who needed money and Bob would always give it to them. He had more important things to think about than money. Bob finally died broke. I don't think it really bothered him to go out like that. He saw plenty of money in his life, but he didn't try to take it with him.

Probably he intends to come back and get it.

A musician always has periods of being between gigs, which means out of work. You've got to be very imaginative during times of no gigs. Up in Fort Worth in the fifties it wasn't all that uncommon for musicians to become gamblers or burglars or pimps or used car salesmen between shows. But there was no way to make a living out of crime in Abbott. They didn't allow crime in Abbott.

So one day I got one of my brilliant business ideas. I went to Frank Clements, who still cuts hair in Abbott to this day, and sugggested I set up a shoe-shine franchise in his barbershop. My gimmick was I would sing the song of the customer's choice after I polished his boots or shoes.

The way I figured it, my fame as an entertainer would spread, because downtown Abbott and the barbershop were on the Interurban line that ran from Dallas to Waco. The Interurban was a great thing, an electric train that carried people up and down Texas and back and forth between cities like Dallas and Fort Worth before the government started paving the country with interstate highways after World War II. As much as I love hopping into my car and driving fast and feeling free, the old Interurban was a cheap, easy way to travel. Go to Switzerland today and you'll find the country crisscrossed with electric trains like our old Interurban.

The Interurban Station in Abbott was close to the cotton gin as well as the barbershop, the cafe, the churches and the elementary school. I thought people would come pouring off the Interurban to do business and be drawn like flies to honey by the sound of my voice and the sharp crack of my shoe-shine rag.

After the first day's operation of Booger Red's Shine n' Sing, I went to Mr. Clements to collect my share of the gate.

He gave me fifty cents.

"This ain't right," I said. "You must owe me at least two dollars."

"Willie, I didn't even make two dollars today my own self," Mr. Clements said.

I closed up shop and went to work baling hay.

But Bud Fletcher, who was tall and good-looking and slicker than bacon grease, started talking club owners into hiring our band on a fairly steady basis. We would play any kind of music the club wanted, whether we knew how or not. Sometimes we didn't succeed and were never invited back. Usually, though, we were a hit. If we didn't know the music they requested, we would fake it. It wasn't that hard. Bud didn't know hardly any music at all, but Bobbie knew nearly everything from "Stardust" to "My Bucket's Got a Hole in It" and I was learning more music every day.

Bobbie and I had been well grounded in music by our grandparents. Dad and Mom Nelson told us how the fiddle and the mandolin and the guitar had always dominated the old folk music gatherings like sewing bees or barn raisings or picnics. The oldest country music recordings I heard were fiddle bands like Sid Tanner and the Skillet Lickers, and the Fiddling John Carson group. When solo vocalists started making records, they didn't seem to care much about instrumentation. They were backed by just a guitar or two and maybe a fiddle. It wasn't until the 1930s that you heard a full band playing on a country record.

Musicians moved from the country to the cities and took their country music with them but wrote songs about city life. When they returned to the country, they brought their experience of Memphis blues or New Orleans ragtime and jazz or maybe the wild mix of music styles of Dallas's famous Deep Ellum Street.

It never occurred to my grandparents that music could make money. Except for minstrels or traveling medicine shows, music was played for fun and for spiritual purposes. The radio and the recording industry changed all that.

No single person did more to make country music popular all over America than Ralph Peer of RCA Victor. Peer was a New Yorker, but he took portable recording machines into the South and set up studios in hotel rooms. Peer was the first to record Fiddling John Carson, who surprised RCA Victor by selling a lot of records and showing there was a big audience for country music. Peer set up his studio in Bristol on the Tennessee-Virginia border and invited country performers to audition. Over a period of what might be the four most important days in country music history, Peer made the first recordings of both the Carter Family and Jimmie Rodgers.

Jimmie Rodgers was the original country superstar. He died of tuberculosis the year I was born. But even before Jimmie Rodgers, a fellow who called himself Vernon Dalhart picked up a national audience on RCA Victor. Dalhart grew up in East Texas as Marion

Slaughter and went to New York City to record for Edison as an opera singer. He convinced RCA Victor to let him make what was then known as a "hillbilly" record. Slaughter chose a stage name by combining two Texas towns—Vernon and Dalhart—and cut the two songs "Wreck of the Old 97" and "The Prisoner's Song." That record sold an unbelievable six million copies. Vernon Dalhart went on recording for every new record company that popped up, singing under twenty or thirty different names.

The big radio stations started "barn-dance" programs on WSB in Atlanta, WLS in Chicago, WBAP in Fort Worth, and WSM in Nashville, where the Grand Ole Opry began in 1925. Most of it was live music in the early days, before the radio stations and record companies realized they weren't competitors but were, instead, in bed together. By the time I started living with my ear against our Philco, the giant X radio stations were in full swing just across the border in Mexico. These stations, which all had X in their call letters, were 150,000 watts. Their signals reached all over the United States and much of Canada. The X stations broadcast country and gospel music along with a crowd of evangelist preachers. You could tune in any time of night and hear the Carter Family, the Chuck Wagon Gang, or the Stamps Quartet.

They didn't start calling it country western music until the singing cowboy movies of the thirties and forties. This was not real country or cowboy or western music, for the most part, that Gene Autry or Roy Rogers and Dale Evans or the Sons of the Pioneers sang around their movie campfires. These were movie tunes by pop songwriters who tried to sound country. But it all began to blend with the real country music of Red Foley and Ernest Tubb, and with the bluegrass music of Bill Monroe—who gave bluegrass its name from his band the Bluegrass Boys—and the innovative banjo picking of Earl Scruggs, and by the fifties you hardly ever heard us called hillbilly musicians.

By the 1970s Gramm Parsons, a country boy, came along playing rock and roll with a country heart. The Flying Burrito Brothers and the Eagles played rock and roll country. The Band did country lyrics in a sort of rock and roll hillbilly style. We got the Allman Brothers, and my friend Leon Russell, and God knows who all else, and by now country music is mixed up in everything.

But it was Bob Wills who put it all together for me, and it was our old Philco radio that taught it to me.

As Waylon said, Bob Wills is still the king.

In high school I loved sports and won letters from the Abbott Fighting Panthers in baseball, basketball, football, and track. I didn't have a dream, though, of going on with an athletic career and playing third base for the New York Yankees. Staying up late in honkytonks was not the ideal way for a young athlete to keep in shape.

I mopped the cafeteria floors in school for a free lunch, and Bobbie and I held a variety of odd jobs around town. For a while we worked the night shift as Abbott's telephone operator—actually it was Bobbie's gig, but she cut me in on it—which was interesting, because we listened in on all the conversations.

Bud Fletcher kept getting us more and more jobs. We went from playing places that seated thirty people into huge halls like the Scenic Wonderland in Waco. Bud booked us in there for the gate. The Scenic Wonderland held 3,000 people. We drew our usual number —about thirty—and didn't get invited back. But we were working.

Bobbie was still feeling guilty about playing music in joints that sold liquor. It was so much against the way we were raised. In the eyes of the real staunch church people, we were sinful.

At that time a lot of people thought professional musicians were kind of a shiftless lot in a way, like actors. It was like on some of the old military bases where they had signs that said *Sailors and dogs stay off the grass*. The same thing applied to musicians.

But when Bud wangled us a job playing on KHBR radio in Hillsboro, I thought I had reached the highest stardom this world could offer. This was the ultimate. We had our own radio program, we were getting paid to play and sing on the radio, just like Ernest Tubb and my other heroes. I was famous, I thought. I was already a legend in my own mind. I was a teenager and people were asking for my autograph. My head started swelling immediately.

I thought I was a star because I was treated like one. If you're the only guy in town who can pick and sing, you receive the star treatment early in life. Same way right now. If you're the only guy in the barracks in the army who can pick up a guitar and sing a song, then in that particular barracks you're the star. A local star is just as happy as a national star. Maybe happier, because there's less responsibility.

I had found out early that a guitar would draw girls. I don't like to admit it, but if a girl baited her trap with sex, she'd catch me every time—and it's unlikely this will ever cease to work. As a teenager I already had a fan club. There was a group of girls who thought I was the greatest thing ever. They bought me a uniform, a nice Western suit, and paid for it themselves. They were like groupies. Everywhere I would play, they'd be there.

About this time I found another hero, a fellow named Pat Kennedy. Pat was a World War II veteran who had come back to Central Texas. He was shot up and pissed off. Pat was one of the first rebels that I remember, a real system-bucker. He told everybody in town where to get off. Pat didn't want to do a damn thing except listen to our band and give us advice. He was on disability. People in town made remarks about Pat not wanting to work for a living. Pat didn't give a shit what they thought. So what if they thought he was a no-good drunkard? He'd point at his ass and say, "You all line up and kiss old rosy." Pat did whatever he wanted to do. He seemed like he was old and grown up, but he was in his twenties, a pal of Bud Fletcher's. Pat would stay up all night and play dominoes and smoke cigarettes with me in a clubhouse we built that had a stove and a domino table in it. He would do anything. You could say, "Pat, why don't you just go tell old so-and-so he's a stupid horse's butt," and Pat would get right up and go tell them. I loved this guy.

He fell off a truck and killed himself.

I got out of high school and took a job trimming trees in East Texas with Zeke Varnon. I nearly went the way of Pat Kennedy much sooner than expected.

CHAPTER SIX

S uffering is the wrong use of the mind. The reason I have a bad experience is to teach me not to do it again. Generally the cause of the bad experience lies inside of my own self, in the way I am thinking, and so I bring it on myself. Like, for example, climbing forty feet up into an elm tree with a coil of rope over my shoulder. I didn't really have to do it. But just because the guy who was already up in the tree yelled down that he needed the rope, I decided to show the tree-trimming crew that I was the best athlete of the bunch.

I scooted up that tree like a monkey. It wasn't until I started back down, missed a grip, and found myself falling through the air that I realized this trip had not only been unnecessary, it was more than a little bit foolish.

As I fell I thought, well, Lord, I have done it again, and if You will bail me out one more time I will use the brains God gave me and devote my talents to the musical arts instead of work that You never intended me to do.

It had seemed like a good idea at the time to finance an old car with Zeke on a no-money-down deal in San Antonio and go to Tyler to become expert tree trimmers. This was in the summer of 1951. I was just out of high school. The Korean War had become real to me because of the draft. Now I believe there should be required national service for a year or so for all kids soon as they turn eighteen, with no exemptions. They don't have to go in the army. They could work in hospitals and parks or whatever. This would force kids to realize they have a working stake in our democratic government. I don't believe a democracy should have a totally professional military force. I believe the military should be in large number made up of people who don't want to be there and will help make the generals honest.

But when I drove to Tyler with Zeke, I was too young to understand this. All I knew was that I was 1-A in the draft, prime meat, and the politicians could throw my ass into the infantry and ship me off to war. President Truman had fired General Douglas MacArthur a month before my graduation. I heard MacArthur's "old soldiers never die, they just fade away" speech on the radio. I didn't know what the controversy was all about, but I liked the idea of a general getting fired if the president thought he was fucking up. If I was on my way to Korea, I wanted President Truman to put the best generals over there he could find.

But here I was falling through the air in Tyler and praying, and then I felt a blow as I bounced off a branch and crashed through smaller branches and tangled in some wires that slowed my fall.

I hit the ground and it knocked the wind out of me. My bad back that I'd gotten from baling hay struck me a punch above the right hip as I stood up and laughed and tried to make it look like, why, hell, I can fall forty feet any day, a tough rascal like me.

Inside a voice was telling me, Willie, don't you go back up in no trees, understand?

I walked off that job and enlisted in the air force for a four-year hitch.

This accomplished two things at once. It got me out of Tyler, and it solved the problem of the draft.

The navy didn't appeal to me. I could remember my sailor suit with the blood all over it, and I didn't want to be on the water all the time. The army or the marines didn't enter my thinking. I decided I wanted to be a jet pilot.

The first thing that happened at Lackland Air Force Base in San Antonio was they marched us down a road between rows of tents, heading us straight to the barbershop.

There were hundreds of tents. Everybody was living in tents because they didn't have barracks. Guys were sticking their heads out of the tents and yelling at us. Their heads had no hair on them. The guys were yelling, "You fucked up! You fucked up!"

I'd always had longer hair than other boys. I was a long-haired musician before hippies came along. I would let my hair grow for months, go to the barbershop and get it cut real short, and then let it grow a long time before I got it cut again. It was mainly to save money, but people called me a long-haired musician.

Marching down the road toward the barbers' tent at Lackland, my hair was long enough that if I let it come down over my eyes it covered my face. I brushed it straight back, and it hung down over my collar.

The air force barber sheared me like a sheep.

I had already learned enough about the air force to realize I wouldn't make a jet pilot. It took years of concentrated dedication to be a jet pilot. I just couldn't see my future at the controls of a jet. For one thing, I tend to be a little absentminded. An absentminded guy should not fly a jet.

I marched out of the barbers' tent with a billiard ball for a head, and I knew right then I had changed my mind about being in the air force. I started to figure how I could get out. During my physical, the doctors had spotted on the X rays that I had a lower back problem. I told them, "Yes, I hurt it baling hay." They made a note of it and sent me out to do my basic training.

Going through basic I didn't have much problem with my back because I was mainly getting up at 4 A.M. and doing a lot of running. I had been accustomed to going to bed about the time the air force expected me to get up. The training cadre sergeant would come out of the dark moving into our tent and blow his whistle and shout, "Drop your cocks and grab your socks! Rise and shine, you sorry shitasses!" We'd be off and running for the next sixteen hours.

But there was no lifting to speak of. I was used to running from my glory days with the Abbott Fighting Panthers. Marching didn't bother me a bit. I sort of liked the feeling when the whole platoon was marching in step and the cadre sergeant was calling out the cadence, "You had a good girl, but she left! You're right, she left!" Running long distances with a pack on my back wasn't so bad, either. I would see bigger guys falling out all around me, fainting and throwing up, and I would just grin and keep running. I made it through the obstacle courses—climbing ropes and crawling under barbed wire and all that—ahead of nearly everybody and would look back and see the field littered with the struggling bodies of guys who thought they were star athletes.

I finished basic at Lackland and was promoted to private first class. They gave me one stripe to sew on my sleeve. I had no sooner put my stripe on my khaki shirt than one of the guys smarted off about it. He said there wasn't no little redheaded fucker going to tell him what to do. It pissed me off. I hit him. He got up and hit me back. We got to fighting, knocking over cots and wrestling through the side of the tent.

The air force took my stripe away after one day. That was fine with me. I realized I didn't want to have leadership thrust on me by the military. I didn't want to become a squad leader or any such shit as that. I didn't want stardom in the air force.

They sent me to Shepherd Air Force Base in Wichita Falls for some additional basic training and then stuck us trainee graduates in a bus and hauled us to Scott Air Force Base in Illinois. They kept us at Scott while they tried to figure out what to do with us. "Relocation" is what they called it. All I did at Scott was play poker and run around and drink beer at the Post Exchange.

The air force decided I could go to further training as a regular airman, maybe wind up a tail gunner in a flight crew. Or I could go to the air police or to radar mechanic school or to the medics. I chose radar. They shipped me to radar school in Biloxi. I washed out. It was more mathematics than I could handle. After that, my choices were air police and medics. I didn't want to be no policeman, so I took the medics.

The medics also trained at Biloxi. Instead of teaching me brain surgery or something useful, the medics put me to lifting heavy boxes. My back gave out on me. It hurt real bad. The doctors took more X rays and found the same lower back problem they had found in the first place.

They kept me in the hospital for two or three months, taking more X rays like if they did it long enough my back would get well. I was able to get out of the hospital at night and go play guitar at the Airmen's Club in Biloxi. There were a lot more airmen at the club than there were girls. I didn't care for dancing with airmen. They weren't too pretty and some of them had two left feet. I snagged a few girls out of that club, but none of them was ever a candidate for Miss Mississippi.

An officer called me in to his office. He said, "Private Nelson, you have a lower back problem."

I said, "Yes sir," instead of saying, "No shit."

The officer said, "We are going to put you in the hospital and operate on your back."

I said, "No, I don't want you cutting on me."

"You won't let us fix your back? It's free, you know."

I said, "I wouldn't let you cut on my back for a million dollars," and I meant it.

"Well, we could give you a medical discharge," he said. "But you would have to sign a release so the air force won't be required to pay you disability, since you had this injury before you enlisted."

I said, "Could I use your pen? Where do I sign?"

After nine months in the air force, I was suddenly a civilian again. I rushed straight back to Abbott, put a band together, and started playing beer joints again.

I was eighteen years old and just about to fall madly in love.

Martha Jewel Mathews was tall, slender, black-haired, olive-skinned, just flat out the prettiest girl I had ever seen in my life. She was sixteen years old.

I didn't know if she was Indian or Mexican or what she was, but I was stone in love immediately. Martha was a little bit afraid of me at first. I had started staring at her when I'd seen her dance in dance halls. She knew who I was because usually I was up onstage singing to her. She knew I liked her although we hadn't said a word to each other. I guess my reputation had preceded me and Martha was kind of wary of hooking up with a guy who thought he had a future in show business.

Martha was a real lively party girl. She had a lot of friends and they danced a lot and were always going to the different dance halls around. Martha did love a good time, and we had plenty of them all over the country after we got together. Many of the stories people tell today about Martha and me, they dwell on the hellacious fights we had and the terrible things we did to each other. But there were good times, too, really sweet and wonderful times.

I met her at the drive-in where she was working as a carhop. Lord, looking at Martha parading around the parking lot in her short skirt made my hormones feel like the Flying Wallendas. Martha shot her dark eyes at me and said, hell no, she wasn't getting in no car with me and Zeke, us both drunk. So I borrowed Bud Fletcher's car a couple of nights later and picked her up.

Up close and comfortable, Martha dazzled me. I felt the kind of *in love* when you feel every minute away from your lover is agony. We struck that indescribably delicious moment when we both declared we were so much in love with each other that death couldn't tear us apart.

We ran off to Cleburne and got married.

Martha was sixteen when we married. My mother married at fifteen. My sister Bobbie married at sixteen. My daughter Lana got married at sixteen, and my daughter Susie got married at sixteen. Personally, I don't think that is so unusual. A lot of girls got married when they were young for a lot of different reasons, like to get away from the house early or because they wanted to start their own families. In those days there really wasn't much schooling required for girls. What they mainly wanted girls to learn was how to cook and keep house and be a wife. They didn't figure a woman had that much need for an education.

Martha and I moved in with Mama Nelson, that wonderful lady who was a rock Bobbie and I could run to for shelter. I got a job working at a saddle factory in the daytime, but I cut my fingers sewing stitches in the leather and that threatened my guitar-picking career, which was then not going so well. There wasn't enough money coming in to support Martha and me, and I couldn't put any more strain on Mama Nelson.

Martha and I had already started fighting. It wasn't over money, not at first. The fights were caused by young people being in love and being extremely jealous of each other. Anybody she would look at, I'd get pissed off. Anybody I'd look at, she'd get pissed off. Me being an entertainer, a singer in a beer joint, and Martha being a waitress, sometimes in the same beer joint, was the cause of many problems.

Plus, Martha and I were both drinking too much and seeing just how much we could do to each other and get by with it. That was a stupid test of somebody's love, we both know now. It had the ingredients for disaster if we didn't change our way of thinking.

I realized I had to take my Cherokee beauty out of Hill County if we were going to have any chance of this powerful love not tearing us both apart. There had to be someplace we could go where we could be together in some green and leafy place that would allow us to accentuate the positive and eliminate the negative, as the Johnny Mercer song says.

Where else? We packed up and hit the road for Eugene, Oregon. That's where my mother Myrle—now called Mother Harvey by the family after her lasting marriage to Ken—had established her latest nest.

I couldn't wait to show my mother what a beautiful, lively girl her boy had married.

The Chorus

MARTHA JEWEL MATHEWS

One story everybody thinks they know about Willie and me is the one about me catching him passed-out drunk and sewing him up in a bedsheet and then beating the hell out him with a broom handle.

For years I've been hearing and reading that story. People who've never so much as said hello to me or Willie tell that bedsheet story like they saw it with their own eyes. They just laugh and laugh, like, hey, that Martha, she was one tough cookie, wasn't she?

Well, it never happened.

How dumb would I have to be to try to sew Willie into a bedsheet? You know how long that would take to sit there and take stitch after stitch?

The truth is, I tied him up with the kids' jump ropes before I beat the hell out of him.

I scooted the jump ropes underneath him while he was asleep and knotted them up on top. I tied him up as tight as I could. The kids were waiting outside in our getaway car. I started whipping Willie pretty good, and he commenced yelling, and I was crying and cussing. Oh, it was quite a commotion, but nothing our neighbors at

Martha is Willie's first wife and the mother of Lana, Susie, and Billy.

Dunn's Trailer Park in Nashville hadn't heard coming out of our trailer before. Hell, we were just kids trying to deal with being married and having babies but no money and no home life to speak of—just one beer joint after another, sleeping under a different roof every few months, drinking way too much whiskey. Neither me nor Willie knew what to expect from marriage. We thought being young and in love was all we needed.

My mother didn't want me to marry because I was so young so Willie and I just decided to run off. We went to Cleburne and had a friend sign a paper that said I was the friend's sister and of legal age. Willie had a driver's license that showed he was nineteen, fresh out of the air force.

We went down to the basement of the courthouse. It was cold, but they had a big old wood stove fired up. The justice of the peace would stop and spit on the stove while giving us our vows.

"Do you, Martha Jewel Mathews take this"—ping, he'd spit—"take Willie Hugh Nelson"—spit again, sizzle. Willie and I started laughing at this judge standing there spitting on the stove. We thought that was the greatest.

Willie had a friend in Dallas who fixed us up with a deal to deliver a car out to Oregon, where Willie's mother, Myrle, was living. The only problem was we had to show $100 to the company that owned the car, to prove we were substantial people.

Of course we didn't have anywhere near $100. But Willie knew a fellow who drove a milk truck and carried money with him every day. He met us at lunchtime and loaned Willie $100. Willie showed the cash to the company and got the car. We chased down the milk truck, gave the $100 back, and lit out for the West Coast with a total fortune of $24. When you're young and in love, the last thing you worry about is money.

We rented a house and were going to live happy ever after. But we weren't making any money, and I got pregnant, and we drove back to Abbott to see what was going on in Texas. My folks said they didn't want to have anything more to do with me for running off so we moved in with Mom Nelson, Willie's grandmother. Willie started playing music in clubs on the weekends. He was drawing $26 a week on the GI Bill—that bought the groceries. In those days, you could eat good on $20 a week.

When I went into labor, Willie had been real sick with the flu for three days. He climbed out of bed and cranked up the car and drove me to the hospital in Hillsboro. The minute we got to the hospital, the nurse saw how sick Willie was and started taking his temperature and fussing over him. She gave him two shots while I laid there and suffered. Willie didn't smoke no pot back then and those shots made him high as a kite for about a day and a half while Lana was being born. That's no joke.

We took baby Lana back all the way out to Portland, where Mother Harvey was living. I got pregnant again. Willie found a job as a disc jockey on radio station KVAN in Vancouver, Washington. He was making a living, more or less, and playing music on weekends. Our daughter Susie was born in Vancouver.

But it became obvious the radio job and the weekend gigs weren't going to lead to where Willie wanted to go, so we decided to give Texas another shot. I was pregnant again by then.

Our son Billy was born in Fort Worth on May 21, 1958. We were living in our own place when we could afford one and with Willie's sister, Bobbie, when we couldn't.

It was about that time Willie and I started really getting into fights over money. Willie had never made enough money anywhere we were, and I worked hard as a waitress and didn't bitch about money. But now we had three little children to feed and put clothes on their backs.

I was trying to talk Willie into going to Nashville. I knew if there was any way for him to make it in music, we had to go to Nashville. I always worked as a waitress, anyway, and he stayed home to babysit during the week. On weekends when he played in a band, we usually didn't have a dollar to spend on babysitters. I wanted to go where Willie was playing. I wanted to get out and dance, have some fun. But we couldn't afford for me to do it and feed the kids, and we kept getting madder and madder at each other.

I Love Lucy was big on TV then. Friends said we reminded them of Lucy and Desi Arnaz, because of the way I'd do Willie. I would raise hell with the ornery asshole. He pulled his shit on me but I threw it back at him. One day we were sitting at breakfast eating biscuits and gravy that I'd made. Willie loved sausage with his biscuits and gravy, but we couldn't afford sausage that day. Johnny Bush, who later wrote "Whiskey River," was there, looking red-eyed and lousy. They'd been drunk a day or two. Willie was being a real smart-mouth, real nasty. So I just dipped a biscuit in the gravy bowl and planted it right in the middle of his whiskey face. Willie kept on eating like nothing had happened, with gravy running down his nose and chin. None of us laughed. That was awful, that nobody cared to laugh. Later when I threw the goldfish down the toilet, nobody laughed. It was just another bummer. Being broke for years on the road can ruin your sense of humor.

Willie finally took off for Nashville and left me in Waco with the kids. He moved in with Billy Walker and his wife, Boots. Willie and I kept fighting on the long-distance phone about one thing or another, but pretty soon I followed him to Nashville on a Greyhound bus with our three kids, three baby bottles, three little blankets, and all our stuff.

The Walkers had four little girls of their own, which made quite a crowd in their little house. Willie and I rented a mobile home at Dunn's Trailer Park out on Dickerson Road by the graveyard. There was a sign in front: TRAILERS FOR SALE OR RENT. You might recognize those words as the first line of Roger Miller's big hit song, "King of the Road."

I got a job at a bar called the Hitching Post right across from the Grand Ole Opry. Faron Young kept coming in there and all the girls just fell all over him. Faron thought this was the greatest thing in the world, because he had this big ego, being a star and all. I would never mention Willie to anybody. I figured Willie would get out on his own and make it, now that we were in Nashville. But one night Faron had been sitting in the Hitching Post for hours and hours. Finally, I said, "You know, my husband has written some pretty good songs. You could take time to listen to one of them."

Faron said, "I don't take time for nothing." Then he sat a while longer before he said "What is your husband's song about?"

I said, "It's called 'Hello Walls.' He's over at Tootsie's Orchid Lounge right now if you want to hear it.

"I ain't interested," Faron said, and he walked out.

Later that night a girl came across the street from Tootsie's and said, "Faron's over there listening to some cat from Texas. Boy, you ought to hear those songs this guy is singing."

Faron walked back into the Hitching Post and said, "Hey, I got me a new song called 'Hello Walls.' " The dumb ass still didn't connect me with Willie. But he went to the studio and cut "Hello Walls," and we began waiting for our royalties. It took a long, long time.

Billy Walker cut "Funny How Time Slips Away." Patsy Cline put out her hit of Willie's song "Crazy." We didn't mind at all that it was another singer, not Willie, who made a hit out of "Crazy." People started getting interested in Willie. But Willie was playing with Ray Price's band by then, going on the road with the Cherokee Cowboys, acting like he could play bass, and Willie's attitude was now that he had a job with Ray Price he didn't give a damn what anybody thought of his music. He couldn't be bothered, now that he had some hit songs. He acted so independent you might have thought he was the king of Spain. He'd do what he damn pleased and blow his money on hotel suites and airplanes if he wanted. Willie was being so damn cool it would make you throw up.

As Willie kept going on the road, our problems at home got worse and worse. Even if Willie hadn't been a musician, we might have had the same problems. But Willie being on the road all the damn time didn't make it smooth for us. At last enough money started coming in from the songs that a little seeped down to us before Willie could spend it. A little money seemed like a lot to me and the kids, and I was glad about it. I didn't realize how fast things were changing with Willie and me.

I got to know that anybody who has problems at home should not go to Nashville. I learned more in Nashville in our first year than I had learned in my whole life. Somebody goes to Nashville and the music people think, well, here's just another picker with a guitar in his hands. And nine out of ten of the pickers don't rise above that level. But you never know, do you?

On one of our early Christmases in Nashville, little Billy wanted a stick horse real bad. We couldn't find one and didn't have the money to buy one anyhow. All we had was a pot of soup that I fixed for Christmas dinner. I had to work until 3 A.M. on Christmas Eve. When I came home Willie was sitting there making a stick horse for Billy.

Willie cut off the straw of my broom. I had three pairs of underwear, and Willie took two of them and made a head for the stick horse. We couldn't afford a new broom. You should have seen Billy's face when he saw that stick horse, he was so happy and proud. It really was a perfect stick horse.

A fellow named Bif Collie and his wife Shirley came to Nashville. Bif was so friendly, and he was going to plug Willie's records. He was totally devoted to Shirley, who was a singer. I mean, you could see how in love with her Bif was. And I thought, why don't Willie treat me as good as Bif treats Shirley?

I'm psychic in a lot of ways. From the beginning, I felt there was something about Shirley that she was after Willie. Bif went back to California. Willie didn't come home that night or the next day or the next night. Then somebody told me Willie and Shirley were staying at a hotel in downtown Nashville, and they wasn't accepting calls.

I went straight to the hotel. I did everything I could to get in that room. But the hotel people wouldn't even let me on the same floor as Willie and Shirley, because they knew I was going to tear the place up.

Willie was always messing around with somebody and he'd come home and tell me he hadn't done doodly shit. He'd have lipstick smeared from one end to the other. I done everything to stop him. I hid in the trunk of the car and nearly smothered to death. I would jump on the hood of the car and ride two or three blocks before he shook me off. I did everything but threaten him with a gun.

Willie came in off a trip on Ray Price's bus. Somebody had already called and said, "Shirley's with Willie on that bus. Don't you dare meet it."

Ray always parked the bus at the service station on the highway. I was just home from having surgery in the hospital. Willie didn't send so much as one flower for that. He came sailing in the house and says, "I want the keys to the car."

I said, "You ain't getting no keys to no car to go nowhere with no bitch."

The musicians on the bus thought Willie was going to whip me to get the keys. But he knew better than to try it. In a head-to-head fight, I stood an even chance of whipping Willie, and had proved it.

Like one night I had been working as a bartender at the Wagon Wheel, and I got mad and started throwing glasses at Willie. One of them hit the railing on the stairs and crashed and cut Hank Cochran's face pretty bad. Ruined his acting career, I guess. That fight went on for an hour. Somebody hit poor Ben Dorsey in the back of the head and put him in the hospital. I ran into Ben on the street a few days later and said, "Why, Ben, what happened to your head?" He told me he'd been in a bad car wreck. I said, "I want you to remember what you just told me. It was a car wreck, and don't you forget it."

Willie and I were in Fort Smith, Arkansas, shortly before the end. I knew the end was near. I had been feeling sad the whole trip, because I knew, well, this was it, there wasn't going to be any more. I had driven to Fort Smith with two or three of the wives of the musicians in Ray Price's band, feeling sad all the way. When I got to Willie's room, the phone was ringing off the wall. I answered it.

Some gal said, "Do you know what time Willie and I are supposed to eat?"

I said, "I don't know, but I sure will ask him. Leave me your number." And she did. It made me furious.

Willie acted like he didn't know the girl who had called. We argued and carried on out back of the club where they were playing. I had a whiskey bottle in my hand and started swinging it. Me and Willie had a hell of a fight.

The police came and hauled me off to jail. Not Willie. Me. Because I was whipping Willie over the head with a whiskey bottle. First damn time in my life I ever been to jail.

Jimmy Day, who played in Ray's band, was waltzing up and down in front of the jail cell saying, "Marsha, Marsha, sweetheart, everything's gonna be all right." Jimmy always called me Marsha because he said Martha was too old-fashioned a name for me. Anyhow, I was crying. There was one bed in there that I was afraid to sit on, and one old toilet I didn't want to get anywhere near. I was scared and upset, and I heard Willie tell the jailer, "We're with Ray Price. We'll pay the fine. It don't make a damn what it costs." They charged $200, and I hadn't done nothing but slap Willie with that whiskey bottle. Didn't even bother him.

On my way back to Nashville, I made my mind up. I would not put up with no more crap, no way you fix it. I wasn't going to overlook another thing from Willie Nelson. And I didn't.

And that's why, I guess, I 'm sitting here in Waco listening to "She Thinks I Still Care" on the record player, and knowing Willie and me are probably better friends now than ever.

MARGE LUNDE

Willie Nelson was just a little bitty redheaded pissant when he first came around the Nite Owl not too long after me and my late husband, U. J. Lunde, opened the place in 1943. He was too young to drink beer legally, and I sure as hell wouldn't sell it to him. But him and his sister Bobbie took to coming in there later and playing music with Bud Fletcher's band the Texans.

Many's the night Bobbie would be onstage playing the piano in the Nite Owl and I'd be babysitting her two little babies. Before I knew it, her kids would wet in my lap. But that was okay, we were all young—I was in my twenties and Bobbie and Willie in their teens —and having a big time. You could relax and have fun in the Nite Owl and nobody would ever bother you as long as you didn't get too drunk and show your ass. If you did that, I would throw you out the door before you could blink an eyeball. You could get as drunk as a dog in the Nite Owl as long as you didn't bother nobody. But there is a certain stage of drunkenness that will make anybody show their ass—and out they went. In forty-four years of owning the Nite Owl —running it all by myself after U. J. died of the sugar diabetes in 1969—the law has never had to close my doors for so much as a single night over any kind of trouble. I handled it myself.

Marge Lunde for forty-four years has owned the Nite Owl, a beer joint where Willie and Bobbie performed as teenagers.

After Willie and Bobbie moved on to the big time, we stayed friends. We didn't check on each other all the time, but we knew where each other was and what was going on even if we was miles apart.

I'd go see them when I could. One night I heard they was playing at a bar a Dallas Cowboy football player named Dave Manders owned outside of Dallas, so I drove up there. Well, that night was the worst damn brawl I have ever seen in any drinking joint in my life. Some 300-pound gorilla drop-kicked a woman off the balcony and she fell right at my feet. I thought she was dead. The ignorant bartenders began grabbing whiskey bottles off the display cases behind the bar and conking people over the head. In my joint I never hit anybody with a bottle. I could do the job with a fist or a forearm. But these Dallas idiots was bashing people in the skull, glass flying everywhere. I pulled Bobbie behind a post and said, "Stay beside me, honey. We're gonna call a cab to the Holiday Inn."

Willie says that is the only night in his whole career, in all the thousands of joints he's played and fights he's seen, that the barroom brawl was so bad he quit playing music and got his band and us together and run out the door before he could finish his music. Good thing, too. As we was running out, the law was running in.

A good friend is somebody that's there when you need them, like Willie was for me a few years ago when I shot and killed my brother-in-law.

I had woke up on the couch in the middle of the night with my brother-in-law pounding on me with his fists yelling he was going to kill me.

I twisted away from him and got my pistol out of my purse at the end of the couch and shot him twice.

My poor sister was laying in the other room. She was an invalid, paralyzed on her right side. Somebody had hit her a blow on the head with a blunt instrument that caused a blood clot the size of a half-dollar. After surgery she was paralyzed. I took care of her.

Now I don't know if it was my brother-in-law who hit her. But he was a Korean War veteran who was being treated at the VA hospital in Waco for what they called paranoid schizophrenia. The doctors made him take Thorazine and other powerful tranquilizers. For three days before he attacked me, he hadn't been taking his medication. I don't know if that caused it, but I knew I was defending my life when I had to shoot him. I didn't have any other chance against him, because I was weak and recovering from gallbladder surgery on my own self.

They hauled me to jail and charged me with first-degree murder.

First thing after I got out on bail, my phone rang. It was Willie calling from the other end of the country someplace.

"Don't you worry about nothing, Marge," he said. "I'll be right there as soon as I can."

Willie flew down here and testified for me as a character witness. I said, "Willie, don't you tell no lies on my behalf." He said, "Marge, I don't need to tell no lies."

He told that jury of six women and six men that he had known me since he was a child, and if I had killed my brother-in-law, I must have had a damn good reason or I'd never have done it.

The jury decided it was self-defense from the word go.

Back in 1946 when Bud Fletcher and the Texans began playing at the Nite Owl, they was a hell of a show. Couldn't no girl pound the piano keys like Bobbie—except for Sissy Elaine Nix, a little-boned person like Bobbie—and Willie was just as cute as he could be. Bud, he was a story all his own. Couldn't sing or play, but he was the big bullshitter at the microphone who made people laugh and dance. Bud stopped many a potential brawl with his wisecracks from the stage. That Bud, he could talk a fur coat right off a grizzly bear.

Willie used to bring his first wife, Martha, in the Nite Owl when they was courting and for years after they got married. Martha was the sweetest, most beautiful girl you ever saw unless you made her mad. If you pissed her off, you had a Cherokee on the full warpath.

I have seen a lot of people grow up in the Nite Owl, and seen their kids grow up, too, and I've got a world of friends from forty-four years in the beer business. But how many of your friends get to be superstars and go off to Hollywood—and still fly home to help pull you out of a ditch?

That little redheaded pissant, he's a darling, I'll tell you. He never forgets.

ZEKE VARNON

Willie was about sixteen when we started hanging out with each other. I was twenty and just out of military service. What drew us together was we both liked to get drunk and chase girls, and we wore the same size clothes—boots, hat, shirt, pants—so if we wound up staying at my house on Saturday night he could wear my clothes on Sunday.

Zeke Varnon is a close friend of Willie's since teenage days.

We would stand beside the highway in Abbott and hitchhike. If we got a ride heading south, we'd go to Waco. If we got a ride heading north we'd go to Fort Worth. We liked moving around a lot, but we didn't have no car. One time we decided to go to California, so we packed our bags and waited for a freight train coming through. We throwed our bags on a passing boxcar, and then the train started going faster and we run like bastards to catch it but we couldn't. Our bags went to California, I guess, but we wound up at the Nite Owl or someplace.

Willie liked jumping freights. I remember he had a big army coat with deep pockets in it. He was broke and starving to death. He went to a supermarket in Fort Worth and loaded up with sardines and crackers. At the cashier stand, Willie said he had to get his checkbook and would be right back. Instead he run straight to the railroad yard and hopped a freight train bound for California—but it turned out to be a local. The train stopped in Weatherford, Mineral Wells, and all points west. Willie got off and caught a freight back to Fort Worth.

Willie had more moxie in those days than anybody I ever saw. We were sitting in Scotty's Tavern, playing dominoes and watching the Monday night fights on TV. A guy at the bar is making comments like he is some kind of expert. Willie says, "I'll bet you ten bucks on the fighter in the white trunks." They fought another round, and the guy at the bar says, "Let's make it ten more."

Willie says, "Shit, let's make it thirty."

We didn't have a dollar between us. If Willie had lost that bet, they'd have beat the pure hell out of us. I asked him later, "Just what did you intend to do if White Trunks got knocked on his ass?" Willie said, "Aw, I'd have thought of something."

Willie had a job for a while wearing an apron and waiting on tables, if you can imagine such a sight, and he played in a polka band on weekends, and pretty soon we bought us a 1934 Ford that was a running son of a bitch. It was about three different colors with tires so threadbare and slick you couldn't take off without spinning the wheels. Trouble with it was, the gas tank leaked. On a Saturday we went by to pick up Willie's girlfriend at a government housing project. Willie goes inside to wait on the girl and I doze off at the wheel. I wake up to some kid pounding on the window and shouting, "Wake up, your car is on fire."

I jumped out of the damn thing and the gas tank exploded. When Willie and the girl come running out, it was a hell of a blaze. The girl says, "What are we gonna do?"

Willie says, "We're just going to wait around like everybody else and watch this car burn and then go get drunk."

That put us back on foot.

We went into the bootlegging business. You couldn't buy liquor in Waco. We scraped all our money together and went to Fort Worth and bought half-pints of whiskey. Coming back we stopped at the old Yellow Dog beer joint—run by Chief Edwards, who had practically raised me and never been seen to touch his lips to whiskey. We pull out a half-pint. Willie takes a drink. I take a drink. Chief Edwards grabs the bottle and drinks it dry. The Chief lets out a whoop, throws his hat on the floor, and stomps the shit out of it. We pull another bottle and kill it. Eventually we wobble to Hillsboro, where some drunk flags us down and asks if we've got any whiskey. We sell him a half-pint for $2. We got so happy we'd actually sold a bottle, we celebrated and drank some more. Before you know it, we was out of whiskey and had $2 left in the world. Willie and me wasn't cut out to be bootleggers is the lesson to that story. We was meant to drink it, not sell it.

Willie decided to get married. Not to Martha, his first wife, but another girl. Willie's mother, Myrle, come down from Oregon for the wedding. They was to get married on Saturday night. Saturday morning Willie says he needs a haircut. We set off to the barbershop in Waco. But on the way we stop at the Yellow Dog to see the Chief. We got drunk at the Yellow Dog and didn't come back for the wedding. Didn't see the girl again until years later when Willie was playing Panther Hall in Fort Worth. They had a sign outside that said WILLIE NELSON TEXAS. Willie walks up with this girl and asks if I remember her. I say I don't think I do.

"Well, I will sure as hell never forget you," she says. "You're the reason I ain't Mrs. Willie Nelson Texas."

Nothing would faze Willie, and even if it did he'd never let you know it. There was a truckstop near the Melody Ranch where they put hot peppers and homemade chowchow on the tables that would burn the gut out of a locomotive. The first time we went there, Willie ordered enchiladas and eggs. He took a spoon and heaped chowchow on top of his plate and poured hot peppers on top of the chowchow and stirred it into a mess that practically had smoke rising from it. All the guys were watching. Willie ate a bite. He started sweating. Knowing the guys were watching, he shoveled more enchiladas and peppers into his mouth. By now, tears were pouring down his cheeks. But he ate the whole damn thing, sweating and crying and acting like it was delicious. Finally somebody asked if he might like a glass of water. Willie said, "Water ain't the right thing to drink with enchiladas. How about a glass of sweet milk?" He drank a gallon of sweet milk. But all he'd say was, "Man, I love them peppers. I just wish they'd get some hot ones in here."

Willie has a way of wiggling out of tight spots like one of them lizards that you grab and the tail comes off in your hand. We were living at the Grandy Courts in Waco when a guy comes to the door Willie didn't want to see. Willie slithered under the bed. I let the guy in and said, "Willie ain't here, but he should be back sometime tonight. Sit down and wait, why don't you?" So I left, and Willie laid under the bed for hours until the old boy got tired of waiting and finally left. Another guy heard Willie had been messing around with his wife and came looking for him with a gun. Me and Willie borrowed a gun for self-defense from Chief Edwards. We sat in the Grandy with the lights out, watching this fellow parked across the street who had the full intention of shooting Willie full of holes. Eventually Willie decided the wisest thing to do was crawl out the back window and put some healthy distance between him and the Grandy Courts.

I took Willie to Tyler, Texas, when he got out of the air force and introduced him to my foreman, Curly Ingram. I had gotten a job with the Aspundh Expert Tree Company. The Aspundh Company hired Willie for 80¢ an hour. He started off driving a truck and immediately ran over some kid's red wagon, which cost Willie $16—two days' pay.

They put Willie on the ground crew with me. Aspundh is a huge company that does all kinds of things with trees—like cut them away from utility lines and such. As ground men, Willie and I didn't have to do no climbing. But there was one great big elm tree that was interfering with the electric lines and causing no end of trouble. A worker up in the tree hollered down to send up a bull rope. Willie says, "I'll bring it up to you."

He slings the bull rope over his shoulder, climbs up an extension ladder, gets to the top of the tree, crawls out on a limb. The guy takes the bull rope and says, "No need to fool with climbing back down. You just catch hold of this rope on this limb and slide to the ground."

Game for anything, Willie wraps the rope around his hand and bails out of the tree.

But instead of sliding, he got hung way up in the air with the rope twisted around his hand.

Willie starts yelling, "I'm a goner! I'm a goner!"

We yelled, "Hold on Willie."

About that moment the rope comes untwisted and Willie starts sliding down it like a cannonball, the flesh burning off his hands. He hit the ground hard with his hands peeled plumb to the bone, like he'd been sizzled in a fire.

Willie looks at me and says, "Zeke, I don't believe trees is my line of work."

He told Curly to keep his job open for him, and he took off. You know, years later the Aspundh Tree Company offered Willie $100,000 to do a concert for their annual convention.

Willie started making a little money with his records, but he couldn't keep track of it. My brother Cliff was in the real estate and insurance business in Texarkana, which we figured meant he knew all about money. Willie asked my brother if he'd handle his affairs for ten percent. Willie had never met my brother, but they struck a deal and set up a company called Willie Nelson Enterprises. Cliff was to pay the bills, take care of the legal stuff, and I was to get a little cut out of the action. Willie was paying $300 a month in child support, so my brother took over that responsibility. Then I talked Cliff into letting Willie have all his credit cards—Texaco, Diners Club, everything. Willie started running them bills up.

My brother come to me and says, "How well do you know Willie Nelson, anyhow?"

"How come?" I says.

"Well, God damn, they're taking my credit cards away from me because of him."

I called Willie and he came to Texarkana in a brand-new bus that he was driving his own self with his whole band on it. It was summer, the air conditioner was running on the bus, and Willie was wearing a bathing suit. He left the air conditioner on while we got quite drunk. I don't recall exactly how Willie and Cliff worked it out, but I do know it was many years before Willie had another credit card.

After Willie moved to Austin, we opened a pool hall on South Congress Avenue. It was a damn good place. Mom and Pop Nelson came down to help run it. We had a big beer garden in back—the Charlie Peepers Memorial Beer Garden—where we played dominoes and cooked barbecue goats with marijuana sprinkled on them. Every time we played music in the beer garden, the police showed up. Oh, we had fun at that pool hall. One night I lost the keys and had to sleep there on the couch. I woke up at seven in the morning and some girl was using the pay phone. She started living with me that day. Don't fate work in mysterious ways?

We had a big NO SMOKING sign in the back room. Willie would come in and say, "Let's go to the No Smoking Room and burn a reefer."

One day much later, sitting in the No Smoking Room, high as raccoons, we was listening to Leon Payne's old song, "I Love You Because," on the jukebox. That was one of our favorite songs when we was younger. It made me nostalgic.

I said, "Willie, do you remember that old song?"

He looked at me and said, "Son of a bitch, I should remember it. Ain't that me singing?"

Sure as shit, it was.

SYBIL GREENHAW YOUNG

The reason my family came to the Pacific Northwest is we didn't have enough work in Arkansas. My husband and I ran a dairy farm back in Tindall, Arkansas, and there was a bad drought. It took what we made off the milk just to feed the cows. So we finally just settled out here in Washington State.

My sister Myrle had lived in Oregon for a long time. She moved to Washington when her husband Ken just practically went blind. He could hardly see at all. My son went to Oregon and got them and moved them up here. Myrle loved the scenery and the climate in this part of the country. She needed somebody to help her with Ken, but she didn't want to leave this area so she came to live near us.

Back in Arkansas our dad made moonshine mostly for himself and friends. The Greenhaws all played music and could sing, except for me. I happened to be the dumb one, I guess. Dad played the banjo. My youngest brother, Carl, was a really good piano player. Myrle sang and played the guitar like my other two brothers, but I couldn't carry a tune in a bucket.

The Nelson family lived not too far from the Greenhaws in Tindall. They were practically neighbors. The families got together to play music. I guess that's how Myrle met Willie's daddy, Ira. I was only five years old when Myrle married Ira and moved to Texas. We were a poor family, so I couldn't go visit her.

Willie's Indian blood comes from my mother Bertha Greenhaw, who was three-quarters Cherokee. I guess you would say three-quarters because Bertha's mother—my grandmother—was full-blooded Cherokee. My granddad was half Cherokee and half Irish.

So if Willie says he's an Indian, that's a fact. The Cherokees were about the smartest, proudest people that ever lived.

Sybil Greenhaw Young is Willie's mother's sister.

PART THREE

Night Life

Night Life

When the evening sun goes down
You will find me hangin' 'round;
The night life ain't a good life,
But it's my life.

Many people just like me,
Dreamin' of old used to be's.
The night life ain't a good life,
But it's my life.

Listen to the blues that they're playin'
Listen to what the blues are sayin'
My, it's just another scene
From the world of broken dreams;
The night life ain't a good life,
But it's my life.

CHAPTER SEVEN

Even though they had given her the middle name of Jewel, it never occurred to me to wonder if Martha's parents might have spoiled her to the point where she thought she could always get her own way. I didn't consider it because I had been so spoiled my own self that I naturally assumed I would always get my own way.

Bind two spoiled kids together with a marriage license and mix in a heavy dose of passionate love along with a tendency to drink and party all night, and you come up with Martha and me—the battling Nelsons. Young and dumb and in love.

There was a frantic quality to our love. If I didn't know where Martha was at any time, I would get a feeling of anxiety in my stomach. When she walked into the room, my heart would pound like the bass drum in the Abbott High band and I would feel so elated I could hardly breathe. It was a coin toss whether love caused us more pain and anguish than it did pleasure.

Trust was not a part of our marriage. I think we thought we knew each other too well to trust each other. Basically I was just not that trustworthy. When you're young and have a guitar and are playing for dances and all those girls come after you, and you drink a lot, you are going to do things that your wife is not going to like. So I was responsible for our early problems. Another woman would probably have divorced me long before Martha did.

Right from the beginning Martha suspected I was running around on her. She was wrong in the beginning, but she wasn't wrong very long. I accused her of running around on me, too. I don't know if she really was in those days, but she might as well have been because I kept throwing it up to her.

Our journey to Eugene, Oregon, to introduce Martha to my mother was not what you would call a huge success. Going up there, we'd drive a while, fight a while, make love a while, and then drive some more. When we got to Eugene, the only job I could find was as a plumber's helper. For a guy who thought he was a star, crawling under houses with a monkey wrench was not at all what I had in mind.

"You could have stayed home and worked for my daddy if you want to be a plumber," Martha would tell me. She was right. W. T. Mathews was a plumber, and his wife Etta sewed all Martha's clothes. Her being right pissed me off all the more.

Martha worked as a waitress in Eugene. She could always find a job as a waitress anywhere we went, because she was so beautiful and smart and she worked hard. Even if she'd been the laziest-ass waitress in town, they'd have hired her. One look at Martha in her poodle skirt and sweater, bobby sox and loafers, her Cherokee black hair and black eyes shining, her laughter like music, it would have taken a blind eunuch not to hire her. You didn't meet many blind eunuchs who ran honky-tonks.

But I was not put on this earth to be a plumber, much less a plumber's helper. Also I couldn't stand the idea of being supported by Martha. It offended my notion of manhood. The man was supposed to be the provider. And Martha would kill me with her mouth when I laid around the house pickin' the guitar while she went off to work. She might have been kidding, but I was in no mood to take a joke.

Martha had a world of patience with me, and I don't mean to make it sound otherwise. After all, she stuck it out with me through ten years of rough times. So instead of constantly fighting, why didn't we sit down and talk over our problems like calm and reasonable people? Well, the words *calm* and *reasonable* would not have applied to either of us. And us two kids, both still in our teens, didn't realize it but we were facing the number-one problem that nearly all married people face: we didn't know how to listen to each other.

I have to smile when I see all the books and magazine articles that say the biggest complaint most women have against their husbands is that the husbands won't listen to them. The problem is not that husbands don't listen to their wives as much as it is that not many people of either sex really listen to anybody.

There are important things men learn to be afraid to try to tell their wives, and I don't mean sneak fucking. Maybe it's a financial situation the man is ashamed to admit he can't handle. Could be some powerful feeling of insecurity that the man is afraid will make his wife think less of him or consider him an outright sissy. The man really wants to unburden his soul to a woman because he instinctively feels a woman is more sympathetic toward him, like maybe his mother was. What many guys do in this case is go to a bar and get drunk and pick up a woman who will listen to all his shit because she's new and never heard it before and thinks her turn will come to lay her own shit back on him, although by the time her turn comes the guy has usually gone home.

Any prostitute will tell you that they have lots of tricks who come in every week and pay money but don't want sex, just companionship. They need to talk to a woman and know what a woman thinks. She might be telling them only what they want to hear, but they need to hear it. Encouragement from a woman is the most inspiring thing a guy can hear.

Most people think communication is talking all the shit that comes into their heads all the time. They don't understand that they can communicate better if for a change they really listen to where the other person is coming from and give a response that is honest.

It's hard to communicate with somebody when you're screaming at them or have just roared away in the car and left them standing at the curb.

In 1953 Martha and I moved to San Antonio. San Antonio was the biggest city Martha and I had ever lived in. It was a wild, noisy, colorful place with a river that ran past the Alamo. There were five or six huge military bases in San Antonio, so the right nightclubs had a wealth of steady customers. San Antonio had more Mexicans in it than any town this side of Mexico City. Maybe Texas won its war for independence from Mexico, but you couldn't tell it in San Antonio. The streets were full of Indians, too, except they called themselves Mexicans because Texas real estate developers had long ago chased the Indians to Oklahoma. You'd see bunches of Indians on the sidewalks wearing headbands to denote their tribal backgrounds, and they'd hold Indian ceremonies in the ballroom at the old Menger

Hotel, where Teddy Roosevelt had organized his Rough Riders. Maury Maverick, the congressman whose last name has become part of our language, told me in San Antonio one day, "Willie, if all these Indians ever learn to quit calling themselves Mexicans and start voting as an Indian bloc, they could practically take over this town."

I fell in with Johnny Bush at some nightclub. He wanted to be a singer but was learning to play drums because it's easier for a drummer to find steady employment. Johnny and I sat in with Adolph Hoffner's swing band called the Pearl Wranglers (Pearl beer was brewed in San Antonio). Johnny had a big voice. He could have been an opera singer if he'd had the training. I remember hearing Johnny sing "Stardust" one night and marveling at how good he was.

Johnny and I became real fast friends. We were sort of like Zeke and me—semi-insane, drinking a lot, and doing a lot of dumb things. Like traveling around the country without a quarter in our pockets. But we always found a place to play. We'd pick up enough gas money to go on to the next gig.

This was when Johnny organized the Mission City Playboys with me on guitar and him on drums and lead vocals.

Johnny advised me to quit trying to sing. He said I'd never make it as a singer. He liked my guitar playing better than he liked my voice. Plus Johnny was a singer and didn't need two singers in one band.

Always in need of money, I heard about a disc jockey job at KBOP in Pleasanton, thirty miles south of San Antonio. My only radio experience had been performing live music at KHBR in Hillsboro in high school, but I drove down to Pleasanton and met the man who owned KBOP, Dr. Ben Parker.

Dr. Parker asked if I could run a control board, and I told him I was an expert. He showed me the board. It had RCA Victor printed on it.

"That's an RCA board, ain't it?" I said. Dr. Parker agreed that it was. I said, "I've only worked on Gates boards."

I remembered the board at KHBR was a Gates board. Dr. Parker said, "I'll show you how to work the RCA board." He showed me, and then he had me do a live fifteen-minute newscast as a tryout. Right in the middle was a commercial that I will never forget. I had to say, "The Pleasanton Pharmacy's pharmaceutical department accurately and precisely fills your doctor's prescriptions."

Try saying that sometime with a hangover.

But Dr. Parker hired me anyhow. Dr. Parker became a major influence on my life. Just from watching and listening I learned how Dr. Parker thought about things and the best way to handle them.

He paid me $40 a week, but the education was priceless. I would sign on in the morning, do the news, sell advertising time, collect the bills, write copy, do everything there was to do at a radio station.

I kept playing music at clubs in San Antonio. Nights I was lucky enough to get a gig, I wouldn't sleep a wink before it was time to drive to Pleasanton and sign KBOP on the air at 5:30 A.M.

Johnny Bush went to work at KBOP, too. One dawn I ran out of gas on the way to Pleasanton and started hitchhiking. Johnny came along and picked me up. While he was still laughing at me, *his* car ran out of gas, and we both hitched a ride to work.

This kind of schedule couldn't last forever. Martha was pregnant by now and didn't want to have her first baby in a strange town. So we left San Antonio and went back to Abbott long enough for our daughter, De Lana, to be born at the hospital in Hillsboro on November 11, 1953.

Martha said De Lana was a biblical name. I don't know of a De Lana in the Bible. She was Lana to me—a brand-new little old person who had come into our young lives.

Now that we had a baby to look after, I figured I should become more responsible. Martha and Lana and I moved to Fort Worth to be close to my dad Ira and his wife Lorraine and my sister Bobbie. I located a job as a disc jockey in Denton. But Denton was sixty miles north of our house, and it wasn't long until I had the same trouble getting there as I'd had driving to Pleasanton, only sixty miles a day more so. In the fifties the speed limit was 70, but you could drive as fast as you wanted to. It was like a French Grand Prix road race on the Texas highways.

I thought we'd found the answer to my 100-mile-an-hour driving to Denton at dawn when they hired me as a disc jockey on KCNC in Fort Worth, replacing Charlie Williams on a program called the *Western Express.* Charlie had suddenly moved to California.

At KCNC I worked from 6 until 7:45 in the morning, was off for three hours, and then worked until 3 P.M. I had a terrific sign-on that I'd stolen from various disc jockeys, primarily Eddie Hill.

I would sign on with, "This is your ol' cotton pickin', snuff dippin', tobacco chewin', stump jumpin', coffee pot dodgin', dumplin' eatin', frog giggin', hillbilly from Hill County."

Then I was off and running. And running was a good talent to have in Fort Worth, because the town was lighting up with a real Wild West gun-shooting, bomb-throwing gang war.

CHAPTER EIGHT

F red Lockwood.
    Thirty-four years ago I promised Fred if I ever wrote a book I would put his name in it. Fred was the first person who ever gave me a joint, back in Fort Worth in 1954.

Fred said, "Willie, let's blow some tea."

I knew what he meant, of course, but I had never tried it. Marijuana was known as tea or reefer or weed or boo, and you bought it by the lid—a one-ounce Prince Albert tobacco can full—or by the penny matchbox from other musicians. I told Fred I couldn't blow any tea at the moment, but I'd like to take some with me and blow it when I got time.

The truth is I was kind of anxious about what might happen. The U.S. government and movies like *Reefer Madness* said I would go crazy and stick up a bank and rape little girls and murder innocent people if I blew tea. I knew enough musicians who used it to know this was most probably a lie. But there was only one way to be sure.

Fred and I had been sitting in some saloon watching the Army-McCarthy hearings on black-and-white TV and listening to Doris Day singing "Hey There" on the jukebox when he suggested we blow tea. After I turned him down, he gave me a skinny little joint with both ends twisted and told me to get high and be somebody.

On the way home, I pulled my car over to the side of the road and lit up. I smoked the whole joint and waited for something to happen. Nothing happened. I had puffed the joint and blown out the smoke, not taking the smoke all the way down and holding it like you're supposed to. I didn't get even a little bit high. I thought: What's the big deal? If I want to get high and be somebody, I'll drink a quart of bourbon. For six months I bummed joints now and then from Fred and puffed them and still didn't get high.

Finally one night I did it right. Since then, I have made up for those wasted six months.

Fred Lockwood and his brother Ace played in clubs on Exchange Avenue, the Jacksboro Highway, the Mansfield Highway, Hemphill Street, White Settlement Road. Fred was a funny son of a bitch. He would say, "That little gal there is the prettiest thing that ever stepped out of the back of a patrol wagon." He would say, "I ain't ate in three days—yesterday, today and tomorrow," a line I borrowed for a song.

I have borrowed another of Fred's great lines for a song—"I've gotta get drunk and I sure do dread it."

Fort Worth in those days had a population of 300,000, and the *Fort Worth Star-Telegram* had a daily circulation of 250,000. It wasn't because everybody in town read the *Star-Telegram*—though it seemed like damn near everybody did—but because it was the regular morning newspaper for all of West Texas. Most of the news had to do with shootings, stabbings, and exploding automobiles.

A kid named Elston Brooks, who was about my age, had the best-known byline on the *Star-Telegram* because he covered both the nightclub beat and the police beat at the same time. You'd see his name and photo above his column on the amusements page, and then you'd turn to the front page and see his byline on a story that said TWO MORE SHOT TO DEATH ON NORTH SIDE.

This double duty of Elston's worked against country musicians getting publicity in the *Star-Telegram*. He would show up in the press room at the cop shop at 5:30 in the morning and check the desk sergeant's report, homicide and the hospitals first thing. Every morning there was a long list of wounded from the honky-tonks.

So when it came time to write his amusements column, Elston wouldn't even think about going back to the honky-tonks to hear a country band, no matter how good it might be. Instead he would interview a touring movie star or go to a play or catch a pop act in one of Fort Worth's "legitimate" nightclubs. ("Legitimate" frequently meant the joint had strippers instead of country singers.)

Big bands like Gene Krupa or Tommy Dorsey would come to Fort

Worth and play the beautiful old Lake Worth Casino. The Skyliner, the Rocket Club, and the Air Castle offered dance music, jazz music, and strippers. Local pop performers like Charlie Applewhite, Norm Alden, and James Petty worked the clubs on West Seventh and Camp Bowie Boulevard where the level of violence was fairly low.

These were the places and people Elston Brooks wrote about in his amusements column. This meant a country artist could sing his ass off in the Jacksboro Highway dives, but his big West Texas audience would never read about it in the *Star-Telegram* unless he made the police news by shooting the promoter.

Elston didn't get around to writing about me until 1961. I was back in Fort Worth again doing a brief stint as a DJ at KCUL—luck spelled backwards—when Elston called the station and asked me to meet him for coffee at Anders Cafe.

I wore a gray, narrow-lapel business suit, a thin tie that was the style then, and my hair was cut short. Elston wore a fedora hat and had his tie yanked down and a cigarette stuck to his lip, like the newspaper guys did then. He interviewed me about the new song I had written that had just been released and was fast becoming a hit.

The next morning I picked up the *Star-Telegram* and saw my picture and read Elston's column about my new hit song—"Four Walls."

He meant "Hello Walls," of course. "Four Walls" was a hit at the same time and had been written by George Campbell, who had a band in Fort Worth.

But Elston spelled my name right at least (I have a profound dislike for seeing my name spelled "Willy")—and the next day he apologized and printed a correction about "Hello Walls," so I got two *Star-Telegram* columns from Elston for the price of one.

The gang wars in Fort Worth were mainly about gamblers fighting over territory. If a Dallas gambler tried to move into Fort Worth, our local gamblers would get together long enough to shoot him. Then they'd go back to fighting among themselves.

Organized crime didn't move into Fort Worth because the local boys were too tough. Ever since Butch Cassidy and the Sundance Kid hung out in Fort Worth's Hell's Half-Acre, and famous gunfighters like Luke Short roamed Exchange Avenue by the stockyards, it has been a town with a Wild West code.

The gamblers would shoot dice and bet football at W. C. Kirkwood's 2222 Club on the Jacksboro Highway or at Boston Smith's place farther out and then would drop in to where I was playing to listen to country music. It was not unusual for country musicians, struggling to make a living, to fall in with people at the bar and take to pulling burglaries or stickups or running a few whores to supplement their income.

Fort Worth cops had a humiliating routine they would use on you if you got thrown in jail. It was common knowledge on the street. If you had given the arresting officers any trouble, they would first wrestle you into a room behind a steel door next to the booking desk and would beat the shit out of you with belts, sticks, and fists. Then once every eight hours—with each change of shifts—they would roust you out of your cell for a "showup."

Every prisoner had to walk in a circle in front of each new shift of cops while the sergeant read their rap sheets out loud. He'd say, "Look at this sorry son of a bitch, men. Don't you want to puke knowing this ugly shitass is in our town?" If you happened to be a police "character"—a known street tough with an arrest record—the sergeant would say, "This worthless asshole is a pimp, a burglar, and a hijacker. He'd be a killer if he had the guts. Every time you see him on the street, whip his ass and throw him in jail. You don't need a charge, we'll find one." The cops would whack the characters in the ribs or on the butt with their nightsticks while they shuffled in a circle. The sergeant would say, "You lowlife hoods better learn you ain't safe on the streets of Fort Worth. If you want to try to scare people, go to Dallas."

North of the Tarrant County courthouse and south of 10th Street, most of the hotels were whorehouses in which $3 bought a straight date and $5 would take you around the world. I played at the Mountaineer Tavern on 10th Street, where the stage was behind the bar. I played on Magnolia Street and at the 811 Club on Hemphill on the South Side. They all had pinball machines that paid off in cash.

I worked with quite a few black musicians and Mexicans. I played Gray's Bar on Exchange Avenue—where they rigged up chicken wire in front of the stage to protect us from flying beer bottles—with a Mexican rhythm guitar player named Momolita and his Mexican bass player, Moose. They were great musicians. I played lead guitar and sang and fronted the band. We played jazz, we played "Little Rock Getaway," "Sweet Georgia Brown." When the joints closed I'd get with the Mexicans and blacks and jam until the sun came up.

Busy as I was playing music at night and spinning records and playing live music on the radio by daylight, I still wasn't making enough money to support Martha and Lana and me, and I felt my career as an entertainer was at a dead end if I didn't get out of Fort Worth.

Like Charlie Applewhite, Charlie Williams, Norm Alden, and dozens of other young guys in Fort Worth at the time, I decided my next stop into the future lay on either the Left Coast or the Right Coast. I chose the Left Coast.

We hit the road again.

We stopped first in San Diego where Martha got a job as a waitress. I went to every club in San Diego trying to find work playing music. But none of the bars would even let me audition, because I wasn't a member of the union. To join the union, you had to pay $100 for initiation and dues. I didn't have $100 to pay the union and couldn't raise $100 unless I could work, which I couldn't. I was just shit out of luck in San Diego.

It hurt my ego for Martha to be supporting Lana and me. I got tired of it.

In the middle of the night without telling Martha I was leaving, I put $10 in my pocket and hitched up to Orange County and L.A. and started hitting the bars looking for work. But it was the same story as San Diego.

A couple of girls picked me up and took me to every club they knew, but there was no work for me. We went to the house where the girls lived. I was tired of lugging my fucking suitcase everywhere I went, so I left it with the girls and gave them my mother's name and address in Portland. The girls promised to send my suitcase to Portland, but I never saw it again.

I went out and tried to catch a ride north. About two o'clock in the morning I gave up and found me a culvert to sleep in. It was cold. I found newspapers and kindling and built a fire in the culvert to keep me warm while I slept. The smoke damn near asphyxiated me. I woke up coughing and stomped the fire out. In the morning I caught a ride to the railroad station and hopped a freight toward Portland.

Somehow I got off the train outside of Eugene. A guy picked me up and gave me a ride to the bus station. Just out of the goodness of his heart, he bought me a bus ticket to Portland. My stepdad, Ken, met me at the bus station and drove me home.

When I finally walked into my mother's house in Portland, there stood Martha waiting for me with Lana in her arms.

Soon as I'd turned up missing, Martha had called my mother. It wasn't hard for them to guess where I was heading. Mother sent Martha some money, and Martha and Lana caught the next plane to Portland. Beat me there by days.

Things started turning around for me. I got a respectable job as a disc jockey in Vancouver. My show was on from 10 A.M. till 2 P.M., all country music. I was head up against Arthur Godfrey in that time slot, but I started drawing good ratings. I was a very successful disc jockey in Vancouver. We had radio personalities like Shorty the Hired Hand and Cactus Ken. I was Wee Willie Nelson.

I played with a couple of bands around Portland and Vancouver. Martha was staying home taking care of Lana and becoming pregnant again.

On January 20, 1957, our second daughter, Susie, was born in a hospital in Vancouver in the middle of a snowstorm. Martha's parents, W. T. and Etta, came up from Waco to help with the babies.

In the fall of that year I made my first record. I cut it using the equipment at the radio station. The A side was "No Place for Me," written by W. Nelson, sung by W. Nelson, produced by W. Nelson, performed by the W. Nelson Band for Willie Nelson Records. The lyric said, "Your love is as cold as the north wind that blows/and the river that runs to the sea . . . There's no place for me." The flip side was "The Lumberjack," written by my friend Leon Payne. I was twenty-four years old.

I hammered that record hard on the radio. For $1 you could get the record by mail with an autographed 8 × 10 photo of W. Nelson, star and recording tycoon. I sold out my first pressing of 500 records and eventually sold 3,000 of them.

Things were going unusually well in Vancouver. I guess I couldn't handle such good fortune. Elvis Presley had started bombarding the charts with "Heartbreak Hotel," "Blue Suede Shoes," "Hound Dog," and "Love Me Tender"—it was like an atomic bomb falling on the music world. That same year the Russians put up *Sputnik*, the first satellite. I used to look up at the night sky, trying to spot the little machine that circled the earth every ninety minutes. It was exciting to think mankind had taken a step into space, where both the future and the past lie for us. I dreamed of going to the moon, but I didn't dream men would be walking on the moon in only ten years.

Mae Axton came to Portland and Vancouver. Besides being the mother of Hoyt Axton, Mae is a top songwriter. She wrote "Heartbreak Hotel" among others. I asked her for advice, and she told me to get the hell out of Dodge.

Working in Vancouver, Mae said, was not the way to become a star.

By now I was beating Arthur Godfrey in the ratings with my DJ show. I was a local celebrity. I walked into the station manager's office at KVAN and demanded a $100 a week raise. "Pay me what I'm worth, or I'm taking a hike," I said.

He told me not to let the doorknob hit me in the ass on my way out.

CHAPTER NINE

W e stopped off in Springfield, Missouri, in my new red Cadillac and stayed with Billy Walker and his family for a few weeks. Billy was working on the Ozark Jubilee on the radio. Martha took a job as a waitress and I hired on as a dishwasher in a cafe. Billy and I talked about the Nashville music situation and depressed the shit out of each other. I got the feeling that if I went to Nashville right then I would have been like a chigger on the butt of the Abominable Snowman. The music at the top of the national charts was Pat Boone, another North Texas boy, singing "Love Letters in the Sand," and Debbie Reynolds singing "Tammy." I couldn't see any future for me in that direction, and Nashville thought my songs were not straight-ahead country enough to be recorded.

Martha was pregnant again. I already knew I couldn't support a wife and two babies—let alone three—on what I could earn as a musician. Two times in my life I decided to give up playing music for a living and get a regular job. This was the first time.

We moved in with Ira and Lorraine back in Fort Worth, and I took a job selling encyclopedias door to door.

I am a good salesman. The first thing you learn playing music on the stage is you have to sell yourself before you can sell the song to the audience. I figured it would be the same with encyclopedias.

The Encyclopedia Americana had a smart pitch that worked almost every time. We had an inside connection at the phone company to get the new listings of young people and newcomers who had just applied for phones. Several hundred people a month got new phones in Fort Worth. We would call them up and give them our pitch.

I would say, "Hello, this is Mr. Nelson. I'm with the Americana Corporation. I'm sure you're familiar with us. We own, publish, and sell the Encyclopedia Americana. However, I want to put your mind at ease. This call has nothing to do with the regular sale of the Americana. We're interested in people who would like to own the Americana without the expense normally involved in buying it. Is this something you'd love to have in your home without the normal cost involved in buying it? Oh yes? Well, what time does your husband come home?"

Each salesman would make six appointments for the day and then go call on them. Of the six, you ought to sell three.

My first day out I borrowed Hall Trace's old beat-up panel truck. I wouldn't park the truck in front of the house because I didn't want the customer to see what kind of car this big executive was driving. I'd park a block away and walk to the house and knock on the door.

I didn't memorize the pitch that first day, but it was written on a piece of paper in my pocket.

My first customer met me at the door and said, "I can't afford it."

I said, "Let me see what the company says about that."

I pulled out the piece of paper and said, "I'm supposed to tell you that you can't afford not to have it. An educational system like this can be yours for the price of a package of cigarettes a day. It's not a question of can you afford it, it's something you should have. Think of your children's future." If the guy had another objection, I had another answer.

The first time out I sold three sets.

I sold a set of books to two newlywed kids who didn't have a stick of furniture. Just a mattress on the floor. They signed up for $400 worth of encyclopedias and had nothing in their icebox but a quart of ice cream.

My conscience started bothering me about selling books to people who couldn't afford them. Since then, that sales pitch has been outlawed by the Better Business Bureau, but back then it was perfectly legal. It was called the negative approach. You started out saying, "I'm not a salesman and I can't sell you anything. So don't try to buy these books. I can't sell them no matter how much you need them."

I got fed up with myself for taking unfair advantage of people. Looking around their houses I had noticed something people in Fort Worth needed more urgently than encyclopedias. They needed vacuum cleaners.

I went to work selling Kirby vacuum cleaners. Now this was really a great product and immediately useful to any family. Kirby's were powerful vacuum cleaners but they were very expensive. I had to have a good story to convince people the Kirby was a better deal for them than a cheaper vacuum cleaner.

I'd go in somebody's house with my Kirby and dig dirt out of their mattress that they had no idea was there. When I got through cleaning their mattress, they thought they were the filthiest people in town. I'd get all kind of shit and corruption out of their mattress and spread it all over the floor. Anybody's mattress has got it, you know, unless you clean it every day. It just accumulates. But you spread all that dead skin and stuff on the floor, it just looks horrible. People think they can't sleep in their bed another night. I'd show them how unhealthy they'd been living. "Do you believe some people actually let their babies crawl on dirty mattresses?" I would say. I sold a lot of Kirbys without it hurting my conscience because I was telling the truth.

But I couldn't stay out of the clubs for long. The nightlife was calling me. Martha would hit the joints with me when we could hire a babysitter or find one among our relatives. She loved the nightlife as much as I did.

I started attending the Metropolitan Baptist Church, where Ira and Lorraine were members. I felt like I made contact with the people at the Metropolitan Baptist, with the Holy Spirit in their presence.

I joined the church and was baptized. Being submerged just happened to be part of their deal, like sprinkling was with the Methodists. I had no objection to it. I figured I could do this just as well without being dunked or showered, but it mattered a lot to the people in the church. And it did give me a kind of wonderful, purified feeling every time I did it.

I began teaching Sunday school. I thought I was a good teacher. I knew my lessons. On Sunday mornings my class would go over our lessons and read the Bible verses for the day. Everybody would kick it around and say what they thought it meant. To me that's what a Sunday school teacher was supposed to do.

Then came one of those unexpected encounters that changes your life.

The preacher at Metropolitan Baptist said he had to talk to me in his office after the service on Sunday. He said, "Willie, either you quit playing in beer joints or else you quit teaching Sunday school."

"You must be nuts," I said.

Some members had told the preacher they heard I was playing in beer joints again.

"It couldn't have been too hard for them to hear it," I said. "I've seen them right there in the audience at those beer joints."

The preacher didn't back down. He had been put into the position of choosing between satisfying the congregation—including the hypocrites—who put money in the collection plates on Sunday to pay his salary, or siding with some redheaded musician who drank and smoked and cussed and picked his guitar and sang in dance halls. We all knew that on Sunday mornings when I would be teaching my class, the swampers at the dance halls would be sweeping up the broken teeth and blood off the floor. It was clear in the preacher's mind. He elected to stick with his money supporters. That made it easy for me, too. I decided to stay with the beer joints that paid me money to help support my family. The preacher sounded so wrong to me that I quit the Baptist Church.

I had never really been regarded as a good Methodist since I was a child cedarbark smoker and Bohemian beer-drinking guitar picker. Now I was no longer a Baptist, either. And I was disillusioned with religions that condemned people like me.

But deep inside I had a powerful spiritual urge. You wouldn't call it religious, exactly, because religious meant the Church and following the rules a bunch of people in authority had dreamed up to keep their subjects in line. These religious Church rules frequently had nothing to do with anything Jesus taught. I mean, you see a church hitting on its members for more and more money so the church can buy real estate and tear down grocery stores to make parking lots and erect carnival rides on top of good farmland and pay big salaries to the preachers and their staffs who go to church conventions to pass more rules and think up new ways to make money—and you say, "I ask you, Jesus, is this how You want it done?"

If you really seriously in all faith get quiet and pray and ask Jesus, He will answer you. This is the truth. He won't necessarily set fire to a bush or send a bolt of lightning. Instead the answer will come through your inner voice, your conscience, your divine spirit.

My inner voice told me the Methodists and the Baptists didn't have a hammerlock on God. My inner voice said there were millions of people in the world who felt the same as I did. I went to the Fort

Worth Public Library and began reading every book on religion I could find. I discovered the world was full of people who believed in reincarnation. Soon as I read about reincarnation it struck me just the same as if God had sent me a lightning bolt—this was the truth, and I realized I had always known it.

The world was full of people that believed one time through life ain't it. Sure, by the beliefs of the Church, a guy could go maybe eighteen years and be the wildest kid on the street and get hit by a train and get sent to hell and that was it, no more Jimmy Blue. I just didn't think that could be right. I believed the guy should have had another chance before he got sent to hell, he was only eighteen, and who were these people to say that what he was doing was wrong, and how did they know what caused him to do it, you know? I was asking a lot of questions myself as a kid and I just couldn't believe the answers the Church gave me. What made sense to me was reincarnation, which says no matter how many times you fuck up, it's up to you, you're still going to have to come back, again and again, until you get it right, until you get a passing grade. That started making sense to me, a lot more sense. And then I started finding other people who believed that way and I felt, well, I'm not in this alone. I started listening to people who knew a lot more about it than I did and I found out that it has progressed leaps and bounds in the last hundred years. Probably right now, more than half the people in the country believe in reincarnation. Fifty years ago, it was less than ten or fifteen percent.

You know when you hear a song and it hits you immediately—hey, that's the *truth?* You know it instinctively? The same thing happened when I read the *Aquarian Gospel*. There's a part in the *Aquarian Gospel* about the life of Jesus that tells where He went during the long period between his childhood and his last ride to Jerusalem when He disappeared. The King James version of the Bible was later rewritten to cover up the fact that Jesus had discovered reincarnation. He learned about it in his travels to Egypt and India. One of His lessons was the lesson of divine love, where He met this beautiful lady in the chambers and she was playing on a harp and she was the most beautiful creature He'd ever seen in His life, and He fell in love with this girl. It's the most beautiful story in the world about how Jesus overcame carnal love and retained his divine love because that was His reason for being here, to show divine love to all mankind. Here He was being tempted by this most beautiful creature on earth, but He remained strong. He stayed Jesus, and stayed divine love personified. I realized it would take many more reincarnations for me to triumph over my lustful urges, but at least I knew I was on the right path.

On the back page of the *Aquarian Gospel,* I wrote a list of commandments to myself. I realize now they were much like the statements my mother wrote me in her letter all those years ago about the kind of person she wanted to be. I was writing them down to make them come true. Visualization. Rosicrucians and other mystical societies teach you to do this. If you want something to occur, write it down and read it over and over, and according to the law, it will happen. The *Aquarian Gospel* had a great impact on me. It all came together with that book. Explained everything to my satisfaction.

I became interested in these secret societies, these secret orders that people belong to. My daddy Ira was a Mason, but he wouldn't talk about it and I didn't know that a Mason is much the same as a Rosicrucian, although the Masons demand secrecy while the Rosicrucians want to share their knowledge with people who are ready to receive it.

I wanted to know what these big secrets could be. There are so many things that I don't know. Like I don't know, really, how many vibrations per second is this pen in my hand, or how many vibrations per second is this particular air I am breathing. The only difference between the pen and the air is the number of times they vibrate. And the only difference between anything is where it's at on the vibrating level. We know little about that.

Martha gave birth to our son, Billy, on May 21, 1958, in a Fort Worth hospital.

Once again our lives had become one of those deals where I owed more than I was making. We loaded the family in the car and took off for Houston.

We didn't have any money, but I did have some new songs I thought I could sell to somebody.

Driving on the highway into Houston, we passed the Esquire Club. It was afternoon, and we stopped in there to listen to Larry Butler rehearsing with his band.

When they took a break I got Larry off to the side and told him I wanted to sell him some songs. I told him I'd take $10 apiece for them. I sang him "Mr. Record Man" and some other good songs. Larry listened real close, and when I finished I said, "How many do you want to buy?"

Larry said, "You mean you would sell 'Mr. Record Man' to me for ten dollars for me to put my name on it and claim I wrote it?"

I said, "Sure."

The way I looked at it, songs for a songwriter were like paintings for a painter. You finish one and you sell it for whatever you can get and then you do another.

Larry said, "I ain't going to buy your songs."

"You don't like 'em?"

"Hell, I love 'em," he said. "These songs are too good for you to sell like this. Hang on to 'em and one of these days they'll be hits."

"But I'm broke."

"Here's a fifty-dollar loan," Larry said. "Go get some food for your kids and rent a house to put 'em in, and come back here to the Esquire Club. I want you to play in my band."

We found an apartment in Pasadena, east of Houston. I had a gig six nights a week at the Esquire Club. On Sunday mornings I worked as the sign-on DJ for a Pasadena radio station.

Things were looking up again. I ran into Pappy Dailey, who had started a record company in Houston called Starday. Pappy had put out two hits so far—"Y'all Come" by Arleigh Duff and "Why Baby Why" by George Jones. About the time I met him, Pappy was forming a new label he named D Records.

I cut two 45-rpm records for Pappy Dailey. One had "The Storm Has Just Begun" on the A side and "Man with the Blues" on the flip. The credits on the record said "Willie Nelson and the Reil Sisters." The other record I did for Pappy was "What a Way to Live" backed with "Misery Mansion."

It was a thirty-mile drive from our Pasadena apartment to the Esquire Club. I had plenty of time to think making the round-trip six nights a week. One night driving to work a lyric popped into my mind:

When the evening sun goes down
You will find me hanging 'round . . .

Driving home again, another line came to me:

The night life ain't no good life
But it's my life.

I finished writing the song and put it in my stack of unpublished work.

They fired me at the radio station for being late to work, hired me again, and then fired me again. I wasn't making much money at the radio station, but I needed even more than they'd been paying me. What I took home from the Esquire Club wouldn't tote the load.

I ran into Paul Buskirk, a fine musician I had known for a while. Paul hired me to teach at the Paul Buskirk School of Guitar. He hired me on a Thursday, then spent the weekend teaching me what I needed to teach the students on Monday.

I had about fifteen students and managed to stay a lesson or two ahead of them. Every now and then I would hit a lick of "Wildwood Flower" or "Under the Double Eagle" to dazzle them with my footwork, but I think they knew I was sort of faking the lessons as I went along.

Paul Buskirk was my mentor. He taught me a lot about life and about music. He's one of the top musicians I've ever seen in my life. He knows his instruments and knows what he's doing and is able to tell you what he's doing and then play it again exactly the same way, if he wants to. That comes from knowledge and training. I, like most guys who play, have no idea where I'm going or what I'm gonna do and sometimes it comes out right, but I wouldn't know how to do it a second time. My playing is a lot of leaping off into space and seeing if I can hit the ground running.

I called Paul aside one morning and offered to sell him "Family Bible." He paid me $50 for it. Then I sold him "Night Life" for $150.

"Family Bible" was recorded with Claude Gray singing it. It rose to number one on the country charts. The credits on the song went to Buskirk and his pardners Walt Brelin and Gray. My name wasn't even on it. But I was really glad to know I could write a number-one song. Up until then I didn't know if I could write a song that was commercial or even acceptable. After "Family Bible" hit the top, I knew then that all my other songs were good. And, believe it or not, I never harbored any resentment toward Paul. I needed that money in a big way when I sold those songs, and I was real glad to get it. I appreciate that Paul and his pardners knew a bargain when they saw it.

"Night Life" had been turned down by D Records and the Pappy Dailey people as not being a country song, even though I owed D Records some songs. I knew "Night Life" was good. I sold it to Buskirk for enough money to go into a studio and record it. Pappy Dailey heard what I was doing and threatened to sue me, but I didn't care. I just changed my name.

The record we put out was "Night Life" by Paul Buskirk, performed by Hugh Nelson and Paul Buskirk and the Little Men.

"Night Life" is now one of the most-recorded songs in history. It's been performed by more than seventy artists from country and blues and jazz and pop all the way to opera singers. "Night Life" has sold more than thirty million records. All I got out of it was $150. But so what? At the time I needed the money. Suppose I'd been stubborn and waited and maybe never sold it at all? The fact that both songs became hits encouraged me to think I could write a lot more songs that were just as good.

Finally the time had come for me to go to Nashville.

Martha packed Lana, Susie, and Billy into our 1950 Buick that I was five payments late on. I drove them to Waco and left them with Martha's parents.

With an Oklahoma credit card—a syphon for stealing gas—I drove that Buick to Nashville wondering, all the way, at exactly what moment the car would fall apart.

The Buick took me as far as downtown Nashville and then belched smoke and kind of sighed like an old horse and laid down and died.

But I was in Nashville at last, ready to shoot it out with the big boys. I was going on toward my twenty-seventh birthday.

The Chorus

BENNIE BINION

The first time I laid eyes on Willie Nelson was at a honky-tonk outside of Fort Worth about thirty-odd years ago. It was a rough joint full of real rough characters. I mean your tough guys of the old school: gamblers and whores and pimps and cowboys out for a wild time. There was enough guns in this place to invade Korea. Willie was singing his songs for this crowd. I knew right off Willie would be a star because everybody was listening to him and feeling his magic. I damn sure felt it—kind of like the pull of a magnet.

There's two people I know of who have magic that strong—Willie Nelson and Billy Graham. Willie might make a great preacher, I don't know. Billy Graham would sure as hell make a great entertainer.

I don't believe in preachers. I'm a Catholic and to me religion is too strong a mystery to doubt. No smart person would doubt it no way. No preacher, priest, rabbi, or nothing knows any more about

---

Bennie Binion is a legendary Texas outlaw character who was one of the founders of Las Vegas as a gambling resort. He was arrested for murder—"It was self-defense. He shot me, so I shot back. He missed. I didn't." He owns the Horseshoe casino and hotel in Las Vegas.

God than I do. I'm eighty-two years old. I've died three times and done went to heaven once.

I was in the hospital with heart failure the time I went to heaven. I spoke to each member of my family in different parts of the country after my soul left my body, consoled them, told them I was fine and everything was all right. And God damn, first thing you know I'm up on stage with Jesus. Some other people that have died and come back say they went through a tunnel. But I just popped up on the stage in an odd bright light, and there stood Jesus. I asked him, "Are you Jesus?" He said, "Yes." I said, "Well, I've always believed in You and God, but I really ain't ready just yet. I sure would like to go back." So He let me come back. It's like this guy that went into a saloon and said everybody who wants to go to heaven line up over here. They all lined up except one fellow on a bar stool. Guy says, "Sir don't you want to go to heaven?" Fellow says, "Yeah, but not if you're loading up to go right now."

I'd just as soon Willie don't become no preacher, just keep on with what he's doing, making people so God damn happy they jump up and holler. Colonel Tom Parker, that used to manage Elvis Presley, is a smart son of a bitch, and he thinks Willie is overexposing himself with all this TV and Picnics and Farm Aids and what all. That's the Colonel's opinion, not mine, and maybe the Colonel don't know what the shit he's talking about. The Colonel would never let Elvis do a God damn thing he didn't get paid for. He said an entertainer has got to be paid, because they'll play out eventually. They got to get all the money they can while they're on top. But I think you've got to do a whole lot more than sing to draw packed houses night after night. It's personality. The people must love you and believe in you.

When Willie was getting ready to shoot his movie *Red Headed Stranger,* I heard he wanted a buffalo coat. I had one made for him at Green Furrier in Anchorage, Alaska. Shipped it to Willie and he wore it in the movie. Some people thought I skinned one of my own buffaloes off the ranch, but that's not the case. I have 1,400 buffaloes, and they're the worst thing to handle, mean and ornery. You can't turn a buffalo like you can a cow.

Willie has got some buffalo in him. You know why that big fur is on a buffalo's neck? Because when it storms, a buffalo faces the storm and goes straight into it instead of running from it. In other words, if the storm keeps coming and coming, the buffalo turns straight into it so he goes through it quicker. Otherwise, if the buffalo ran from the storm, he'd have nothing to show but a furry ass.

I can tell you, Willie understands buffaloes.

MAE AXTON

In 1957 I was doing PR for Colonel Tom Parker, who was managing Hank Snow but had taken over Elvis Presley. So the Colonel and Hank were coming to a parting of the ways, and I was asked to finish promoting a tour for Hank in the Pacific Northwest.

I stopped at a radio station in Vancouver, Washington. This young kid who interviewed me was very shy and clean-shaven. His jeans were worn and patched. He had a butch haircut. I thought he was a local boy. He told me he played every record of mine on the air, and I thought, this kid is all right.

Then he said he read every story he could find that I wrote in magazines. That blew my mind. He said he'd written some little songs that I'd never heard of. He didn't know if he had a chance to be a top songwriter, but did I have time to listen to one of his songs? He looked poor from hunger and so sweet. He was shy but when he looked at me he looked directly at me with those eyes that show straight into his soul.

I said, "Son, I've got a plane to catch. But I'll take time to hear your music."

In the lobby of the radio station, this young Willie Nelson turned on a little tape player. The first song he played was "Family Bible." It took about four bars before my chin hit the proverbial floor.

I kept listening to his songs until finally I said, "I've gotta run for the airport. But I want to tell you two things. One, if I could write half as well as you I'd be the happiest woman on earth. Two, you quit this job and go to Texas or Tennessee and write. I know you couldn't be making much money. So here's my unlisted phone number. I can always raise a couple of hundred dollars. Call me."

Later when he started turning out hits he began sending me flowers. The first ones I got from him I still have, pressed between the pages of my memory book.

Many years down the road from Vancouver, I went to see Willie perform in London. You talk about a great communicator. Willie knocked them out. At the break I went backstage and hugged him and said, "Willie, you've won them." This big grin spread across his face. There was a flash of delight in his very peaceful, penetrating, wise eyes—he knew he'd gotten through to people who were not from his country, but they understood his message and they cared.

Mae Axton is a noted songwriter—she wrote "Heartbreak Hotel" for Elvis—and mother of singer-actor Hoyt Axton.

Those eyes. They really show everything he's feeling. In Austin I was in a hotel room with Willie and his lawyers and some guys from a record company in Germany. These Germans were embroidering things, laying the con on Willie, telling him he had to do it their way and it would be so great.

Willie sat very quietly, but I was watching his eyes. The Germans were trying to take him for all he was worth. They thought they had him totally outsmarted. But I saw dark clouds forming in his eyes, a fire starting inside his heart, close to anger. I could see him thinking: Do they really believe I'm this dumb?

When the con men finished their pitch, Willie turned his eyes on them for a full minute. Then he said, "Okay, if that's how you say it has to be, then we won't do business together." He walked out and left them with sauerkraut on their faces. They thought they were dealing with some stupid hick from Texas, and suddenly they realized he'd let them talk their way out to the street.

I booked Willie on a big package show with Patsy Cline at a hotel in Stafford, Arizona. The entertainers all stayed in free rooms at the hotel. After the show, Willie said he was getting ready to go to his room and wondered if I had anything he could read. I said, "Willie, the only thing I have is a book of poetry I'm working on, just a manuscript stapled together."

"Would you mind?" he asked.

Willie writes poetry. Willie himself is poetry to me. His loyalty, friendship, caring, his love of people, all those things make great poetry come out of him. The next morning he gave me back the manuscript. On it he had written, "While reading this book and the thoughts contained I find myself saying, these are thoughts that I have but never quite seem to transfer them from my mind to paper. My hat is continued off to Mae B. Axton. Sincerely, Willie Nelson."

That page is kind of yellowed, but I have it framed on the wall of my den.

Not long ago we held a press conference for Willie. The room was crowded. Willie came in while I was talking. He wore his shorts, a tank top, a baseball cap, and tennis shoes. And he reached out his hand to me and said, "Mae, I just want you to know that I need that two hundred bucks now."

CHARLIE WILLIAMS

I was doing a radio show in Sherman Oaks when a good friend of mine, Joe Allison, asked me to write the liner notes for the first album of a new singer-songwriter named Willie Nelson.

I went into the studio that day in 1962 expecting to find the usual nervous rookie at the microphone. Instead, there was Willie, clean-shaven with his hair slicked back, perched on a high stool with a cigarette in one hand and his chin in the other, calmly recording his own songs as though he'd been doing it all his life.

He sang, "Stop here, across the way on your right. That's where my house lives. Sometimes I stayed there at night."

A very far-out opening line for a song. The way Willie sang it, though, it seemed the most logical and poignant thing for a heartbroken man to say. There's an excitement that runs through the engineers, the musicians, and the spectators when a recording session is really working. I felt the thrill of being there as a new star was being discovered. Willie sang "Touch Me," "Wake Me When It's Over," "Hello Walls," "Crazy," "Funny How Time Slips Away," "The Part Where I Cry," "Mr. Record Man," "Darkness on the Face of the Earth," one after another, and by the time he finished Willie was the only calm person in the studio.

Willie and I liked each other and started hanging out together. When he'd come to L.A., he'd call me and we'd go holler whoopie after his show. We went to a lot of guitar pullings together over the years.

One guitar pulling I remember most vividly was a night in Willie's suite at the Spence Manor in Nashville—Willie was a headliner by now—and about ten of us met up to show off our new stuff.

Johnny Darrell was there, blind running drunk. If you've never seen Johnny Darrell drunk, you have missed one of the . . . well, no, never mind. You haven't missed a thing, now I stop and think about it.

Anyhow, Johnny was real drunk. He snatched up Willie's old Martin guitar—the famous one he picked so much he wore a hole in it, the one with all the names signed on it—and was reeling around with the guitar saying he was going to sing a song.

Very nicely, Willie said, "Johnny, if you don't mind, would you please use another guitar?"

Charlie Williams is a country music veteran DJ, songwriter, manager, and producer—and former business partner of Willie's.

Johnny ignored him and went right on tuning and flogging the guitar and stumbling around.

Willie said, "Johnny, please. There's plenty of guitars in this room, but that one is very special to me. I'm afraid you're gonna break it."

Darrell whirled on him and said, "What's the matter? You become too God damn big a star to let me use your guitar?"

Willie was off that couch like a shot and across the room and grabbed Darrell and pinned him against the wall in the corner and said very quietly but forcefully, "Put that guitar down and do it now."

Johnny immediately put down the guitar. Willie went back and sat on the couch, gave one of his serene smiles, and said, "Now, then, I'd sure like to hear your songs, Johnny."

I wonder if Willie is afraid of anything. It seems to me he's so together, so full of complete and total confidence, that nothing can shake him ever. I'd like to believe that's true, but it can't be. There's got to be times when he says, "Whoa, this really is hard to figure." The man is human, after all. He's got to be scared of something. But I can't imagine what the hell it might be. If I have seen it, I didn't recognize it.

PAUL ENGLISH

I was born in Vernon, Texas, in 1932. After I finished high school in Fort Worth, I hit the street.

I joined the North Fort Worth Boys Club when I was about nine years old. My mother and dad was Holy Rollers. They started the Northside Assembly of God. I played in the band. I played down on the Exchange on North Main on the corner on Sundays, and I couldn't go to a movie or anything like that, but I could go to the Boys Club so I started boxing at the Boys Club. I turned into a rough little character in order to survive. I never saw a movie till I was fifteen. I went to the Star Theater on 10th Street and saw a movie at the Star Theater. When I got out these boys accosted me. They were the Peroxide Gang. I whipped three of them and they said, "My God, you're great. You know, we'll make you our leader." So I was introduced to a brand-new thing—girls. I said, "How about this? A whole new life has opened up for me." I had all the girls I wanted and was the head of the Peroxide Gang.

Paul English is Willie's drummer, business partner, and close friend of twenty-two years.

I wasn't a big known character. I was just a kid. But I knew some big characters. I started making the papers in 1956 when the *Fort Worth Press* started running a "10 Most Unwanted" list. I made it for five years in a row. They said, "if Paul wasn't there he just left," meaning, whenever there was a murder, if I hadn't been there I'd just left. I was involved in three murder trials, but they never led to anything. I was the kind of guy they were always trying to stick charges on. One of the murders the police tried to blame on me, there were six guys shooting at each other. One guy ran out of bullets and got killed. But that ain't murder—not in Texas, anyhow.

My friends and I started beating pinball machines and slot machines. Back then even a little old drugstore would have four or five pinball machines. We'd just get a drill and some piano wire and drill them and put a Crayola on the side of them and run up big scores and get paid cash.

In '55 I started running girls. This went on for a long time. I ran it like a business. I had it fixed so customers could charge it to their hotel as entertainment expense. I worked call service. When the Western Hills Hotel opened as the world's first drive-in hotel, I started working out of it. The base was $50 and up. Even the Westbrook Hotel uptown on 5th Street worked girls on calls. It was a good business but you had to work hard.

I ended up in jail in Waxahachie in 1952. I was headed straight for the penitentiary then. I had become really adept at picking locks. Matter of fact we had a contest on how many daytime burglaries we could pull and I think I pulled twelve. I was always scared but that was part of the fun. I don't think I was ever legitimate until I started playing drums for Willie in 1966.

In 1968, we needed uniforms. At that time all the bands wore uniforms and Willie said, "In our band everybody wears something different." We went Hollywood, right? I had this beard similar to what I've got now, and everybody would say, "Anybody ever tell you you look like the Devil?" They'd say, "I don't want to hurt your feelings, but anyone ever tell you that?" And I'd say, "Well, you're not going to hurt my feelings because the Devil was the prettiest angel in heaven." I considered it a compliment. We saw this cape in the window and Willie said, "Aw, you got to have this." I did think I looked like the Devil and so I bought the cape. You know, a $29 cape in Hollywood? Then we played Panther Hall and I'm from Fort Worth, right? I've been with Willie for two years already and when I got off stage that night, there were about fifteen girls waiting for my autograph, and so the cape stayed—for a long, long time. I finally went to where I had about seven capes and then I went to full length with velvet and silk lining. I had started always wearing black, like I do now.

Willie feels safe with me behind him. I carry two guns, for one thing. When the TV show *20/20* interviewed me they didn't believe I actually carried a gun and so the interviewer asked to see it. I said, "Which one?" The TV person like to have fainted.

At one time I had five rent houses and lost them all helping out while the band was in financial trouble. As late as 1973, I was making $175 a week and I had $5,250 coming in back salary. Now I'm in the *Guinness Book of World Records* for being the highest-paid sideman drummer.

I always loved Willie, you know. When I was in Houston working girls I'd always go see him. Willie asked me how he could get hold of a certain drummer, and I said, "Well, I can play better than him." He said "Yeah, but you wouldn't work for thirty dollars a night." And I said, "For you I would." And I did. He was the only one I would have ever worked for. Had it not been for Willie, I would be dead or in the penitentiary.

Willie Nelson is my best friend by far. I'm probably closer to him than I am to anyone. When we were driving the station wagon around the country together, we stayed in the same room together. I have one good eye and one glass eye, and he'd forget which was which. I'd be driving and he'd say, "Now, tell me which eye is out. I want to make sure you're awake." Willie and I make a good pair because he's the eternal optimist and I'm the kind of guy who figures out all the angles.

When times were rough, Willie would say, "One of these days, Paul, I'll make all this up to you." And he has. I own twenty percent of Willie Nelson Music, his publishing company, and I make about $56,000 a year just off of that. It's enough to retire on. I'm just bragging on him being true to his word.

PATSY BUTLER

Willie walked out of the Esquire Club behind us one night in the late fifties. We got in our car and looked over and Willie had two flats, not one, but two. Larry and I pulled over to help him. We opened up the trunk to get his spare out. The spare was flat, too. We

---

Patsy Butler is a close friend whose bandleader husband Larry gave up half his own salary to hire Willie at the Esquire Club in Houston.

just closed the trunk and told Willie, well, we'll just take you home —thirty miles to Pasadena. It was late when we got to Willie's house. He said, "Y'all come in with me. If you don't come in, Martha's gonna kill me. Y'all are gonna have to explain to her what happened, cause she's never gonna believe me." Larry and I got out and we went in and it was late and we woke Martha up. I said, oh, Lord, and we went in and talked to her for a minute and she was hot at Willie. So Willie come out the door and got back in our car. He said, "I'm going home with y'all."

That night Willie got one of those little ten-cent spiral notebooks. He started writing songs and wrote way on up into the morning. Next night, Willie come back home with us again, still hadn't got his tires fixed. He started writing again. There was about five songs that Willie wrote in this little book that's never been recorded. I put the book up for him and for the last twenty-five years, every time I've seen Willie, I've said, "Willie, you've got some songs. I kept them for you." There was people calling me after Willie got to be such a big star trying to get the songs from me and I wouldn't let them have them. They told me that they own this and that of Willie's songs, and I said, well, you're not gonna get them, these songs go to Willie Nelson, nobody wrote them but Willie and if they're yours, well, when Willie comes after them, he can give them to you. But I'm not gonna let anyone have these songs but Willie Nelson. They're his. I took these songs up to Willie in 1985. He looked at them and he said, "Well, I'll be damned. Where'd you get these?" I handed him the book. We walked out of the studio and Willie turned to me and he said, "Would you do me a favor? Hold on to them for me." If Willie ever needs songs, he knows where they're at.

In October 1960, Larry and I went to the DJ convention in Nashville. In the lobby of the Jackson Hotel Ralph Emory was set up with his radio show for the entertainers that had new records or wanted to come up and be interviewed by Ralph Emory. But you had a time, like George Jones was at 3:00, Faron Young was at 1:00, everybody had a certain time to be up there. You had to wait till that time come, because Ralph was interviewing everybody. Larry's time was at 2:30 in the morning, and we had messed around, we had walked all over Nashville, we got back, it was late, God, we were tired when we got back to the Jackson Hotel. A lot of people were mingling in the lobby. Ralph Emory was sitting over to the very far right. We was standing in line talking to some musicians and Larry said, "Pat, that's Willie over there. That man laying on the floor, that's Willie." I said, "How can you tell it's Willie?" He was curled up in a little ball, had his back to us. He had his arm over his face. When I got close enough where I could see who the man was laying on the floor, I fell right on top of him. Willie turned over and he looked at me. I said, "What in the world are you doing?" I said,"Willie, what are you doing laying on this floor?" He said, "I'm trying to sleep." I asked Willie how he got to Nashville. He said he walked. He had this record he wanted Ralph Emory to play. And Ralph wouldn't put him on. I said, "Well, just wait around. Larry goes on at 2:30. You go on up as soon as Larry goes up." So sure enough, we waited and Willie stood up there with us but Ralph wouldn't interview Willie. Ralph just turned Willie down flat, wouldn't let him play the record he had with him, "Night Life."

In 1985 we was visiting with Willie in Austin. We got to talking about the fun times we'd had and laughing about some of the incidents that had happened and Willie looked at me and said, "Pat, how long's it been since I played your club?" I said, "Well, a good while, probably the last time was 1969." That was the night he first met Connie. Willie came to Cut 'N' Shoot the following Friday and did me a show. I don't guess I've had anything make me feel so good. And Willie never took a nickel for the show.

PART FOUR

Write Your Own Song

Write Your Own Song

You're callin' us heathens with zero respect for the law.
But we're only songwriters, just writin' our songs that's all.
We write what we live and we live what we write. Is that wrong?
Well, if you think it is, Mr. Music Executive, why don't you write
    your own song.
An' don't listen to mine
It might run you crazy
It might make you dwell on your feelings a moment too long.
We're makin' you rich
An' you're already lazy.
Just lay on your ass and get richer, and
Write your own song.
Mr. Purified Country, don't you know what the whole thing's
    about?
Is your head up your ass, so far that you can't pull it out?
The world's gettin' smaller and everyone in it belongs.
And if you can't see that, Mr. Glorified Country
Why don't you write your own song?
An' don't listen to mine
It might run you crazy
It might make you dwell on your feelings a moment too long.
We're making you rich
An' you were already lazy.
Just lay on your ass and get richer, and
Write your own song.
So just lay on your ass and get richer, and
Write your own song.

CHAPTER TEN

B undini Brown, who used to be in Muhammad Ali's corner during his heavyweight championship years, believes powerful thoughts and sounds are always passing through us in radio waves, and what we must do is learn to listen. Bundini's classic line, "Float like a butterfly, sting like a bee," popped into his head through radio waves, he says. He recognized it as inspired advice for Ali to adopt as his philosophy in the ring. Bundini believes God is in the radio waves that our conscious minds too often choose to tune out. I agree with him about all of that, as you know by now, but for the purpose of talking about songwriting we will stick to the part about inspiration.

Countless poets, authors, and composers have reported with a feeling of awe that when their best work came it seemed as if some force beyond their control was dictating what they wrote. I don't know if Shakespeare ever said as much, but I am sure he felt it. Closer to home, one of my favorite writers, Hank Williams, used to say, "I pick up the pen and God moves it."

If God—or for now let's say creative imagination—is whispering into everybody's ear all the time, why is a Shakespeare or a Hank Williams such a rarity? Why can't everybody write *Hamlet* or "I Can't Help It If I'm Still in Love with You"? As Bundini says, the trick is being able to tune in instead of tuning out. The deeper you can learn to listen to the sounds and thoughts that are always passing through you, and the more you can learn to trust what you are hearing, the more likely you are to write something good.

Of course, there will always be people who will hear or read what you write and say, "What a piece of shit." Speaking as a songwriter of long experience, I can assure you that you will never encounter a shortage of critics.

The only answer to critics—and this may be the most important quality for you to develop if you desire a career as a writer of any sort —is perseverance.

I don't mean just to outlive your critics. It can't be done. New critics are constantly arriving to shove old critics away from banquet tables where they feast on roasted writers.

By perseverance I mean determination, sincerity, devotion, dedication, tenacity, willpower, self-assertion, firmness of spirit, ruthlessness when necessary, obstinacy, even selfishness.

In other words, "Fuck 'em if they don't know it's good."

It amuses me the people who set themselves up as critics. Not just the critics in print or on TV but also the critics who have titles at music publishing companies and movie studios. What do they know? They may have the power for a while to pull down their pants and shit all over you. But if you listen to your inner voice and refuse to quit doing your best, in the long run you will be the winner even if you don't turn out to be Shakespeare or Hank Williams. Being true to the heart of your own self puts you way ahead of the game no matter who thinks they're keeping score.

But the assholes can sting you anyhow. Why I should remember this for so long, I don't know, but I opened a show for George Hamilton IV in Canada about twenty years ago, and a critic wrote, "Where on earth did they dig up this freak Willie Nelson, who can't sing and is an illiterate songwriter?"

Maybe I wasn't as sure of my singing twenty years ago as I became later when my voice grew stronger, but being called an "illiterate songwriter" pissed me off profoundly.

Ever since then, I have never really worried about critics, because if this was the mentality of people who criticize other people, then fuck them.

If there is one thing I have known I am good at since I was old enough to catch the first thoughts and sounds that passed through me, it is songwriting.

There are millions of things I can't do, but songwriting I can do.

Melodies are the easiest part for me, because the air is full of melodies. I hear them all the time, around me everywhere, night and day. If I need a melody, I pluck one out of the air.

For example, I was on a plane with Sydney Pollack and Jerry Schatzberg shortly after I signed to do the movie *Honeysuckle Rose.* Sydney was the executive producer and Jerry the director, and they were talking to me about the music. They wanted a song.

"What kind of song?" I said.

Either Sydney or Jerry said, well, some kind of song about people traveling all over the country making music.

I said, "You mean about being on the road again?"

They said yeah, that's it.

I like to show off occasionally. I picked up an envelope, or maybe it was an airsick bag, and wrote:

> *On the road again.*
> *I just can't wait to get on the road again.*
> *The life I love is making music with my friends.*
> *I just can't wait to get on the road again.*

"How about this?" I said.

It was just one those things. As soon as I wrote "On the road again" the rest of the words simply flowed as if someone else was moving my pen.

Even if I had already thought up the song before I got on the plane, I wouldn't have admitted it to Sydney and Jerry. I liked seeing the surprise in their faces. But the fact is, it had never occurred to me until I said those first four words.

"How about the melody? What does it sound like?" Sydney asked.

I said I didn't know, I would work on the melody later. I didn't give any more thought to the melody until months later, the day before I was going into the studio to cut it. I saw no reason to put a melody to something I wasn't ready to record. I knew I wouldn't have any problem pulling the melody out of the air.

Every song doesn't come that easily. From the middle fifties until the middle seventies, I wrote way over 2,000 songs. I have hundreds of songs stashed here and there. Some I recorded for myself or friends but never released. Others I have never even put on tape, but I could pick up my guitar today and play and sing any of those unrecorded songs if I wanted.

After the middle seventies, I stopped churning them out because I no longer felt the *need* to keep writing constantly. When my family and I were hungry and the rent was overdue, that was a real need. There is nothing that quite compares with being broke and desperate to make a real writer keep working.

Now I write for two reasons. One is when there is a specific need for a song, as there was for "On the Road Again." The other is when an idea comes to mind and I know it must be a song because it's too good to throw away.

If I've gone a long time without writing a song, I don't worry about it. I know something will come up. As Roger Miller says, sometimes the well runs dry and you have to wait until it fills up again before you have anything else to say. In my hungry days, the landlord didn't give a shit if the well was dry, he wanted his money. Maybe that's why my well never ran dry in those days.

Some of my best writing, I think, is done when I'm driving down the highway by myself. My mind is clear and open and receptive. Then something will happen. Could be it's something I hear on the radio for real, or something I pick up through the radio waves that fill the universe. A song will start. The good ones come quickly, and in a few minutes it's over. I almost never write them down when they first come to me. One test I use is if I forget the song, it wasn't worth remembering.

If the song sticks in my mind, I will write it down days or months later. I'll add a second verse, add a bridge. Once I pick up my guitar, the songs may change some more. I might put it in a key that calls for a different melody than the first one I hear. But usually when I come to the point where I write down the lyrics, the song is basically done.

I seldom used to have the leisure to write this way. As a young man I made being broke and desperate into a life-style. I guess I could have retired modestly at the age of thirty off of royalties from songs like "Crazy." I might have had to live on a houseboat, but I would have had enough money coming in to provide me with potted meat sandwiches for the rest of my life. But I enjoyed playing music too much to consider just retiring to the life of a writer. If I had quit playing professionally I would have been out every night sitting in with somebody anyhow. Working the road kept me organized. If I have to be somewhere tomorrow, I won't fuck up too bad today. It's when I have too much time on my hands that I really get in trouble.

I chose not to live off my royalties but to keep myself in a condition of being close to broke and desperate—not as much as when I was in my twenties, which I think is the most difficult age for most people to grow through because you feel like you'll be trapped in your twenties forever—but close enough that the old feeling of need was a fairly constant companion.

I remember one night in 1973, when I was forty years old, I felt almost as desperate as I had felt back in the early Nashville period. I got so drunk and discouraged that I laid down in the street in the snow late at night in front of Tootsie's and waited for a car to come along and run over me. Luckily no cars came, or else they missed me, and eventually I began to feel stupid and got up and went and bought another round of drinks.

At the age of forty I had come a long way and was successful by most any standard. So why did I do that? Because I knew I could become broke and desperate again in the time it takes to snap your fingers. Anybody who went through childhood during the Great Depression—when broke and desperate described nearly the whole country and certainly the farm folks of Central Texas—grew up knowing financial security is an illusion. No matter how high you stack up money in the stock market or a bank vault, they can take it all away from you in an instant. Of all the low points I hit in Nashville, laying down in the snow and wanting a car to run over me had to be lowest.

One night I was in a studio in New York City recording my first album for Atlantic Records under my new deal with Jerry Wexler. I had never recorded in New York before. I had my own band with me, which was a good thing. The labels I had worked for previously would never let me use my own band. I would go to the studio and have three hours to record four songs with studio musicians that maybe I had met before and maybe I hadn't. They were excellent musicians, but some of them had already done three sessions that day and were tired, and none of them had played with me enough to know what I felt and how to follow me.

But Atlantic was letting me use my own band at last. We did have a lot of good musicians sitting in—Doug Sahm, Leon Russell, Jimmy Day, David Bromberg, and others—so that the big guys at Atlantic felt more comfortable. Still, things were not clicking like they should.

I walked out of the studio and back to the hotel. In my room I paced from corner to corner, listening to the radio waves, the old sensation of need surging through me. Then I went into the bathroom and sat down. I saw a sanitary napkin envelope on the sink. I picked up the envelope and started writing:

> *Shotgun Willie sits around in his underwear,*
> *biting on a bullet, pulling out all his hair.*
> *Shotgun Willie's got all his family there . . .*

Kris Kristofferson told me later the song "Shotgun Willie" was "mind farts." Maybe so, but I thought of it more as clearing my throat.

I went back to the studio session with the sanitary napkin envelope in my hand, we cut the song, it became the title song of the album, and Atlantic sold enough of them to put out announcements that *Shotgun Willie* was my "breakthrough album."

In fact, my breakthrough album, *Red Headed Stranger,* was two years in the future on CBS. Atlantic went out of the country music business right after they released my *Phases and Stages* album, and didn't spend any money trying to promote or sell it. But *Shotgun Willie* had assured me once again that when I was under pressure to write songs in a hurry, I could still do it. I wrote, and we recorded, that whole album in about a week.

When I went to Nashville in 1960 as a young songwriter with ambition to be a singer, it was because Nashville was where the store was. If I had anything to sell, it must be taken to the store. Nashville, New York, and L.A. were the big stores. There was hardly any demand for me or my music outside of Texas, and I knew if I was going to be recognized widely I would have to make it in Nashville.

I didn't try to change my lifestyle when I hit Nashville. I enjoyed fooling around with the phrasing, but it made my sound noncommercial for all those Nashville ears who were listening for the same old stuff and misunderstood anything original. They didn't know what to do with me. I wasn't country like Roy Acuff was country.

If a song had more than three chords in it there was a good chance it wouldn't ever be called country, and there was no way you could make a record that wasn't called country in Nashville at that time. I had problems immediately with my song "Crazy" because it had four or five chords in it. Not that "Crazy" is real complicated, it just wasn't your basic three-chord country hillbilly song.

"Crazy Arms" by Ralph Mooney was a three-chord country classic. A song like "Stardust" has a lot of chords. My songs are somewhere between them. For a while my songwriting career became a matter of arguing that I wasn't this and I wasn't that—so what the hell was I? They couldn't define the songs I was writing, and I was too stubborn to tailor my stuff for the country music market.

Even though I was writing a country song, I wasn't singing it in the traditional way. Not that I couldn't. I just wanted to phrase it the way I felt like phrasing it. I could sing on the beat if I wanted to, but I could put more emotion in my lyrics if I phrased in a more conversational, relaxed way. I found I could get ahead of the beat or fall behind the beat and still make it all work out in the end without breaking meter. People who really didn't know much about music lost their beat in their own minds, so they thought I was breaking meter.

Sometimes I did break meter, but I knew when it happened. It would be a mistake caused by taking chances. Maybe I would wind up with more words than I had time to sing in a particular measure, so I either dropped the words over or added a measure. If you add a measure, you break meter. I never intentionally broke meter, but I did intentionally phrase dangerously close to it.

The nitric acid test for a songwriter—where the inferior materials dissolve and leave the gold—is what we call guitar pulling.

A guitar pulling is where songwriters gather in somebody's room and fight it out for attention and approval. You might say it's like a bunch of Old West gunfighters coming together to see who is best—only instead of slapping their holsters and coming up with six-guns blazing, they unsnap their guitar cases and come up singing.

This would be a room full of real piranhas, too. Picture a dozen novelists getting together in one room, and each in turn reads his latest chapter out loud to the others, who are all competing for the same publishers and audience. That would be a novel pulling. You can imagine the tension in the room, scornful glances, the caustic remarks—but you can also imagine the tremendous feeling of pleasure when the other writers couldn't help but break into murmurs of respect.

There's a certain openness and honesty between songwriters, I think. There should be. There was with us. Anyone was fair game. We were trying to prove we were writers and get our songs recorded. There was a gang of us living in Nashville together. It was very competitive. Whoever had a recording session that week had better watch out, because he was going to get swarmed by a lot of songwriters. We'd find out who his A&R man was, who is publisher was, where his house was. You could try any way you wanted to get your song to him.

Hank Cochran, Kris Kristofferson, Harlan Howard, Roger Miller, a bunch of guys like that, would gather at guitar pullings to see what the other writers were writing as well as to show off their own stuff. You had better have a lot of stamina, because guitar pullings turned into long nights. And even if you had the best song, you might not get it recorded. Plugging songs and pitching songs is an art in itself. Besides being a hell of a writer, Hank Cochran is one of the greatest song pluggers who ever lived. I mean, Hank could sell 'em. You could be the guitar-pulling champion of the month, and just because your peers liked you was no guarantee that the big boys at the record companies would even hear you.

"Go home and live with the guy until he publishes your song," is what Hank Cochran used to say. That theory worked for Hank many times. Let's say Burl Ives was coming to Nashville to hear some new songs and asked Hank to get six or seven writers together for a guitar pulling.

Hank wanted Burl to record Hank's songs. Hank didn't care anything about Burl recording my songs or Kris's songs. But being a good song plugger and a professional, Hank would call a few of his writer friends together and say, "Burl wants to hear your songs." He'd get me and Roger and Mel Tillis and whoever in a room with Burl Ives. We'd pick our best songs and start singing them to him. Burl would sit there and listen to all of us sing. Hank would wait. After we had sung every song we knew, they would all be running together in Burl's mind. About the time the songs all sounded the same and Burl was thoroughly confused and we had run out of songs anyway, Hank would sing his own songs. Hanks' songs would be the last ones Burl remembered when he went into the studio.

There are songwriters like Billy Joe Shaver or Lee Clayton who can knock the room on its ass at a guitar pulling but have never been able to keep steady employment with the record companies. They'll write fine songs like Billy Joe's "Honkytonk Heroes" or "Black Rose" or "Old Five and Dimers" or like Lee's "Ladies Love Outlaws," but it's usually somebody else who cuts the record and makes the money.

It's always been fashionable for the record companies to find a good songwriter and sign him to a contract for his songs. That ain't a bad deal for a guy who only wants to be a songwriter. But I wanted to cut my own songs, as well. So they grudgingly allowed me to sing as long as they could cover up my voice with horns and strings and hope the songs were strong enough to carry the album. They didn't bother trying to promote me. They figured, hey, when we need a good song for one of our twenty other singers we'll just go pick one off of Willie's latest album and people will think it is new work.

There wasn't much other choice. Other than signing with a publishing house or recording label, you could sign with a middleman who usually called himself a producer or a manager. The middleman would sign the artist for everything—management, publishing, and booking. Then he'd sign the artist to a record company and pay him three or four percent out of the ten percent the label paid the middleman.

They'd give the artist a small amount to sign and tell him his three or four percent came out of royalties. They'd promise the artist all kinds of things, put out his record, and send him a statement at the end of six months.

The statement was always an incredible document that was impossible to read. The record company would take a reserve of fifty to seventy percent of the records shipped and say that the artist owed the company for the reserve. They held back money from the artist to cover "breakage." That arrangement started when records were 78s made out of glass and sometimes actually broke, but it stayed the same old shitty deal even when everybody switched to LP albums that were made out of vinyl. You could drop a vinyl LP out of a ten-story window and not hurt it. There ain't been a broken album in thirty years, but they still try to hold out ninety percent of the "breakage" reserve. The statement charged the artist for everything in sight. Stuff you thought you were getting free—telephone calls, a bar tab, room service, postage stamps—they charged you for all of it.

You'd get your statement and be excited and open it to see how much money you had made—and find out you owed the record company $50,000. Instead of being semi-rich, you'd suddenly have to scramble for money to pay your income tax.

What you'd do then is go to the middleman or the record company for an advance on the next album which you needed because they hadn't paid you any royalties on the last one. They knew you wouldn't be there asking them unless you were broke.

So before they'd give you money in advance they'd try to renegotiate your contract, sign you up an extra two years at a worse deal. For years we didn't know how to read our statements and we didn't know enough to hire our own lawyers to negotiate our contracts. The record companies and the middlemen would tell us, "You don't need a lawyer. You're a good old country boy, and I'm a good old country boy. We're just good, plain, honest folks. Be nice to us. You know we wouldn't screw you, hell, we're a big happy family here. Sign this contract and let's go have a beer, pal."

Waylon to this day says when somebody calls him "pal" it makes him paranoid.

Waylon got screwed as bad as anybody ever did, because Waylon is truly a good old honest country boy who wants to trust people. Once Waylon put out a new album, went on the road for about 180 days, came back to Nashville and opened his new statement—and discovered he owed the company something like $31,000.

He went in to get some money to pay his band, and they wound up signing him to a new five-year deal starting at the oldest, lowest rate. The way they got him signed was by sending the contract option pickup in care of Waylon Jennings at their own record company address. Then they signed the receipt for the option pickup themselves, and it was the same as if Waylon had signed it. After a short waiting period—which Waylon didn't know about—the contract automatically went into effect. The shock of this gave Waylon the idea of hiring a sharp New York lawyer to look after him. He signed with Neil Reshen. Neil put the record company through an audit and found 200,000 albums not accounted for. The company said, "Well, you're right, but we'll settle for fifty thousand dollars. You don't settle, we'll suspend Waylon, which we can do because he's got a new contract with us." They would keep reserves going back fifteen years on some artists.

Songwriters might write cynical worldwise lyrics and constantly talk about money, but most of us are downright naive when it comes to business. A songwriter back in Nashville would stroll up to me and say, "I just made a deal with X Music Company and they gave me half the publishing royalties."

I would say, "Great. What does that mean?"

He'd say, "I don't know, but it sounds good, don't it? I just ordered me a new Cadillac."

What it really means is the writer gets half the publishing royalty and half the writing royalty—which is his right according to copyright law, but they make him feel like he's getting a generous deal.

If you should write a song that sells a million records as a single, you enter the arena where mechanical royalties become very important. Mechanical royalties mean the A side and the B side of the record earn the same amount. Let's say the A side is a hit. After the record sells 100,000 copies or so the company can drag out another old song of theirs and stick it on the B side with your hit on the A side. Your hit then has to split royalties with both B sides.

It should be split 50–50, but it never used to be split that way when we let the company lawyers negotiate our own contracts. The publisher would wind up with seventy percent of your A side hit after "expenses," and maybe own all of the B side.

The writing and publishing royalties can turn into a bonanza if you are shrewd enough or powerful enough. Take the *Tonight Show* theme. It was written by Paul Anka and published by Shanka Music, which is owned by Paul Anka and Johnny Carson. Every time the *Tonight Show* theme is played, Johnny Carson gets half the writer's royalties and half the publisher's royalties. We're talking about more than $300,000 a year in royalties for the *Tonight Show* theme. And how many years has it been on the air now? Twenty some-odd? I am not implying there is anything illegal or immoral about this. It's a case of smart show business.

What I am saying to all you songwriters is to get yourself a good Jewish lawyer before you sign anything, no matter how much the company says they love you.

A songwriter never knows where a hit is liable to come from or how long it might take.

Merle Haggard and I were doing a session in 1982 at my studio in Austin with Chips Moman as the producer. Chips brought in a guitar player named Johnny Christopher. Along with Wayne Thompson and Mark James, Johnny had written a song years before called "Always on My Mind." They told me Elvis had cut it, but I had never heard it.

Johnny sang the song for me. I wanted Merle to hear it to see if maybe he and I would do it together. Merle didn't particularly like the song. He didn't hear it well enough, I think. As soon as Merle and I finished our album—*Pancho and Lefty*—I stayed in the studio with my band to do a few more tunes. I wanted to see how "Always on My Mind" would sound with just me singing it.

My album with "Always on My Mind" as the title song sold triple platinum, more than three million units. We'll never know what would have happened if Merle had really heard the song right.

"Always on My Mind" bowled me over the moment I first heard it, which is one way I pick songs to record. It could be any kind of song that touches me. There are beautifully sad songs that bowl me over, like "Loving You Was Easier (Than Anything I'll Ever Do Again)" by Kris Kristofferson and "Turns Me Inside Out" by Lee Greenwood to name just two. Haunting melodies you can't get out of your mind, with lines that really stick. Waylon and I cut the Simon & Garfunkel song "Homeward Bound" and the Eagles' song "Take It to the Limit" because they bowled us over. We didn't know if they were old songs or new songs. Waylon and I cut a song called "A Whiter Shade of Pale" because we loved the melody soon as we heard it. I didn't know what the lyrics meant. The melody was infectious and the lyrics were weird and far out enough that I thought they were bound to be good. I couldn't wait for somebody to ask me what the lyrics meant. Each time somebody did, I would make up a different story. I had no idea when we recorded the song that it was already a rock classic by Procol Harum.

Then there was the time I thought I discovered Julio Iglesias. Connie heard this guy singing on the radio and said, "Hey, Will, listen to this." I listened and thought, wow, I've found somebody here! The next day Connie went out and bought a Julio album. I listened to the whole thing. I phoned Mark Rothbaum and said, "Try to find out who Julio Iglesias is and see if he wants to cut a record with me." Mark found Julio in Los Angeles. Julio said, sure, he'd like to do a song with me.

I didn't know Julio was selling more records at that time than anybody in the world.

Julio flew to Austin and came to my studio out at the golf course.

He had found a song he liked, called "To All the Girls I've Loved Before." We cut a track of it in my studio in about two hours, mainly to put my voice on it. Julio took the tape back to L.A. and redid his part a few times to get the English down better.

Julio and I performed it together on national TV at the Country Music Association Awards show. A few weeks later the single came out. It was a monster hit.

With Julio, it was his singing that attracted me. But as a rule it is my feeling for the song itself that urges me to cut it.

A song came to me once that I knew would be huge. It was a story song that grabbed you right away with a sharp hook and a powerful message and a chorus that everybody could remember and sing along with.

I turned it down. I was already doing a long story-song sequence, "Red Headed Stranger," in my shows. I knew if I recorded this new song it would be such a hit the audience would insist on hearing it every show. There simply wasn't enough time in the show for me to do two story songs.

So I sent "The Gambler" over to Kenny Rogers.

One of the most beautiful songs I've ever heard is "Moonlight in Vermont." The words don't rhyme at all anywhere in there, but it's still poetic.

I always wanted to record "Moonlight in Vermont," but I didn't really feel I was musically qualified to do the arrangements. Then I happened to be living in the same condo complex in Malibu as Booker T. Jones. We became friends. I asked him if he would work up some arrangements for me on "Moonlight in Vermont" and "Stardust." Booker T. came up with sounds that I loved and I could perform. I asked him if he would produce an album for me.

"What kind of album?" he said.

I decided I would select my ten favorite songs of all time. We started with "Stardust."

"Stardust" was one of those songs I heard all the time on the radio when I was young. We had the sheet music for it as kids, and Bobbie played it on the piano. I tried to figure out the chords to play it on the guitar, but it was real hard and took a long time to learn. I needed a producer with Booker T.'s skill as a musician to show me how to do it. There's a saying I believe in: "When the student is ready, the teacher will appear."

Next after "Stardust" I chose "Georgia on My Mind," "Blue Skies," "All of Me," "Unchained Melody," "September Song," "On the Sunny Side of the Street," "Moonlight in Vermont," "Don't Get Around Much Anymore," "Someone to Watch Over Me."

The *Stardust* album sold triple platinum in 1978. It was really my "crossover" album. I remember the first night I sang "Stardust" with my band at the Austin Opera House. There was a kind of stunned silence in the crowd for a moment, and then they exploded with cheering and whistling and applauding. The kids in the crowd thought "Stardust" was a new song I had written. The older folks remembered the song well and loved it as much as I did.

"Stardust" is my favorite song, but I'm just as glad Hoagy Carmichael and Mitchell Parish wrote it instead of me. Because maybe then they would have written "Night Life" instead of me.

I guess my three favorite songs that I have written so far are "On the Road Again," "Angel Flying Too Close to the Ground," and "Healing Hands of Time." The first one is a good happy song. The second is a good love song, and the third is a good philosophical song like "One Day at a Time" and "It Should Be Easier Now." These are songs of a very personal nature, but everybody can apply them to their own situation. I wrote "Angel" during a time when Connie and I were having personal problems, but people related it to their own love affairs or even to someone who had died. It was the same with "I Still Can't Believe You're Gone." I wrote it about Carlene, Paul English's wife, when she died, but it has a lot of different meanings to a lot of different people who have no idea why I wrote it.

What this should say to songwriters is there is no formula for writing songs. If a song is true for you, it will be true for others.

If I were just starting out today and I had a song I thought was good, I would go to Nashville. That's still where the store is.

I would go around to all the publishing companies in Nashville and talk to all of them and take them a tape of my song. The publishing companies will open their doors to a guy who walks in and looks and acts like he's got something they want. If they're really in the publishing company business and really looking for writers, they'd be dumb and unprofessional not to give a writer a chance. It's not that hard for them to say, "Sure, we'll take your tape, leave us your phone number and we'll call you." They have people to listen to new material, because it's their business.

If you have a good song, the odds of you finding somebody who will like it and record it are good. If your song is mediocre, the odds ain't so good. If you've got a real great personality and a piss poor song, you might get signed up for life by the publishing company because they like you. I know a lot of guys who ain't that great as songwriters but have good jobs with publishing companies because they're good talkers and good at pitching songs.

I will never say anything to discourage a songwriter who is out there knocking on doors, trying to get heard. But if you are a real songwriter, nothing I could say would discourage you, anyhow. If my opinion could change your mind about being a songwriter, then you really weren't a songwriter to begin with and I would have done you a favor by making you look for a different career.

If a real songwriter happened to hear from somebody else that I didn't like his work, he would say, "What the hell does Willie Nelson know? Fuck Willie Nelson."

You can't tell a real songwriter he ain't any good, because he knows better. And he'll keep hacking his way through show-biz hell until he proves it.

CHAPTER ELEVEN

The roughest part of my life with Martha was our time in Nashville.

I picked up Martha and our three kids at the bus station about two weeks after I'd arrived in Nashville and drove them to our new home —a little green trailer house at Dunn's Trailer Court on the east side of town. There was a used-car lot on one side of Dunn's and a veteran's cemetery on the other. About thirty trailers sat on concrete blocks behind a headquarters house with tall stone pillars. There was a pay phone on a post in the middle of the yard. The rent was $25 a week, which was about $10 more than it was worth.

Martha went right out and got a job mixing drinks at the Hitching Post. It was on Broadway, across the street from Tootsie's Orchid Lounge, where I hung out with the other broke pickers who were trying to sell songs. Being the hard worker that she is, Martha quickly became manager of the Hitching Post and began working a second job at the Wagon Wheel.

Martha had two jobs and I had none. For eight years she had been going around the country with me and it seemed like every time we took a step forward we fell backwards six feet. After all her years of hard work, we had landed in maybe the shabbiest place we ever lived. Martha's Cherokee temper was getting the best of her, and she was drinking a lot more. My Indian blood was being mixed up with too much whiskey at Tootsie's, and my old manhood hang-up kept telling me only a worthless asshole would lay around drunk playing the guitar while his wife worked two jobs to support the family.

I could see Martha and me pulling apart from each other. I saw us growing in different directions and wasn't wise enough to keep it from happening. In the back of my mind I'm not sure I really wanted to keep it from happening. I think we may have had so much water run under the bridge by the time we reached Nashville that when things started going bad it was too late for us.

Martha found out I had been running around on her while I was in Nashville by myself. Then I found out she had been running around on me, too. To my way of thinking it was okay for me to cheat on her, but it sure as hell wasn't okay for her to cheat on me. That's how I thought a man should look at it.

The first thing a man in Texas was trained to do was to find the guy his wife was running around with and kill him. I didn't know who Martha was seeing on the side, so I went looking for a lot of suspects. I always carried a gun back then. It was part of the uniform. You carried a gun, you looked mean. Everybody I knew carried a gun. You stuck it in your boot or in your belt if your shirttail was out.

I was mad enough to shoot somebody. But the circumstances never quite called for it. Sometimes if I had showed up an hour earlier, no telling what might have happened. If the other guy had said, "Okay, Willie, I'm Martha's boyfriend, so go for your gun," then at least one of us would have gotten shot. Fortunately the guys I was after had a little more sense than I had, or else they didn't want to get shot over a piece of ass.

It's strange that this is how I was raised, coming from a strong church family. But I was taught you had to at least whip a guy who flirted with your wife, and you had to shoot him if he went far enough to threaten your family. One of the greatest laws, I thought when I was growing up, was a Texas law that made me real proud to live in the state of Texas. I understood that it was just in Texas that it was legal for you to kill anybody you caught screwing your wife or husband. You could kill them both and legally walk away free. I always thought, boy, what a great law that is. I never thought what might hapen if I was the one who got caught in bed. It turns out the Texas law didn't exactly say you could kill your mate's lover. But I do know some people who got killed doing things like that, and nobody went to prison.

In Nashville my fighting with Martha became more and more physical, as if we had screamed all we could stand. Martha was a tough old girl. She fought like a tiger. She took a lick pretty good, and she dealt one out even better. One time I had my hand around her face and she got my little finger in her mouth and bit it to the bone. Slowed up my guitar playing. My voice went about four octaves higher when I'd hit a chord.

Hank Cochran rescued us from Dunn's Trailer Court. He asked me to go with him to Pamper Music in Goodlettsville about twenty miles north of Nashville. The owner of Pamper Music, Hal Smith, listened to my songs, and nodded and said he'd call me. I went back to Dunn's to wait. Hal told Hank, who was his top writer and song plugger, that he liked my stuff well enough but couldn't afford to hire me. Years later I heard Hank said Hal could take the $50-a-week raise Hank had just received from Pamper and pay it to me as an advance against my royalties.

Hank drove back to our trailer to tell us the news. He had an easy time finding the trailer because Hank and Roger Miller had both lived in our same trailer earlier.

When Hank said I at last had a real job that paid a real salary for writing songs, I broke down and cried.

Martha cried, the kids cried, Hank cried. We were so happy. It was a real big deal for me—my first job as a professional songwriter.

We moved to a nicer place in Goodlettsville and I started working in a garage at the Pamper office. There was just a door, a window, a guitar, and the walls. I started talking to the walls, like I had done when I was a child in Abbott reading the pages of the *Star-Telegrams* that kept the wind out. Hank walked into the garage, and on a piece of cardboard I had written "Hello Walls."

Faron Young cut "Hello Walls" and it sold two million copies. Suddenly, my world started spinning. In 1961 Patsy Cline recorded "Crazy," Billy Walker recorded "Funny How Time Slips Away," and Ray Price recorded "Night Life." All four made the Country Top 20. "Crazy" and "Hello Walls" cracked the Pop Top 40.

Chubby Checker had started a new craze called the Twist at the Peppermint Lounge in Manhattan that year, the Berlin Wall was built, the Bay of Pigs happened, and Roger Maris hit sixty homers for the Yankees. But for me 1961 was the year I started making it as a songwriter.

Faron Young had loaned me $500. When I got my first royalty check of $3,000 from "Hello Walls," I ran to Tootsie's and found Faron sitting drinking at a table and kissed him flush on the mouth I was so excited. I tried to pay Faron the $500, but he wouldn't take it. "I don't want your money, son," he said. "Wait till you can afford it and then fatten a steer for me or something."

It took years, but I finally paid Faron back by giving him a prize bull my son Billy bought at a livestock auction for $38,000.

After "Crazy" and Hello Walls" were recorded, I heard Ray Price's bass player Donny Young—now better known as Johnny Paycheck —had quit. I talked Ray into hiring me to play bass with the Cherokee Cowboys. Ray didn't ask if I knew how to play bass, which I didn't.

The Cherokee Cowboys hit the road. Johnny Bush, Roger Miller, Darrell McCall, Buddy Emmons—they all played for the Cherokee Cowboys. I was making $25 a day faking it as bass player, but more royalty checks started coming in. I blew the money as fast as I could. Every time the Cherokee Cowboys pulled into a town, Ray would put us all up at a Holiday Inn. But I'd get the biggest, most expensive suite they had—a penthouse if there was one—and have a party for the boys until the money ran out. Between Jimmy Day and me and a couple others, the money just disappeared. I even took to flying commercial airplanes to the next gig instead of riding the bus.

You can imagine how this went over with Martha. She was getting some of the royalty money, but not as much as she should have.

Martha and I had advanced into the worst type of marital discord. There wasn't so much hitting each other any more. Now it was fighting with cruel words that once you say them you can't ever take back. If you hit somebody, or they hit you, it's over with. It's out of your system. But if you speak mean angry words, it goes to the bone and stays there. Just your tone of voice can do damage. Maybe you hardly notice how harsh you sound, but the other person never forgets it. They'll always hear your words and your tone and remember what you meant. You are what you are thinking and what you say is what you mean in those situations. You've got to watch that. It's heavy shit.

I bought Ray Price's 1959 black Cadillac with fishtail fins, a classic car, and gave it to Martha. She would get drunk and terrorize Nashville in that car. I was so worn out from being jealous and macho that I got to where I barely cared any more if Martha was carrying any boyfriends in the Cadillac.

There was a rumor I heard on the road that Roger Miller and Martha had something going. I never did ask either one of them if it was true. But Roger wrote a song called "Sorry, Willie." Actually I was with Roger the night he wrote the song someplace outside of

Tulsa. By then, Martha and I were separated and I didn't care to know what might have happened between them.

In fact, I recorded "Sorry, Willie" on Liberty with Joe Allison. Roger was at the session. It wasn't that I had become broad-minded about such shit as that, but, you know, I wasn't sure of anything. And art is art wherever you find it.

I went into Tootsie's one night toward the end of our marriage and tried to talk to Martha. We were both drinking. She didn't want to hear any more of my crap. She started throwing glasses at me. One hit the wall and shattered and cut Hank Cochran's face pretty bad. I took him to the hospital, but I was wiseass drunk and wouldn't let the doctor touch Hank, whose face was a mess of blood. I kept telling the doctor, "If you're a good doctor, how come you're working at this hour of the night?"

Hank said, "Willie, shut your fucking mouth and let him sew me up before I bleed to death."

One night Hank showed me an 8 × 10 glossy photo of a girl singer named Shirley Collie.

She was already pretty well known. Shirley was a regular on the old Phillip Morris road show with Red Foley and a bunch more. She was an old pal of Grady Martin, one of the world's best guitar players. Shirley was—and still is—one of the finest female vocalists and yodelers and probably the best harmony singer I've ever known. When we worked together, Shirley sang as close harmony with me as anybody possibly can. She second-guessed me. Like with my band today, they always guess where I'm going to go with a song. Shirley could sense that, too. Shirley and I were pretty much on the same level of thinking, music-wise, whatever that was. However low or high that was, we were very close.

Shirley and I cut duets of "Willingly" and "Touch Me." Both records reached the Top 10 in 1962.

It was the final blow for Martha to find out I was seeing Shirley, who was married to a DJ friend of ours named Bif Collie. Martha packed the kids into her black Cadillac and took off for Las Vegas in 1962 to get a divorce.

You hear stories that when I married Shirley I thought she had six months to live. It's true she had told me she had a terminal disease called lupus. If she had it, she got over it. But that had nothing to do with why I married Shirley.

Shirley traveled with me for quite a while singing and playing bass. I had left the Cherokee Cowboys, and it was me and Shirley with

Jimmy Day playing steel guitar, just the three of us. I would follow her every night on stage. She'd sing "Penny for Your Thoughts" and then she'd do "Bet My Heart I Love You," which is a yodeling song. Shirley tore the house down yodeling. I mean she was great. The last time I saw her, a year or so ago, I invited her onstage and she yodeled and tore the house down again. She's still great.

I had learned from Ray Price to sing songs the crowd is familiar with if the crowd is not familiar with you. But this didn't prevent me from trying to do it my own way when I started a band called the Offenders. We didn't really intend to offend people, but it seems like we always were. Maybe it was our attitude. It could be that because we fancied ourselves as the Offenders, we naturally became offensive. We played jazz and things that people who had come to dance didn't want to hear. We played whatever we wanted to play.

Finally we broke up that band and I started singing songs the audience was familiar with. I did "Fräulein" and "San Antonio Rose" and "Columbus Stockade Blues" and all the old favorites that got their attention. The same music that got the crowd up on the dance floor would get them out of their seats in an auditorium. Once I figured that one out, it was pretty simple. I discovered "Rolling in My Sweet Baby's Arms" was just as hot in a concert as it was in a dance hall. That was a big revelation to me. I had always been told you couldn't play that kind of music in an auditorium because people came to listen and they didn't want a lot of yelling and screaming, they wanted to hear the record just like it was when you made it. But this wasn't necessarily true, and it opened up a whole new area to work in.

In 1963 Shirley and I went to Reno for her to get a divorce. I took boxing lessons while we waited. Then Shirley and I married and returned to Nashville. On the day President John F. Kennedy was shot, we found our dream house. It was a house thirty miles east of Nashville on a farm that we called Ridgetop. I was eating liver and onions in a restaurant on the Gallatin Highway with Shirley when we heard the awful news about President Kennedy. I decided to quit the road and settle down with Shirley at Ridgetop and be a farmer. I was thirty years old, and I had retired from the road. I thought it meant a major change in my life.

CHAPTER TWELVE

I just wanted to write songs for a while. I wasn't making any money on the road, and I really wasn't having no big fun, and I just figured it was time I got off somewhere by myself and wrote some songs.

I decided if I took myself off the market for a while, maybe when I did go back out, I'd be able to draw more money, and as it turned out, it was true. I had a great time, doing nothing but raising hogs.

We had Lester and Earl, the Foggy Mountain Hogs. On our mailbox it said WILLIE AND SHIRLEY AND MANY OTHERS. We had all kinds of dogs and cats and horses. The old man that used to work for me, Mr. Hughes, was a great colorful old guy. A clever horse trader, he'd buy horses for me, and buy cattle for me, and run the farm. His wife was named Ruby. Ruby was a big old gal, and Mr. Hughes was a tall skinny old man that didn't weigh hardly 100 pounds, and she weighed close to 200.

He used to come in and I'd leave a bottle of whiskey down in the cabinet so he could get to it. He was always sneaking whiskey. I'd notice every day there'd be a little gone, a little more gone, and I'd always keep a full one, so when he'd run out, I put another one in there. And we used to sit down and drink a lot together. We'd get pretty loaded, and he'd say, "Well, I'm gonna go home and if Ruby's got me a steak cooked, I ain't gonna eat a bite of it, and if she don't have me one cooked, I'm gonna kick her clothes off." He was a funny old man.

Shirley loved farming as long as I was there with her. But then when it come time for me to go back on the road, she had to stay home. I knew that was probably the wrong thing to do. I should have taken her out with me again. So pretty soon, I was out on the road, and Shirley was home taking care of Lana, Susie, and Billy, who'd come back to live with us. She became a mother. I'm not sure that's what she had in mind in the beginning, but she did great, and it worked out fine for a while. Then she got restless, and the marriage started going downhill after that.

I didn't lose much money farming, but the fact that I lost any money at all was hilarious. I was making a little money writing songs and raisings hogs was just a hobby for me, to give me something to do.

Johnny Bush and I went out and bought seventeen weaner pigs. Paid 25¢ a pound for them. In the sleet and the snow, we built a pigpen and throwed them in the pen. But what we'd done when we built the pen, the bottom plank was just about a fraction of an inch too high. Soon as we turned the pigs loose, they went right out under that bottom plank and into the hollow down there and it was cold and sleeting and we chased them God damn pigs all over that hollow. We wouldn't have worked that hard for no man alive. Ever. But we finally caught them, every one of them, and got them back in there, and I put them on a feeder where all they had to do was eat and get their bellies full and go over there and get them a drink of water and go back over there and eat some more.

But I should have put their water farther away from their food so they'd get a little more exercise. What they did was sit there and get so fat that some of them actually ruptured themselves. They ate so much, they got so fat, that their whole ass end fell out because they were just too lazy to go get exercise. I fed them like that for five months, took them to the market, and sold them. By then the market had dropped so I only got 17¢ a pound for them. But I couldn't keep them because when it comes time to sell a hog, it's time to sell a hog. I didn't want to put more feed money into them. On that one little batch of hogs, I think I lost about $5,000.

We had some chickens at Ridgetop, some laying hens, because I like fresh eggs. Shirley named them like pets. She had eight or nine hens that layed every day. Ray Price kept fighting roosters back then, though their fighting ability was debatable. Some people said he had running roosters and fighting horses. Anyway, Ray called me and said he had a rooster that he wanted to put out on my farm to exercise. I said, "Sure, but Shirley's got some laying hens out here, and I don't want them bothered." He said, "Any problem, I'll come get the rooster." So I said okay. About the third day, one of Shirley's hens was dead. I called Ray and I said, "Ray, we've got a problem. Your rooster's killed one of Shirley's hens." Ray said, "Oh no, I'll come and get it."

But he didn't come that day, and he didn't come the next day. The next day after that, there was another dead hen. This time Shirley is hot. She's going in the house looking for the shotgun. Rather than turn her loose in the barn full of horses and chickens with a double-barrel shotgun, I decided I would do it myself. I took the gun and I killed the rooster and I gave it to our maid who took it home and cleaned it and had a big rooster dinner.

I called Ray and told him what I'd done.

I think everything Ray was trying to say kind of got clogged in his throat. Finally, he said that he would never record another one of my songs for doing that. It was the end of everything between us. My answer was that there wasn't a fighting rooster in the world that was worth one good laying hen. It took him years to get over it but we laugh about it a little bit now.

During those days Webb Pierce built himself a guitar-shaped swimming pool. His neighbors complained. I think it was Ray Stevens and a bunch of guys that got up a petition to try to keep the tourist buses from driving through their neighborhood. The buses went by Webb's house to see his pool, and when they came by Webb's, they went by everybody else's house, too. In response to the petition Webb said, "Fuck them. That's what they get for moving next door to a star."

I just threw in that Webb Pierce story because it says so much about show business.

In the six years I lived at Ridgetop, we gathered quite a family around us. Lana, Susie, and Billy had come to live on the farm even though I never did get legal custody of them from Martha. But that was all right with Martha, because she divorced her second husband in Las Vegas and married Mickey Scott, a guy she had known in Waco, and they moved down the road from Ridgetop. My dad Ira and stepmother Lorraine took up residence on the farm. My stepbrothers, Doyle and Charles, moved onto the land with their families. My sister Bobbie Lee divorced her second husband who had run a used-car lot in Fort Worth and brought her new husband, Jack Fletcher, and her three boys—Randy, Freddie, and Michael—to Ridgetop. My mother Myrle and her husband Ken moved into a red-brick house five miles away. Wade Ray, who played music with me for years, moved across the road with his wife, Grace, a great woman. Wade and Grace belonged to a mystery school called Astara, and I studied their lessons with them. After he joined my band in 1966, Paul English came with his wife, Carlene, and settled at Ridgetop. Frank and Jeannie Oakley opened the Willie Nelson General Store in Madison. The farm was 400 acres in the Cumberland Gap. We accumulated 25 brood sows, 800 Duroc and Poland China hogs, hundreds of white Leghorns and other chickens, ducks and geese, 9 horses including 3 Tennessee Walkers and 2 Palominos and 2 ponies for the kids and a quarterhorse named Preacher for me. The farm produced oats, clover, grazing grass for 200 head of Black Angus cattle. I took up calf roping. Every time I'd rope and tie a calf, somebody would yell, "That's one in a row."

I gained thirty pounds and took to smoking a pipe and wearing bib overalls. On November 28, 1964, I made my first appearance on the Grand Ole Opry for which I was paid $35. I began co-hosting a television show with my old hero Ernest Tubb. The whole enterprise was being supported by my songwriting royalties.

Ray Price had cut a record of "Night Life" and used the song as his intro. He would say, "This song was written for me by a boy down in Texas. It's not like the songs I usually do, but I hope you'll like it." Instead of fiddles, Ray was using violins in his band. (When Ray recorded "Make the World Go Away" by Hank Cochran, he filled it with violins and said, "I believe the symphony audience wants to hear country music.")

This may sound like I had it made.

But I was starting to feel like a minnow in a dipper. My songs were selling, but my records weren't. I needed to jump back in the lake and keep swimming.

On a running tour in 1965 I stopped in Phoenix, where the hottest act in town was a kid named Waylon Jennings. I went to catch his show, and afterwards we shared a bottle of tequila and he asked my advice on his career. "Whatever you do, Waylon, stay away from Nashville," I told him. "Nashville ain't ready for you. They'll just break your heart."

Upon hearing my advice, Waylon did what any good songwriter would do. He went to Nashville.

Crash Stewart came to Nashville in 1966 to plan a Texas tour with Ray Price. Before they could set their tour, Ray got a better offer and pulled out. I told Crash I would step in and take Ray's place. "Willie, I love you, but you ain't nowhere near the equal of Ray Price when it comes to filling dance halls," Crash said.

I agreed. But I had an idea. "We'll hire another big name—like Marty Robbins—to replace Ray. We'll fill out the show with Stonewall Jackson, Jeannie Sealy, Hank Cochran, and Johnny Bush and my band. But we'll call it the Willie Nelson Show."

Using all that advertising on the radio around the country would be a great way to get my name out to people who'd never heard of me. The crowd might say, "Who the hell is Willie Nelson?" But by the end of the show, they would know. It was a trick I picked up from Colonel Tom Parker. When Colonel Parker was managing Eddy Arnold, he paid somebody $50 a week to phone airports and hotels all over the world and page Eddy Arnold.

Crash bought the idea. He hired one more singer for the package. The new singer was Charlie Pride.

It may not seem like such a big deal twenty years later, but Charlie Pride is black. I told Crash I didn't think we should put Charlie in our show. We were going into South Texas and Louisiana. I could foresee major problems with bringing a black country singer onstage. I said, "This is too big a risk. It's our promotion. We could lose money and make people mad."

Then Crash played me Charlie's record "Snakes Crawl at Night." Hearing Charlie sing made all the difference. Charlie was in.

The first night Charlie played with us was in Dallas. He went out onstage and said, "Well, I guess you're probably surprised to see me singing country music with this deep suntan I got, but I love country music and hope you'll listen and enjoy it." Charlie was real humble and nice and Uncle Tommed the shit out of them. He sang great and they loved him.

One night during that same tour, we had a night off and I went over to Dewey Groom's Longhorn Ballroom in Dallas to hear Johnny Bush. Charlie Pride was just sitting at a table. I got drunk at the party and got up on Dewey's stage and told the crowd they ought to hear my new friend sing. That's when I called Charlie out of the audience and brought him to the microphone. I could hear gasps from the partygoers, and especially Dewey Groom, who had said he would never book Charlie Pride or any other black musician at the Longhorn Ballroom.

I knew something special was called for at that moment, so I grabbed Charlie and laid a big kiss on his lips, and once the crowd recovered they listened to Charlie and went crazy over him.

After the show me and Charlie Pride and Dewey Groom and a bunch of us went over to the motel room and partied and played songs all night long. Dewey got drunk and wound up passing out in the same bed with Charlie. I said, "Look at Dewey. He's trying to change his luck." Dewey woke up with a smile on his face, and Charlie was happy, and they've lived together ever since. I'm kidding about living together, of course, but Dewey sure never had no more prejudice about booking Charlie Pride.

I was making about $100,000 a year from my songwriting royalties, but me and my band was always right on the edge of broke. We bought an old bus and started touring the country. Shirley hadn't wanted me to go on the road. Particularly for a month at a time and without her. She was a performer and a good one and wanted to be part of the show. But I needed her to stay home with the kids. She did a good job of it for a long time before she got bored and pissed off and our marriage fell apart.

Anyhow, by 1968, my life with Shirley had turned into blithering hell. She helped me fall through a plate-glass window one night when I was too drunk to walk straight. We had a lot of terrible, nasty fights. Shirley was boozing as bad as I was and we were all swallowing enough pills to choke Johnny Cash when he was at his worst.

Then one night I looked down into the audience while I was performing at Larry and Pat Butler's 21 Club in Cut 'N' Shoot and saw this tall blond knockout sitting at the band table. It was classic eye contact, lightning across a crowded room. I told Jimmy Day, "Get that blond for me." After the show, there she was. Her name was Connie Koepke. We didn't have time to do much but gape at each other before the band took off for our next gig. But I got her phone number. I called her the next time I was in town and first thing I knew, I was stone in love again.

Connie was in her early twenties and had never been married. She had been raised a devout Catholic girl, and her family didn't think highly of her running around with a married man. But Connie was in love with me, too. We were very happy. She traveled with me some, and it was a great time for both of us. Back at Ridgetop, Shirley had no idea Connie existed. Shirley and I were into a very bad pe-

My sister Bobbie Lee and me, when we were four and two.

The old family place in Arkansas.

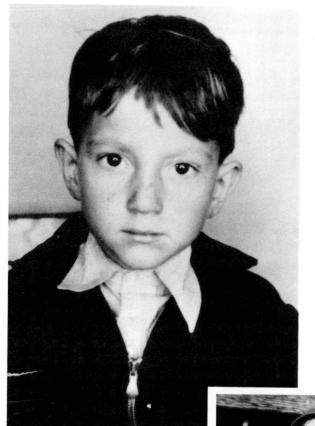

My second grade school photo.

Mama and Daddy Nelson in front of their old house in Searcy County, Arkansas, just before they packed up and moved to Abbott with my parents in 1929.

An outing to the park in Waco with Mama Nelson. We could hardly wait to get to that watermelon.

Me, Mama Nelson, Bobbie, and one of the Nelson cousins.

The Abbott City Hall.

CITY HALL
ABBOTT, TEXAS

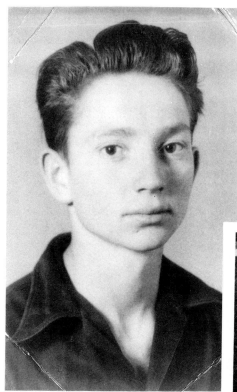

8

This photo is from my junior year at Abbott High in 1949.

All dressed up for a school dance (and a pretty girl).

9

Mama Nelson and me in the old porch swing in Waco.

10

11

Me, my dog, and Bobbie in front of our house with our friends.

Bobbie and me.

12

The gang posing on our front lawn.

13

*Just hanging around
Abbott High.*

14

The sophomore football "star" of the Abbott High Panthers.

Me, Bobbie, Bud (on the fiddle) and my pop, Ira, (on the guitar) perform at the local radio station.

Ira performing on stage in 1977.

My mother at one of my shows in the '70s.

The dashing Air Force man in uniform.

Onstage with Larry Butler, who gave me a job in his band so I wouldn't have to sell my songs away.

20

At 18, with Joe Massey and the Frontiersmen.

MEL'S RANCH MARKET

EVERY SATURDAY NITE · 9:30-10 p.m.

Hear it on KUGN·590 Kc.

21

*Couples' night out on
the town. That's Martha
with me on the right.*

*In the studio, working
on my first album.*

Lana and me.

Susie, Lana, and Billy moved in with Shirley and me in 1965.

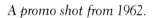

Me and all the ladies down at the radio station.

A promo shot from 1962.

My first two albums,
with Liberty Records in
1961.

28

Shirley and I got married in 1962.

The house at Ridgetop, outside
Nashville. When it burned down at
Christmas time in 1970, we all
moved back to Texas.

29

30

Me as a pig
farmer, 1963.

31

With Paul English in 1965.

Signing on with Haze Jones and Ott Devine of the Grand Ole Opry, in 1964.

On tour in 1968 with
Paul English, Jimmy
Day, and David
Zentner.

Mama Nelson at one of
our shows in the '60s.

riod, having terrible fights, breaking up and getting back together, and then breaking up again. With me and Connie, though, every day we saw each other was like going on a honeymoon.

I was sitting in the living room at Ridgetop reading the paper one afternoon in November of 1969 when Shirley walked in with a handful of mail.

Shirley opened an envelope and stared at a piece of paper like she couldn't believe what she was reading. "Willie," she said. "This Houston hospital has sent us a maternity ward bill that says you and a Mrs. Connie Nelson have a baby daughter named Paula Carlene, born October 27th, 1969!"

A lot of thoughts went through my mind all at once. What a dumb fucking thing to do was one of them. I had put my home address on the registration forms when we checked Connie into the hospital. But I ain't stupid. I must have been tired of the secrecy and wanted to get this out in the open.

It was definitely out in the open now.

Well, Shirley took to cussing, screaming, fighting, threatening to sue, calling my sorry ass every name she could think of—and Shirley was an eloquent lady with plenty of insults in her repertoire. She did all the normal things a woman would do under the circumstances.

What could I say? My only defense was the truth—that Connie and I were in love—but this didn't calm the atmosphere at Ridgetop. Finally I got on my high horse and acted outraged and offended and stomped out of the house.

Connie and I got married at a wedding chapel in Las Vegas on my birthday, April 30, in 1971.

There was one little matter I neglected to mention to the preacher.

I was still married to Shirley.

Shirley and I had been split up for a year and a half. After our bitter battles the first couple of months following the hospital bill, Shirley moved out of Ridgetop and I didn't see her again for ten years. In my mind, my marriage to Shirley was over long ago.

I don't know whether Connie realized I was still married then or does now or really cares that much. I think she knew in her mind, too, we felt the same way. We always have felt that when we got married, we blew it. We got along so great when we were just hanging out, living together, and having a good time and she was following me around all over the country and she was my lover. When we got married, she became a wife with all the definitions that go with it.

Every time you see a joke about marriage, it's about either his infidelity or hers or he's no good, she's no good, all the nagging connotations that go along with a marriage, a husband and wife. We hated that. We didn't want to be that, and then we got married and we became that. We became a husband and a wife and all the things that go with it.

I think the paperwork in marriage means more to women than it does to men. I've always felt that a marriage contract was in the minds of the people that did it and not on a piece of paper. A judge somewhere in some courthouse had no right over me and over my mind, over my thoughts and feelings for another person. That's why, probably, they call me a rebel. I don't believe that one person can judge another person's actions. I don't think a person should say, well, okay, you're legally married or you're legally divorced. That has to be between the two people, and Shirley and me were divorced in my mind. I had divorced myself from the Shirley situation, and that was good enough for me.

Shirley was granted a divorce from me in Nashville on November 2, 1971, six months after Connie and I had our ceremony at the wedding chapel in Las Vegas.

Connie being a Catholic could have presented obstacles that we couldn't overcome in the eyes of her church, but our love was stronger than anything. All she asked of me was to agree that Paula Carlene—and Amy when she was born nearly two years later—be raised Catholic.

In 1978 Connie and I had a second wedding. It was like a reaffirmation of our love and commitment. Our second wedding was held on June 10th in the Las Vegas home of Steve Wynne, who owned the Golden Nugget. When people asked why we wanted to get married again, Connie said it was to change the date of our anniversary.

"Will is always working on his birthday," she said.

Connie came to Ridgetop before Christmas of 1969, as soon as Shirley left. Suddenly Lana, Susie, and Billy had not only a new stepmother but also a new sister, Paula Carlene.

Connie and our baby arrived just in time to get into the middle of what our family has come to call the Great Ridgetop Shootout.

My daughter Lana had gotten married at age sixteen to a country boy named Steve Warren who was in his middle twenties. They lived a few miles away with their kids. Steve and Lana stopped by Ridgetop one morning, but Lana stayed in the car. Susie went out to talk to her sister. After Steve drove Lana away, Susie told me Lana had two black eyes and bruises on her face. "Steve beat up Lana," Susie told me.

I ran for my truck and drove to the place where Steve and Lana lived and slapped Steve around. He really pissed me off. I told him if he ever laid a hand on Lana again, I would come back and drown his ass.

No sooner did I get back to Ridgetop than here came Steve in his car, shooting at the house with a .22 rifle. I was standing in the door of the barn and a bullet tore up the wood two feet from my head. I grabbed an M-1 rifle and shot at Steve's car. Steve made one pass and took off.

I drove straight back to Steve and Lana's. Steve had come home and taken their son Nelson Ray and left again. He told Lana he was going to get rid of me as his top priority.

Thinking Steve would come to Ridgetop to pick me off about dusk, I hid the truck so he couldn't tell if I was home. We laid a trap for him. I had my M-1 and a shotgun.

He drove by the house, and I ran out the garage door. Steve saw me and took off. That's when I shot his car and shot out his tire.

Steve called the cops on me. Instead of explaining the whole damn mess, the beatings and semi-kidnapping and shooting and all, I told the officers Steve must have run over a bullet.

The police didn't want to get involved in hillbilly family fights. They wrote down what I told them on their report and took off. Then we turned back to the immediate problem of seeing to it that Steve wouldn't mistreat Lana again.

It was kind of an unusual introduction to our family, but Connie reacted like a real trouper. She's a strong person, Connie is, really good and dependable. I admired the way she handled herself at the Ridgetop Shootout.

My records still weren't selling, and we had wrecked five cars in three months. Down in the basement of the Ridgetop house we had a crude little recording setup where the guys and I would get drunk and write songs day and night. The week of Christmas in 1969, Hank and I wrote "What Can They Do to Me Now?"

On the night before Christmas Eve, I was at a party in Nashville when I got the news that the Ridgetop house had just burned to the ground. Connie and Paula Carlene were home when the fire broke out, but they were safe.

It was a horror to see the smoking black skeleton and smell the burnt wood that sizzled in the water from the fire hoses.

I ran into the smoking, stinking debris and kicked through the ashes until I found an old guitar case that contained two pounds of Colombian tea.

I stuck the case under my arm and went back to the car and sighed with relief. In 1969, you could get life in prison for being caught by the law with one joint. In Louisiana you could get the death sentence.

I was glad to find my stash before the authorities did.

CHAPTER THIRTEEN

T he Happy Valley Dude Ranch was closed for the winter, but Crash Stewart arranged for us to move the whole family there after the Ridgetop fire. Happy Valley is near the town of Bandera, about fifty miles west of San Antonio. The country is rolling hills and cedar trees and pure flowing creeks and springs bubbling out of the limestone everyplace. As spring came to the Hill Country, the land was a riot of wildflowers—bluebonnets, Indian paintbrush, desert willow, and primrose. The afternoon sky was bright pastel blue. The way mountains of white clouds built up above the hills, looking like snowy peaks, you could imagine you were in the Rockies.

Connie and baby Paula and I moved into the ranch foreman's house. The other kids and relatives and friends and the band and their families scattered out into clapboard guest cabins. The Happy Valley Dude Ranch was a great location for us. We had an Olympic-size swimming pool, tennis courts, stables, and a nine-hole golf course. Although I had batted the golf ball around a little before, it was living on the Happy Valley golf course that started my addiction to the game.

I was reading Edgar Cayce, the healer and prophet. The poems of Kahlil Gibran made sense to me. Gibran said life on earth is a quest for returning to God.

I started working on the *Yesterday's Wine* album, though I wasn't ready to record it then. *Yesterday's Wine* was my first concept album, an album that tells a story. It's about a guy—imperfect man—watching his own funeral and reviewing his life.

Yesterday's Wine starts off "Do you know why you're here?"

Yes, there's great confusion on earth, and the power that is has concluded the following:
Perfect man has visited earth already and his voice was heard;
The voice of imperfect man must now be made manifest
And I have been selected as the most likely candidate.
YES, THE TIME IS APRIL, AND THEREFORE YOU,
A TAURUS, MUST GO.
TO BE BORN UNDER THE SAME SIGN TWICE
ADDS STRENGTH AND THIS STRENGTH, COMBINED WITH
WISDOM AND LOVE, IS THE KEY.

After the *Yesterday's Wine* album came out a friend of mine got a call from a hippie fan in San Francisco who said, "I'm worried about Willie. He thinks he's Jesus."

I got a kick out of that. Just last year one of those supermarket newspapers had a full-page story about the face of Jesus suddenly appearing on the outside wall of a grocery store in South America after a dramatic rainstorm. Hundreds of people came to pray to the image of Jesus, and some of the sick went away cured. A few days later, following another thunderstorm, a new figure appeared on the wall beside Jesus. It was Julio Iglesias.

What had happened, the rain had washed off the coat of whitewash that had covered a poster for "To All the Girls I've Loved Before."

The supermarket headline said:

THAT'S NOT JESUS—IT'S JUST OLD WILLIE

Well, this imperfect man in *Yesterday's Wine* was just old Willie. In the song "Goin' Home," it's just old Willie who observes his own funeral and sings:

The closer I get to my home, Lord, the more I want to be there.
There'll be a gathering of loved ones and friends, and you know I want to be there.
There'll be a mixture of teardrops and flowers,
Crying and talking for hours
About how wild that I was
And if I'd listened to them, I wouldn't be there.

Well there's old Charlie Tolk, they threw away the mold when they made
him.
And Jimmy McKline, looks like the wines finally laid him.
And Billy McGray, I could beat any day in a card game.
And Bessy McNeil, but her tears are real, I can see pain.
There's a mixture of teardrops and flowers,
Crying and talking for hours
About how wild that I was
And if I'd listened to them, I wouldn't be there.

Lord, thanks for the ride, I got a feeling inside that I know you,
And if you see your way, you're welcome to stay 'cause
I'm gonna need you.
There's a mixture of teardrops and flowers,
Crying and talking for hours
About how wild that I was
And if I'd listened to them, I wouldn't be there.

I think it's one of my best albums, but *Yesterday's Wine* was regarded by RCA as way too spooky and far out to waste promotion
money on.

The *Willie Nelson and Family* album came out in 1971 and went
into the dumper, commercially.

I was in sort of the same situation I had been in ten years earlier.
My band would fill a Texas dance hall. We were stars in Texas. But
in Nashville, I was looked upon as a loser singer. They wouldn't let
me record with my own band. They would cover me up with horns
and strings. It was depressing. But as some athlete said, I hung my
head high.

The Ridgetop house was rebuilt and we all traveled back to Tennessee.

For the Country Music Association Awards party week in 1971,
Harlan Howard arranged a guitar pulling at his house. The rules were
simple—just singer and guitar on a stool in front of a gas-log fire in a
big room full of record executives, songwriters, and disc jockeys.

Naturally I had my favorite Martin guitar. I had already worn the
hole in the body of the guitar because classical guitars like my Martin
are not meant to be played with a pick. The hole looks soulful, but
it's just a hole. I didn't have all the autographs on the guitar that
night at Harlan's because Leon Russell started the autographing two
years later.

I had been playing electric guitar early in the noisy beer joints. I had a Fender Telecaster and a Fender Stratocaster. Those Fenders had much smaller necks than a classical guitar. Baldwin then gave me a guitar and an amp. I still use the amp, an aluminum job made in 1951, but I busted the Baldwin guitar at John T. Floore's one night. I sent the guitar to Shot Jackson in Nashville. Shot Jackson took out the guts, took out the pickup, and put them in a Martin classical guitar and set the whole bastard instrument up.

I've got such a terrific tone out of this guitar because it was a good guitar to begin with and then putting all that electronic equipment in it just happened to work exactly right, and there is just enough beer spilled in the amplifier to give it the perfect tone for me. I've never changed guitars or amps since Shot fixed up this Martin for me.

It came my turn to sing about two in the morning. The party had halfway thinned out. Most of the food was gone but there was plenty of booze. I climbed on the stool with my old Martin and sang all the songs I had written for a new album I called *Phases and Stages*. The concept is a look at marriage and divorce from the man's point of view on one side and the woman's point of view on the other. Considering the puzzlement with which Nashville had received *Yesterday's Wine*, I didn't know how this new concept album would go over. The song I started off with that night was "Bloody Mary Morning."

When I finally finished, a stranger came up and said, "I'm Jerry Wexler. We're starting a country division at Atlantic, and I run it. I'd love to have the album you just sang."

I said, "I have been looking for you for a long time."

Jerry let me bring my own band in to play on my albums for the first time. *Shotgun Willie* came out first and sold more than any album I'd ever done. *Phases and Stages* followed and sold much better than *Shotgun Willie*. My third Atlantic album was *The Troublemaker*, mostly gospel songs, and by then the company had decided to drop country music and wouldn't do any promotion.

But I was long gone from Nashville by then. As soon as I signed with Atlantic, I moved back to Texas, looking for something like the Happy Valley Dude Ranch.

First we had to pick a town for headquarters. We considered Houston. I even put a deposit on an apartment in Houston. But then I went up to Austin and looked around. My sister Bobbie was playing a gig at a piano bar on the top floor of an apartment building near the capitol. She and her husband Jack were living in Austin with their kids, Freddy, Randy, and Mike.

The more I got to thinking, I liked the idea of living in Austin more than Houston. Who wouldn't? Houston was too hot and too crowded. Austin was a very pretty place. My friend Darrell Royal was the football coach at the University of Texas, and he told me I'd be crazy not to move to Austin. He said Austin had a lot of people like me, brothers under the skin, and I would find it out.

Austin had lakes and hills and plenty of golf courses, and it also had Big G's and the Broken Spoke and other good halls to work.

And Austin had a new redneck hippie rock and roll folk music country venue in an old National Guard Armory. They had painted the walls with portraits and scenes by Jim Franklin, Gilbert Shelton, Michael Priest, Jack Jaxon, and other Austin artists who were becoming well known in the hippie underground. My friends in Mad Dog Inc. had an office near the stage where they did "indefinable services for mankind." The roof was hung with acoustic shields, and the crowd mostly sat on the floor like at the Fillmore in San Francisco.

There was a strong Austin to San Francisco axis in those days. The towns reminded me of each other. If San Francisco was the capital of the hippie world at that time, then Austin was the hippie Palm Springs.

This new Austin hall I'm talking about was sort of like San Francisco, but at the same time it was pure Austin.

It was called the Armadillo World Headquarters.

You need to understand what Austin was like when we moved there in late 1971 and rented an apartment on Riverside Drive.

If you stand downtown and look west across the river to the limestone cliffs that rise up abruptly on the other shore, you are looking at the place where the West literally begins.

The cliffs are a tall wall of rock that runs in an arc from Waco south to Del Rio. The old cotton economy of the South ended where it struck those limestone cliffs. Farther west beyond the cliffs is the Hill Country, which used to be the Comanche territory.

Built on seven hills in a river valley where pure artesian water flowed from the rocks and with a mild climate and deer and other wild animals roaming through the oaks and cedars, Austin was like Palm Springs for the Comanche nation long before the Anglo real estate developers turned it into a town in 1840. Houston had been the capital of Texas until then. The brazen act of building a new capital right in the middle of the Comanche's centuries' favorite resort started the bloodiest Indian war in Texas history.

You know the Indians lost, but it was hard to tell in Austin in the early seventies. A hell of a lot of young people wore feathers and beads and necklaces and bells and doeskin pants and skirts with fringes and moccasins and long hair and headbands.

It was cheap living. Low taxes, no traffic to speak of. Billie Lee Brammer, who wrote *The Gay Place*, a novel about Austin, was legally blind without his glasses, but Billie Lee was forever taking a bunch of acid and losing his glasses and driving safely all over town in the middle of the night. Austin was a stable place that depended on the state government offices and five universities for much of its economy.

There was no way to get rich in Austin. Only half a dozen houses in town would be allowed in Beverly Hills. People who did have money didn't show it off. Car dealers and beer distributors were big socialites.

You couldn't legally walk around Austin smoking weed or eating acid or mescaline or peyote—dope was very much against the law in Texas—but it seemed like you couldn't walk around Austin for very long without at least being offered a joint.

Every few blocks in Austin you saw some new, unexpected vista— a Victorian house framed against the water and the purple hills, a pair of hawks circling above Mount Larsen, a Mexican family eating dinner on the front porch of a house painted pastel yellow with statues of Jesus and the Virgin in the front yard behind a little iron fence.

Barton Springs was the greatest outdoor swimming hole in the country. You could fish and swim in the river right beside your house. You could go out on Lake Travis in a houseboat and putter around hundreds of miles of shoreline for days before somebody found you.

For a population of about 250,000, Austin was a real piece of paradise, an oasis, the best-kept secret in America.

The most famous musician in Austin when I got there was Jerry Jeff Walker. Janis Joplin had sung for years at Kenneth Threadgill's place in Austin, but she'd gone to San Francisco to make her reputation. Jerry Jeff and I had some wild nights and days partying and picking in joints and people's homes around Austin. Everybody wanted Jerry Jeff to play his classic "Mr. Bojangles," but he never did like to be told what to play or when to play it. If some host asked Jerry Jeff to play "Mr. Bojangles" or anything else at the wrong moment in the wrong tone of voice, he was liable to whip out his dick and piss in the potted ficus plant, and the fight would start.

There was more live music played in joints in Austin every night of the week than in Los Angeles.

Rock bands like Shiva's Head Band, the Conqueroo, and the Thirteenth Floor Elevators were going from Austin to San Francisco and back to the Armadillo World Headquarters. The Armadillo World Headquarters was a center for the arts. You could buy jewelry and leathergoods there as well as beer and good food cheap. They booked acts from the Austin Ballet to Ravi Shankar to Bette Midler. Eddie Wilson, who was the ramrod of the operation, would try anything. Rednecks and hippies who had thought they were natural enemies began mixing at the Armadillo without too much bloodshed. They discovered they both liked good music. Pretty soon you saw a long-hair cowboy wearing hippie beads and a bronc rider's belt buckle, and you were seeing a new type of person.

Being a natural leader, I saw which direction this movement was going and threw myself in front of it.

My first show at the Armadillo World Headquarters was August 12, 1972.

In the spring some promoters had put together an outdoor concert called the Dripping Springs Reunion on a ranch west of Austin. They had bluegrass, Loretta Lynn, Tex Ritter, Roy Acuff, Kris Kristofferson, Waylon Jennings, Billy Joe Shaver, Leon Russell, and me—with Coach Royal onstage. The promotion lost a bundle, but it had the seed of a sort of country Woodstock and got me wondering if I could do it better.

After my show at the Armadillo, I started getting bookings at college auditoriums. A new audience was opening up for me. I phoned Waylon in Nashville and told him he ought to come play the Armadillo. Waylon walked into that big hall and saw all those redneck hippies boogying to the opening act, Commander Cody, and he turned to me and said, "What the shit have you got me into, Willie?"

The Chorus

BIF COLLIE

If there's any man I'd like to have run off with my wife, it would be Willie Nelson. The reason I say that is, Willie already did it. He sneaked Shirley right out from under my eyes. Just like you hear in the songs on the jukebox, I was the last one to know. I might have caught on earlier, except I was too much in love with Shirley to be suspecting anything.

Also, I have to admit Willie didn't pull no gun on Shirley to make her leave with him.

It was a pretty ironic situation all around. Shirley was the first girl I ever really fell in love with, but not the first one I married. My first wife was the ex-wife of Floyd Tillman, who was Willie's idol at one time. I don't truly remember meeting Willie until 1960—after I was married to Shirley—but our paths had kept crisscrossing until we finally collided in a room at the Hermitage Hotel in Nashville.

The year I brought Shirley to Nashville with me for the annual disc jockey convention, Harlan Howard and Hank Cochran showed up at our room with Willie and some more songwriters. They picked and sang and carried on. Little did I know there were seeds being planted in the hotel room between Willie and Shirley. I heard later

Bif Collie is a record executive, disc jockey, and ex-husband of Willie's second wife.

that Willie and Hank had a bet to see which one could make Shirley first.

Shirley and I went back to California after the convention. It seemed like no time at all before Willie came to California for a recording session. Joe Allison phoned and asked if Shirley would like to do a duet with Willie Nelson. This may be the first duet he ever did. The story I got was Willie offered Joe a piece of one of his songs if Joe could put him and Shirley in the studio together.

And I went out and promoted their records. One of 'em was called "Willingly."

I came home one day and there was a note from Shirley on the kitchen table saying she had to go to buy a dress to wear on Allison's *Country America Saturday Night* TV show.

Well, that must have been some hell of a dress, because she wrote the note in 1962 and she ain't back yet.

Days kept going past, and I didn't know where Shirley was. I had no idea if she was dead or alive. Shirley had talked about suicide before.

After three weeks of worrying, I heard she was living in Nashville.

Then Shirley started calling me out of the clear blue sky. It was weird. She'd say, "I just got out of the emergency room again. I'm having emotional problems." I thought, well, sweetheart, so am I.

People knew Shirley was with Willie by now. They weren't married yet. I guess he was still married to Martha. But people would phone and say, "Don't you know that SOB stole your wife? Why do you keep playing his records on your radio show?"

I'd say, "Hell, it's my job to play the best music, and Willie is one of the best no matter whose wife he's with."

I wish I could say I was never mad at him, but that wouldn't be the truth. See, when Shirley and Willie took off, she had my American Express card. They used my card to rent a car and drove it for weeks and weeks. I got a rent car bill for over $2,000. That year Willie probably made $120,000 in royalties while I was making $15,000. But they stuck me with the rent car bill.

American Express took my card away. I never did get it back. Shirley is Willie's second ex-wife.

SHIRLEY NELSON

The day I ran away from Bif, my husband, I flew to Seattle to meet Willie, who was on the road working for Ray Price and the Cherokee Cowboys. The tour was about to take them across Canada for thirty days. I wanted to prove to Willie that I was serious about being with him, so they hid me on Ray's bus while we went all the way across Canada and back into the United States.

Willie and I went on to Atlanta together. We would walk down the streets and look in the windows and laugh and go back to the motel and eat Chinese food or pizza and tell each other who we were and what we wanted to do. We were so happy. Willie was still trying to get away from Martha, and I was still trying to get away from Bif. I wish everybody could experience falling in love the way Willie and I did. It is a magical feeling—totally out of sight.

When we finally got back to Nashville, we took my money I'd made on my TV shows in California out of the bank and used it to live on until Willie could get his royalty checks. We didn't care about money. Willie wasn't such a big success as an entertainer, but we had a great family life at our farm at Ridgetop until things started to fall apart in about 1965 and finally smashed to bits in 1969.

When we first got together and Willie was writing I would get very upset because the way he wrote was he'd lay down across the bed and get real quiet. It frightened me because I thought maybe he was having second thoughts about us being together. In fact, he just withdrew into himself. You would almost have to see it to understand. I didn't realize what he was doing. Later on, he would write when I was in bed. When I got into writing a little bit, I would put things down on the recorder and then when he would come in, he would play those things. I've got some beautiful notes, love notes, that he would leave me—thank you for being the way you are with me and thank you for loving my children and all. They're beautiful love notes.

I called Martha and asked if we could have Billy come live with us first, because he was the youngest. He was like my own little boy to me. I sang him all the songs I knew. We went everywhere together and we played and he was just mine, always. Then his sisters came to live with us at Ridgetop. One night Billy and I were sitting in front of the fireplace and he said, "If you ever leave, if you ever go away from here, would you take me with you wherever you go?" I said yes, I would. I had no idea of ever leaving. But it was a lie that I would take him. I couldn't take him. If I had picked him up and taken him with me, they would have come and got him. He didn't legally belong to me. But I didn't explain it to him. I still have very guilty feelings about Billy. I feel I have added to Billy's problems in life, and I didn't mean to. I pray that one of these days he's going to listen to me and believe I love him.

I prayed that Susie and Lana would become my friends, too, and listen to my side of the story.

Things started coming apart in Ridgetop when Willie decided to go on with his dream of being an entertainer. He enjoyed being a gentleman farmer for a couple of years at Ridgetop, even though he didn't have much aptitude for it. But when he started going on the road for weeks and months at a time, our family life began slipping away. Willie and I began having really terrible fights. He kept kicking down doors—he always had this thing about kicking down doors even if the key was in his pocket. I was hearing rumors that he was running around on me. I didn't want to believe it, but it was tearing me up. One night I got so mad that I actually shot at him a couple of times.

It was only an accident that I found out about Connie. When the bill arrived from the Houston hospital saying Paula Carlene was born, I just couldn't handle it. I thought it was my fault. Maybe I wasn't a good enough mother. I never did think Willie did anything wrong.

When Willie moved the kids out of Ridgetop, I phoned my parents and asked if I could come back home. I've stayed pretty much out of sight since I went home to my folks to get well. I don't want to be on the road. The road is just not my life. I'm a small-town person. It took me nearly ten years before I was strong enough to see Willie again. I sent word to him that I was coming to his show in Las Vegas. He called me out onstage to sing "Amazing Grace" and "Will the Circle Be Unbroken" with him.

Later I told Willie, "You're so thin."

He laughed and said, "Yeah. If I'd stayed with you I'd probably be fat and sitting around the house."

I had been so afraid that the Willie I had known ten years ago wouldn't still be there. I didn't think I had the courage to see him in his beard and earring and all. But he's still the same heart, the same man who's so full of love, the same sensitivity as that guitar picker I fell in love with. I have never come close to remarrying. I can't make a commitment to anyone, because I love Willie. I'm happy with that. At last, I can handle knowing there's nobody else for me.

BILLY COOPER

You think ole Will can't talk to the birds and the beasts and all God's creatures? Well, I'm here to tell you he can do it.

Me and Will was sitting around a campfire one night on the bank of the river in Austin, out back of a house he used to have in West-lake Hills. Just the two of us. We was dreaming up stuff for the first Picnic he was gonna have in Dripping Springs. We was talking about going down to the Armadillo World Headquarters, where Charlie Rich was playing, and asking him if he'd perform at the Picnic. Hell, I think Will had already announced Charlie was coming, but we thought we might as well go ahead and ask him anyhow.

This tree limb had fallen into the water about fifteen feet away. I looked down and saw a snake on the limb watching us. This was a four-foot water moccasin. I don't like nothing about snakes no way. He's got these little bitty eyes, looking at us, and I said, "Oh, Will, that be a snake fixing a stare on us. Maybe we oughta move back a little."

Willie says, "You know, snakes respond to shadows."

I say, "Oh, yeah?"

Will puts his forefinger out in front of him a foot or so and starts making a slow, circular motion, six or eight inches, clockwise. And this old snake raises up off this tree limb and his head starts following Will's finger round and round. Will would start again and the snake would start, his old head going round and round following Will's finger.

The snake finally got spooked, hisself, by Will. The snake run over to the right of us about eight feet and hid behind a log. He'd stick his head up and look at us, but he didn't want no more of Will's finger. That cottonmouth knew he had met his master.

I drifted off to sleep. When I woke up it was early daylight, and hundreds of birds flew into the tree I was sleeping under and set in the branches right above me. I was awful tired and didn't want to move.

I said, "Hey, Will, please tell them birds not to shit on me."

He said, "Go on to sleep, B. C. You'll be all right."

When I woke up again there was birdshit all around me but not one drop on my person. You think I'm lying? Anybody who thinks I'm lying just don't know Will.

Billy Cooper has done a little bit of nearly everything for Willie, including being his bodyguard.

CHET ATKINS

With a record company you can have a whole room full of people who all put their heads together and grind away at a problem and still come up with the wrong answer. One company I was with, we used to have meetings and say, "We've got to stop Dolly Parton from wearing those terrible wigs. She looks like a hooker!"

When we signed Willie on RCA I remember somebody at a meeting saying, "Willie has got to be big. He's got style and he's different and he's a great songwriter and his time is going to come now, damn it. Just like Roger Miller, Willie's time has got to come."

I said, "Well, he sounds great in Texas. What we've got to do is spread him out of Texas."

So that was going to be our thing—promote the hell out of Willie and sell his records all over the country.

But we didn't do it.

I was just about the worst at promotion and sales. I didn't care anything about that part of the business. What time I wasn't working in the studio, I was off somewhere playing my guitar. I would fall asleep playing my guitar. I just didn't have the time—or take the time—to promote and sell records, mine or anybody else's.

It hurt Willie a lot to have a guy with my attitude about sales as the one who was supposed to push his product. I guess the timing just wasn't right. So much of what happens in show business for good or bad is timing.

RICK BLACKBURN

When I came to Nashville in 1976 to run the marketing operation for CBS Records, Billy Sherrill had already brought Willie into the company. The album *Red Headed Stranger* had come out, and "Blue Eyes Crying in the Rain" had been released as a single while I was working across the street for Fred Foster at Monument Records. The single was taking off, becoming a pop hit, and Willie was approaching stardom.

I went over to meet him for breakfast at the Spence Manor Hotel. Willie came jogging down the road at 8:30 A.M., all covered with

---

Chet Atkins is a producer, a former president of RCA Records, and a great guitar player.

Rick Blackburn is president of CBS Records Nashville.

sweat from his five-mile run, and we went inside and ate eggs and hash and talked about music and philosophies of life. And got stoned. Here it was, 8:30 in the morning and I wasn't worth a damn for the rest of the day.

But Willie was already on the rise. It was happening so fast that all I had to do was grab the ring and hold on. *Red Headed Stranger* was a hit for all the wrong reasons. It didn't follow the formula, the fashionable mix of the day. There were 1,000 reasons that record should not be a hit. But the *Red Headed Stranger* project took on Willie's personality and became a hit for all the right reasons—because it was Willie Nelson. It was Willie's statement.

There were at least two Willie Nelsons in the public mind at that time. One wrote this brilliant concept album, *Red Headed Stranger.* Another was the great ballad singer who sang "Blue Eyes Crying in the Rain." It was months before the Willies joined in the public mind so that people who reacted to him as a singer also got interested in the album. Then Willie took on the superstar image he has today.

Willie's contact with CBS Records has been sort of on the run. Three months will go by and we don't hear from him. Then suddenly we hear from him three or four times in a day. But I always take great care to leave him alone to create. With Willie, you just trust him and say, "Go lead us somewhere and we'll follow." The key to the whole thing is Willie is not now, never has been, and never will be predictable. Willie doesn't need advice. It's important for CBS Records to recognize that. I think Willie appreciates our attitude. We appreciate his music. So it works.

A case in point. In 1978 he called me and said he had an idea for his next album. "I'm going to record ten of my all-time favorite songs," he said. "Songs like 'Stardust,' 'Moonlight in Vermont,' 'Sunny Side of the Street' . . . What do you think?"

I said, "I think you're crazy." I gave him typical record executive answers. "You're a great writer. Go write. Do a 'Luckenbach, Texas' or some damn thing. Stay with the mood that's hot."

Willie said, "Great songs are great songs no matter when they're written. The other thing is, my audience right now is young, college age, and mid-twenties. They'll think these are new songs, and at the same time we'll get the sentiment of the older audience who grew up with these songs but don't necessarily know me as an artist. We will bridge that gap."

I heard him out and said, "I still think you're crazy."

People around the company said, "What the hell are we going to do with 'Sunny Side of the Street'?"

Of course, it turned out to be like shooting fish in a barrel. *Stardust* couldn't have been a better project if we had drawn it on the blackboard, which we didn't. Willie had figured it out. That was a pivotal album for country music. It opened up a whole new audience.

Willie has always been a prophet, slightly on the edge. But he manages to keep it in perspective. He takes things right down to zero base.

The night he won Entertainer of the Year at the Country Music Awards, we all rushed backstage and embraced him and smothered him with accolades: "Willie, congratulations! Terrific! You're our guy!"

He looked me dead square in the eye and said, "Rick, I don't know what all this means. Does this mean I'm a better singer than Kenny Rogers?"

He put it in perspective for himself and then turned the page.

We do marketing tests that ask the consumer to associate one word or phrase with various stars. When we hold up a picture of Johnny Cash, they say "Black." Kenny Rogers is usually "the Gambler." You know what they say about Willie? The consumer says, "Free spirit."

DARRELL ROYAL

It was summer in Brownsville, down on the Gulf of Mexico, and it was hotter than hell when the Devil turns the blowers on. Brownsville is the southernmost town in the United States. Willie had a membership at this country club in Brownsville and had asked me to be his partner in a member-guest golf tournament. He had been hanging out at the Kerrville Folk Festival in the Hill Country, where I was going to pick him up in a plane. But Willie said he wanted to drive his Mercedes to Brownsville. So he showed up that morning for golf, having been up at least one night if not two or three, and we teed off with two strangers on a course where the fairways were cut out of a big grapefruit orchard.

I mean it was so hot and sweaty you didn't dare pick your nose for fear you'd slip and put your eye out. Not a breeze stirring, no air at all, no water except for these muddy irrigation ditches they call *resacas*.

We had played about nine or ten holes when Willie hooked his ball into a *resaca* that was pretty wide, almost like a little lake full of

---

Darrell Royal is a legend in sports, a Hall of Fame football coach who won three national championships at the University of Texas.

muddy, gooey brown water. I turned my back to hit my own shot and heard a tremendous splash behind me.

I saw the little white tennis hat Willie had been wearing. It was floating on the mud in the *resaca*. After a minute, here came Willie rising up out of the muddy water, splashing around fully clothed, throwing the water on himself like he was taking a bath.

He waded out and came back to the cart. He pulled his billfold out of his jeans and tossed it in the cart to dry. Willie took his shoes off. That old mud was oozing between his toes and dripping out of his hair and beard. I didn't snap, you know, didn't act like there was anything different about him. He just said, "Hi," which is typical. I said, "How you doing?" He said, "Just fine, thank you."

He walked onto the green to putt. There was a puddle of gook around his feet. With mud and crap all over him, he looked like the Creature from the Black Lagoon. These strangers we were paired with, they couldn't believe their eyes.

Willie pushed his ball to the right off the next tee, which he is prone to do. I sat in the cart while he went and found his ball among the grapefruit.

"What club do you need?" I called.

"Throw me a two-iron," he said.

He was kind of hunkered down on his heels in the old cowboy squat, his elbows on his knees. I took out his two-iron and threw it like a boomerang.

The club went whistling over the trees and hit Willie smack in the head and knocked his ass right over.

I thought: God Almighty, I have killed Willie.

But he rolled around and stood up with the club in his hand and yelled, "Thanks, Coach, I got it."

When he came back to the cart, I said, "Lord, Willie—are you hurt?"

He said, "Am I bleeding out the ears?"

I said, "Naw."

"I guess I'm not hurt, then," he said.

I was taking a lot of heat from the bluebloods for running around with this dope-smoking hippie. My answer to them was, "Willie doesn't fault me for my sins, and I don't fault him for his." And I'd drop it right there. A friend is somebody who's willing to overlook your faults, because we all have faults. Willie doesn't put on airs for anybody. He doesn't try to change to suit a crowd. If he doesn't suit the crowd, he'll just vanish and be gone.

Willie has threatened someday to put his guitar case in the trunk of his car and take off down the highway, just him and his guitar. He said he might start on I-35 and play all the way up the right side. When he gets as far north as it goes, he'll turn around and still be playing the right side on the way back to Texas.

His wardrobe is certainly no problem to him. If I go somewhere, I match up ties and match up socks and plan it so I can change from one rigging to another rigging. But Willie's rigging is all the same. He doesn't try to match his T-shirt to his tennis shoes. He just puts on something clean and goes on down the road. He could pack one duffel bag and stay gone two years and be happy as a lark.

TOM GRESHAM

In about 1970, I'm coming through San Antonio one day and Crash Stewart tells me Willie has moved from Nashville to the Happy Valley Dude Ranch in Bandera.

Boy, it was bleak. No work for anybody. We were sort of burnt out. Willie couldn't get dates, RCA wasn't treating him right. I started booking gigs out of the dude ranch. Willie would work weekends for enough money to pay some of the bills. Paul English, Bee Spears, Larry Trader, myself, Willie and Connie, and some others lived at the dude ranch. We wasn't hippies, but we lived like hippies.

Willie came to me and said, "We ought to put on a picnic on this bankrupt golf course." I thought it was a good idea whose time had not yet come. The guy who could make it happen financially didn't like the idea, at all. But while I was negotiating, Willie's band played a date back East. Driving home, they picked up a hippie girl hitchhiker. We've still got the clean cut look, right? They brought the girl to Bandera for a while and she said she wanted to go to the Armadillo World Headquarters in Austin. We didn't know what the hell it was all about, but we drove her there on the bus. Armadillo World Headquarters was an old National Guard Armory that had been turned into a hippie dance hall by Eddie Wilson, Spencer Perskin and Shiva's Head Band, Mike Tolleson, a group called Mad Dog and a bunch of people who worked their asses off for less than no money. Jim Franklin, the artist, painted beautiful murals all over the building. It was a shameful day for the city of Austin when they tore down the Armadillo World Headquarters and replaced it with just another office building.

Tom Gresham is a Texas music promoter who has done many Willie shows over the last twenty-five years.

The Armadillo was a real eye-opener for us. Willie saw crowds of young people who would be natural prospects for an outdoor music festival. Like a country Woodstock.

Willie borrowed $5,000 from a Houston lawyer, Joe Jamail, the guy who fifteen years later represented Pennzoil in the huge judgment against Texaco. We bought and bagged 20,000 tickets. Larry Trader, Billy Cooper, Gino McCoslin, Eddie Wilson, and I set out to sell the tickets. About that time the *Shotgun Willie* album came out and sold more in Austin alone than most of his previous albums had sold nationwide. You could sense something was about to happen.

The first Picnic in 1973 was a go-for-broke deal. None of us had earned a quarter or had any hope for the future unless the Picnic worked.

Willie wore cutoff blue jeans, sandals, let his hair grow long, grew a beard. He said in effect, "Kids, I'm one of you, and you can be one of me." He didn't lead them, he followed them. And they responded. Here was somebody older, a character, part of another world from the rock and roll world the kids knew. Suddenly the Woodstock kids became the Austin kids. Willie came out of the Picnic a charismatic figure with an enormous audience.

We didn't make much money on the Picnic. Two days after it was over, I took my collection to Bobbie's house and we cut it up. Willie gave me a small part of it—enough to get my car back that had been repossessed.

But the Picnic was a catalytic thing.

Inside Willie's personality is a child, and yet he's an alleycat. He's been bruised, and you can see it in his face, his scars. But the child-like thing in Willie is his optimism, a kind of childlike faith in hisself and the people around him.

When Willie really started taking off and hiring big time managers, they wanted Willie to leave us old-timers in the dust. I never argued that the new management couldn't get bigger, richer shows for Willie than I could. Hell, they had power and money I never had. Willie became very profitable to them. For three or four years I had to fight like a tiger just to hang on to the bones they threw me.

But Willie wouldn't let them leave me. I stayed in his face, kept pushing. I wasn't a big-league player like the new guys, but Willie never put a security guard at the door and said don't let Gresham in. I can go any fucking place I want to if Willie is there. I have held on to my territory, but it has been a struggle.

I don't give a shit what he says, he's getting tired of the road. It's extremely hard to live in the world of Hollywood and Madison Avenue and Broadway and Billy Bob's and the Little Wheel all at the same time. I think Willie might circle back to a life-style he's had before. He's a very spiritual person. He sees his life as a series of circles. That is, he's reincarnated many times in his own life. Once he's experienced all the other life-styles, he'll probably come back to something he's already done before. Exactly what that may be is not for me to guess. I just hope I recognize it when I see it.

SAMMY ALLRED

One of Willie's first Austin business ventures was the Willie Nelson Pool Hall at 2317 South Lamar. His daughter Lana did the books for the pool hall, I ran errands when I wasn't starring onstage or on the radio. Zeke Varnon was the mastermind. Willie let Zeke drive the Mercedes to the bank, and Zeke told them it was his car, so he had a good line of credit for a while. Willie is a genius at knowing when to hang out places. Like before a show, he knows exactly where to go and when. Same at the pool hall. He knew just how often to come by to keep the rumors going. "Hey, Willie's coming in . . . Willie was here."

The year we went and played the "World's Biggest Show" in Terlingua, Texas, the promoter furnished Winnebagos for all the acts. Waylon was there, and Leon Russell, a huge lineup of talent. Except there was a lot more of us than there was audience. We had thought the "World's Biggest Show" would be held at the "World's Champion Chili Cook Off." But the chili deal was three miles away, and the miles in Terlingua are longer than they are anywhere else.

The next day and night we drove 980 miles from Terlingua to the Homecoming Concert in Abbott, where Willie was going to play an outdoor concert for all his old neighbors.

Paul was driving Willie's Winnebago. He came so close to having a head-on collision that it ripped the rearview mirror off the side. We arrived in Abbott about daylight. In those days the neighbors, you know, were afraid of outdoor festivals. They thought Willie and the rest of us was a bunch of hippies. They didn't want crazy-looking people like us threatening their neighborhood.

A guy came up to our Winnebago and said, "I'm from the sheriff's department. I'd like to speak to Willie Nelson."

Sammy Allred is a friend of Willie's, one of the first DJs to play "outlaw" music— and is half of the musical performing act called the Geezinslaw Brothers.

Paul said, "Willie ain't here right now, but I can take care of it for you."

"We need you to sign this paper," the deputy sheriff said.

"What is it?"

"This paper says anybody that sets foot on any property that ain't leased for the Abbott Homecoming Concert, it's okay if we shoot them."

There were pickups pulling horse trailers, going in and out. All along the line you could see more pickups with guys sitting on the hoods holding shotguns in their laps.

Willie wrote out a list of the acts that were supposed to perform at the Homecoming and asked me to be the master of ceremonies.

Billy Cooper's dad—the Reverend George W. Cooper—said a prayer to open the Homecoming Concert. Then they sang hymns. Willie slipped me a piece of paper. "Here's the list of every act that's here," he said. "Anybody can play anytime they want to for as long as they want."

"What'll you be doing?" I said.

"I gotta leave for a while," he said.

So Willie disappeared. I went around to the acts and asked how long they wanted to play, and I introduced them. Things were going great until either Kinky Friedman or Kenneth Threadgill let a couple get married onstage during their set. That kind of threw things out of kilter. Plus at that time I tended to drink a little myself, and I kept getting Asleep at the Wheel mixed up with Greezy Wheels.

People were real congenial for about the first eleven hours before they started turning hostile.

Somehow or other, the poster for the Homecoming Concert had Leon Russell's picture on it. The picture aroused expectation in the crowd that Leon Russell would be performing. Country people are like that—they see an artist's picture on a poster advertising a show, and they don't know no better than to believe that artist will actually be in the show.

About sundown the sound went dead. We had to scrape up $740 to pay somebody to turn the sound back on. When the sound started again, the crowd thought it meant Leon Russell was about to perform. They started chanting. "We want Leon, we want Leon, where is Leon?"

At these outdoor events, right about sundown there is a time when it can go either way—become a real nice concert or else a bloody riot.

People were chanting, "We want Leon!" I kept trying to ignore them. They didn't want to hear that the poster was just a mixup at the printer. "We want Leon! We want Leon!" Louder and louder. Hell, the one I wanted to see right then was Willie. He'd been gone for eleven hours.

People were crowding toward the stage screaming for Leon. They started climbing the fence, like you see at prison riots, or in third world countries where the rich people are having a banquet and the poor people are trying to break down the gates.

Suddenly Michael Murphy—now known professionally as Michael Martin Murphy—came onstage with a red, white, and blue guitar and a four-year-old kid. He plumped that kid in his lap and started playing and singing beautifully—God bless Michael Martin Murphy, I say every chance I get—and the angry crowd began to quiet down.

And wouldn't you know it? Willie comes back. Willie follows Murphy onstage and finishes up the evening to screams and cheers of joy and it all turns out great. His timing is fantastic.

That was the concert where Willie presented a bouquet of roses to Mama Nelson, his grandmother who raised him, and she said, "Willie, you need a haircut."

LARRY TRADER

It wasn't all that easy to book Willie in the late sixties and early seventies, particularly after he grew his hair long and wore an earring. People were scared to death of him. Club owners would say, "We love Willie, but we can't hire a guy with long hair and tennis shoes."

I would say, "What do you think about the man they put up on the cross? Willie is just trying to make a living, there ain't no need for you to kill him."

Willie had a song out then, "Half a Man," which in my estimation was a great piece of work because it described the peaks and the valleys, the highs and the lows that I was going through myself.

It was always something to contend with. I got Willie into a poker game in Louisiana and had to borrow money for us to make it to the next gig. We'd have to push his bus to start it. You'd want to make sure there was plenty of air in the tanks for the brakes, because when you got to the top of the hill and began rolling down you could be in for a hell of an adventure if the brakes didn't catch.

Larry Trader is Willie's close friend and golf pro, as well as a show promoter.

We always left together and counted the money together and came back together. I got so closely associated with Willie—like I had been with Ray Price—that I'd get up and have breakfast when he did, go to sleep when he did, go through every problem with him. I became sort of like a male wife, except there wasn't no romance of course. I didn't have to kiss nobody's butt if something went wrong. I'd just speak my piece, get it out of my craw, and keep moving.

In Bandera, all of us living like a family, I think I became hypnotized by the way Willie could tune a guitar and play it and make pretty music with pretty words. It seemed like magic. At the same time, Willie was amazed by my ability to hit a golf ball. That looked sort of like magic to him. I could hook it or fade it, hit it high or hit it low, come up with any shot I needed. Knock it stiff. Hole the putt. Next case. Willie is my golf pardner, and we challenge anybody. Golf and music are closely related. A large number of musicians are golf nuts, and I believe the reason boils down to one word—tempo.

Whatever you can think of in golf, you can relate to music. You rush your swing, you get it out of meter. You get a half beat too fast with your swing, it's like the drummer is off the beat. If your tempo ain't right you will go home busted.

I became president of Willie's Lone Star Records label as a result of the Ridgetop fire. Willie used to have a little studio down in the storm cellar with a little two-track tape machine. After the fire, Willie's dad, Ira, poked through the ruins and found all these reels of tapes. I took four reels to a studio in Dallas. They sounded great. I told Willie I'd like to clean up the tapes and see if we could use them.

These were tapes made when guys would be sitting in the cellar rehearsing or passing time if somebody didn't show up for a session. There were suitcases and trunks and boxes of these tapes in the cellar when the house burned. They were charred and warped and some came apart in my hands, but they survived.

I figured I had enough stuff saved from the fire to do three albums. I picked out twenty-two of the best songs with the best quality and played them for Willie.

The qualilty was so good Willie thought he'd just finished cutting them. He listened real close, then said, "Why don't we go into the record company business? You're the president."

We opened the Lone Star Records office at the Austin Opera House. I knew as much about how to run a record company as a baby knows about running the circus. Willie was on the road, I was trying to sell records. It got very confusing.

Lone Star Records put out six albums—three by Willie and three by some of the good Texas acts we had signed. We had a terrific roster of artists for Lone Star Records, but we just didn't know shit about marketing records. Finally Willie said, "Let's just shut down the company for a while and see what happens next."

Next, we went looking for a new home. This was in 1979. Willie and I had been to the Pedernales Country Club twenty miles outside Austin a couple of times before we drove by and saw a "For Sale" sign outside. In many ways it resembled the place in Bandera—nine-hole golf course, Olympic-size pool, big clubhouse, tennis courts, a bunch of apartments near the clubhouse. It had a wonderful view to the west across the hills and north to the Pedernales River and Lake Travis, and it was full of deer and rabbits and wild turkeys. Willie told me to make an inventory of the place. The homeowners had tried to take care of the golf course, God bless them, but it was a mess. The facilities were great, but there weren't enough people to support the club or the bar and restaurant.

Willie bought it. He remodeled the clubhouse into a state-of-the-art recording studio with a big office for himself overlooking the pool and the hills, and offices for his assistant, Jody Fischer, and Bobby Arnold and Larry Greenhill, the sound engineers. We fixed up the pro shop. Willie spent a fortune on the golf course putting it into first-class condition.

Now I'm in complete heaven. When Willie is home, we get to play golf every day like we did in the old times. Knowing Willie is happy when he looks at his golf course and is pleased with what we've done with it, that's a big kick for me. When he looks at you with those brown eyes and says, "Boy, this golf course is beautiful," there ain't no higher feeling that that.

I mean we have got it covered.

I could easily have screwed it up the night I broke Willie's neck. We were at a club down in Corpus Christi and I had a little matchbox of pot I wanted to go outside and put away. There was a pole right where you came into the club near the ticket box. They had this long hallway and a ramp at the far end.

We had been drinking. I told Willie I was going outside. He said no, you're not. I said I need to go outside. He said, you stay where you're at. So I waited till he turned around to watch the band, and I eased on out and started walking up the hallway. In a minute I heard running footsteps. Willie was chasing after me. At the top of the ramp I hooked an arm on that pole and swung around—and Willie shot past me and just took off flying from the ramp like a skier. I heard a horrible crash, tables and chairs breaking when he landed on them.

We hauled Willie out of the wreckage and stayed there and partied until he got back on his plane and went to Nashville, saying he thought he had a headache.

The next day he phoned and asked what I was doing. I said I was getting ready to play golf.

He said, "I wish I could be playing with you, but it looks like I'll have to miss a few rounds."

I asked him what was wrong.

"I'm laid up in bed with a broken neck," he said. "What the hell happened in Corpus, anyhow?"

How he keeps coming out of all these wrecks is a wonder to behold. Like down at Bracketville one year, Willie was flying in to the landing strip near Happy Shahan's Western town that they used for the Alamo movie set. Happy is watching the plane coming in, knowing Willie is on it. The plane hits a big chughole in the strip and flips over on its side and crashes.

Happy likes news and publicity, you know, so first thing he does is pick up the phone and call the radio stations, the TV, the newspapers. Happy says, "Willie Nelson's plane just crashed. Y'all better hurry."

He jumped in a Jeep and drove out to the crash to pick up the remains.

And here comes Willie and his pilot, limping up the road.

The media people was arriving by then. They started firing questions at Willie. How did he survive? Was he dying? Was he even hurt?

Willie smiles and says, "Why, this was a perfect landing. I walked away from it, didn't I?"

He's accident prone. This is why you have to be careful around him at all times. I love the man, but you don't never know when something might fall on him.

PART FIVE

I Gotta Get Drunk and I Sure Do Dread It

Gotta Get Drunk

and I sure do dread it,
st what's I'm gonna do;
my money,
ɪoney
gin' the blues.
ole paycheck on some old wreck,
an name you a few
ɪrunk and I sure do dread it,
st what I'm gonna do.

, I can't stay sober
ɡood people in town
ar me holler,
y dollars
hink of lettin' 'em down.
ɪoctors that tell me
owin' it down!
e old drunks than there are old doctors
ɔetter have another round.

CHAPTER FOURTEEN

S itting on the roof of the White House in Washington, D.C., late at night with a beer in one hand and a fat Austin Torpedo in the other, I drifted into a reflective mood.

My companion on the roof—it couldn't do him any good to use his name, except I should say President Carter knew nothing about this and would not have condoned it—was pointing out to me the sights and the layout of how the streets run in Washington.

"That string of lights is Pennsylvania Avenue," my companion would say between drags on the joint and swallows of beer. "The tower all lit up over there is the Washington Monument. You can see Constitution Avenue, and there's the Capitol and the Potomac River, and down a few blocks is the Watergate building . . ."

It was a good way to soak up a geography lesson, laid back on the roof of the White House. Nobody from the Secret Service was watching us—or if they were, it was with the intention of keeping us out of trouble instead of getting us into it.

Downstairs, Connie and our daughters Paula and Amy were excited about spending the night at the White House as guests of President Carter and Rosalynn. Connie and I were given a bed in the Lincoln Room. Paula and Amy were in the Martha Washington

Room. I had played and sung that afternoon in the Rose Garden. The Carters treated us so well, it was like being at our own house.

Jimmy Carter and Rosalynn are like people I grew up with in Abbott. They're so down-to-earth and so nice that they were too good to be politicians. You have to lie a lot to be a politician, and I don't think the Carters are capable of lying anywhere near as much as their high station seemed to require.

So I let the weed cover me with a pleasing cloud and reflected on what a long, strange trip it had been from smoking cedar bark and grapevine at the age of four or five, to getting puke-on-your-shoes drunk with my dad Ira at the age of nine, to sitting on the roof of the White House sharing a number in the warm humid night.

I guess the roof of the White House is the safest place I can think of to smoke dope.

Hell, it had only been a couple of days ago that I was busted and locked in jail in the Bahamas for a handful of weed that I never even had a chance to set on fire.

On account of that miserable little pinch of weed that I never smoked, I was now laying on the roof of the White House with my left foot in a cast.

Me and Hank Cochran had been in the middle of a tour the week before. We got a couple days off, so we decided to go down to Hank's place in the Bahamas and do some fishing, soak up the sun, ride around in Hank's boat.

My luggage didn't make the same flight that I did. We went on to his boat without it. The next day they phoned me from the airport and said my bag had arrived.

Driving to the airport, I happened to remember there might be a little pack of something I had forgot about in the pocket of my jeans in the suitcase.

The thought crossed my mind: I wonder what I'll do if they found it?

When I arrived at the airport and saw the little gleam in the eye of the customs agent, I knew they'd found it, but I still didn't know exactly what to expect.

I went to the room where my suitcase was sitting on a bench. I was wondering—should I try to sneak my blue jeans out while the customs guy ain't looking? Should I just edge over like Sam Spade and grab that little bag of weed? Or were they trying to trap me into doing something really foolish?

"Is this your suitcase, Mr. Nelson?" the customs agent asked.

I noticed my jeans had been moved to the top of the bag.

I said, "Yeah. I sure do appreciate you taking care of it for me. I'll just be on my way, if it's all right with you."

"You won't be going anywhere today, Mr. Nelson."

They searched every item in the suitcase but could ony find that one little bag of weed. We took a ride to jail.

I was stuck into a bare cell with a concrete floor. It was better than a Texas jail, but it was no luxury suite. I was alone for a few hours. By now, Hank had found out I was busted. He came to the jail and smuggled me in a six-pack of beer. Then Hank went out and hustled up somebody with $700 cash to make my bond.

When they opened the door and let me out of jail, I was about half ripped from drinking the six-pack, and I was so happy to be free that I cut loose a big Indian war whoop and leaped off the front porch of the jail.

I broke my left foot.

I hobbled before the judge on crutches. The judge said, "We're going to release you on the condition that you never come back to the Bahamas again."

So there I was, on crutches, on bond, deported from the Bahamas, and flying straight to the White House to see President Carter. A few hours later I was on the White House roof smoking dope.

Marijuana is like sex. If I don't do it every day, I get a headache.

I think marijuana should be recognized for what it is, as a medicine, an herb that grows in the ground. If you need it, use it. People who smoke it and get real paranoid don't need it. People who smoke it and become brain dead, it's the wrong medicine for them. For me smoking marijuana is like eating a couple of Valiums for somebody else. I have a tremendous amount of natural energy, and I need to take the edge off. Friends have told me I don't smoke weed to get high, I smoke it to get on a more level keel and not be like a turkey that's going out there sticking his head in everything. A few beers will calm me down, but beer also puts me to sleep. Whiskey is a totally different story. But the important thing to remember about using any of this stuff is there is always a trade-off. Whiskey will make you not give a shit about your problems, but it will also kill you. Valium is addicting and, like whiskey, can turn into a much bigger problem than whatever you're trying to forget by using it. With marijuana, the trade-off is you can ruin your lungs.

There's been a lot of talk about marijuana being harmless, but I think it's a lot more dangerous to the lungs than dope smokers realize. Especially the strong marijuana that's around these days. Each year it seems to get a little stronger. The wise course is not to abuse it.

Your lungs are not really supposed to breathe anything but oxygen —pure, fresh air. There are always arguments about which is worse for you—marijuana smoke or cigarette smoke? Gasoline fumes or smog or poison gas? There's tons of shit we breathe every day that ain't good for us. But if weed is used moderately, for a purpose, to calm yourself—because there's plenty of us who are very nervous and need more of it than others, and we know who we are—then marijuana is just one more natural blessing that grows from the earth.

I know alcohol is not the answer for me. I enjoy drinking a little bit these days just because I get kind of silly, but my disposition won't handle alcohol on a regular basis. Whether it's my Indian blood, or my Irish blood, or just my blood, I don't know, but alcohol makes me do things that I'm not always proud of.

Whiskey can make me cranky, even downright belligerent. I get into bourbon or gin, I'll start looking to stir up some shit. I'll see things I don't like that I may have not noticed until the booze pointed them out. I'll look for trouble. I grow rabbit ears. I'll get very sensitive about what's said in the room. Tequila has more of a psychedelic effect on me, more like a hallucinogenic. I usually stay pretty pleasant on tequila, but I usually get real drunk on it and don't know what I'm doing after a point. Maybe they'll tell me the next day that I was having a good time and not hurting anybody, so that's okay now and then. With bourbon whiskey, though, I not only can get annoyed real fast, I always get diarrhea of the mouth. I start talking way too much, saying everything that flows off the top of my head. The next morning I suffer what the Coach, Darrell Royal, calls the re-re's: the regrets and remorses. I'll sit on the side of the bed and think, oh my God, did I really say that? Oh God, I didn't really tell them all that shit, did I? Did I really get into a fighting disposition? Did I really start feeling very amorous at the same time I got too drunk to fuck? Oh God. These are the re-re's.

Whiskey runs my mouth the way speed loosens the lips of most people. Speed works the opposite on me—it makes me shut up. My brain is whirling so fast that my mouth couldn't possibly keep up, so I am struck dumb.

While I'm admitting to the contents of my medicine chest of drugs and alcohol, I'll tell you two things you'll never find me doing—smoking cigarettes or using cocaine.

Heroin is so far beyond anything I would use or even tolerate around me that I won't bother to talk about it.

I have one firm rule with the band and the crew regarding cocaine: if you're wired, you're fired.

Anybody in the band or crew who hasn't quit cocaine has at least pulled up hard from the way it used to be. Cocaine is a stupid drug to use. It gets out of hand before you realize what is happening to you. Everybody starts off thinking they can snort a few lines from time to time, get a pleasurable buzz of energy and confidence and a feeling of power. But sooner or later, cocaine will overcome you. Some of the guys in the band and crew were spending too much money on coke, damaging their health and definitely affecting their music. When you're wired, you stay up and party, maybe never sleeping between one show and the next, thinking you're doing fine. But really you think you're making it when you're only faking it. Coke don't even make you funny the way whiskey can do, it just makes you think you're funny. For a singer, Cocaine is a disaster on your breathing and throat. Coke has fucked up many a singing voice. I appreciate that the coca leaf grows in the ground, like a medicine. A cup of hot tea brewed with coca leaves is a good tonic for the blues. Indians in the mountains in South America chew coca leaves to pick up their spirits and keep them going in a hard life. But by the time cocaine gets to the user in this country, it is nothing like the coca leaf you would pull off a bush in Bolivia. The dealers cut the powder with some very poisonous shit. A coke snorter who is moderately deeply into it—like a gram a day—knows damn well he is sticking strychnine, borax, crank, baking soda, all kinds of words that end in -drine, up his nose, but he doesn't care. Coke makes smart guys stupid. He keeps on throwing good money and precious time after bad dope. Eventually he blows his act.

The old joke is that a couple of snorts of cocaine will make you feel like a new man. But the first thing the new man wants is a couple more snorts of cocaine.

One interesting thing that has happened to our band in the last few years is we have picked up our tempo without realizing it.

Sometimes I'll hear our old version of "Whiskey River" played on the air, or maybe "Devil in a Sleeping Bag" or "Shotgun Willie," and I'm surprised at how laid back we used to sound. We tape our road show every night, and there is a tremendous difference to me in our drive and energy now compared with the middle to late seventies.

Probably this has a lot to do with certain drugs we don't take anymore. Our old style was fine for earlier times because everybody was laid back, and we were as laid back as anybody. Austin was a real mellow scene.

There's another big reason that our band has gotten stronger: the musicians themselves. They've been with me so long they've become part of my family. I hired Bee Spears to play bass when he was a seventeen-year-old kid in Helotes playing bass with George Chambers. Jody Payne joined us shortly later. Jody was married at the time to Sammie Smith and playing in her band. We did some dates with Sammie. I would go onstage and join her for a few numbers, which put me on the bandstand with Jody. I really liked the way he played backup, and I liked the way he sang harmony, so I talked Jody into staying with us.

Grady Martin has been my hero forever. There's nobody better to have in the studio than Grady Martin, because not only does he play guitar, he knows what everybody else is supposed to be doing, too.

Billy English came along to help as a roadie first. He had been playing drums with a preacher. Billy's a great musician. He's a guitar player, bass player, drummer, songwriter, you name it. But Paul plays drums with me. Paul won't let Billy play too much because Billy plays too good. Paul will be the first to tell you fuck no, man, I'm playing the drums. But every now and then he'll let Billy jump out in front and play, like on "Milkcow Blues," and he's fantastic, and that's how he kind of got started doing the percussions back there. Billy plays percussions on things like sticks and pipes and bones.

I met Mickey Raphael at a recording studio in Dallas when he was a teenager. He was sitting outside the studio waiting for me and told me he was our new harmonica player. I just said, "Follow us, kid." In a few years Mickey was a star, dating Ali MacGraw and living on the beach in Malibu.

This is our basic stage lineup—Bobbie, Paul, Bee, Jody, Mickey, Grady, Billy, and me. All of them have worked for me in hard times for no money. Zero. Stayed and lived with me when a lot of musicians would have just left. We all supported each other, and that's why we're still together.

When our crowds got bigger our energy level rose up. All of a sudden the people were yelling louder than they had the year before. It fired us up and probably caused us to do more up-tempo shows.

I know our no-coke rule has made us sound better. At least when we're straight we're all playing on the same page. It is hard to communicate with people who are doing coke or pills. It's impossible to play music with them. You have a good tempo going, and then somebody takes the lead and the next thing we're playing a polka. It takes away from the feeling in the music. You lose the ability to let the music rise and fall. If you're on uppers, the music is all up. If you're on downers, the music is all down. I can tell if a musician is fucked up the minute he hits the bandstand.

Coke was never an issue when I started playing my way through the honky-tonks in my youth. But alcohol was always there, right from the beginning. My grandparents were as far from being alcoholics as Billy Graham, but there was always a bottle of whiskey hidden in the barn to use as a tonic for a chest cold or sore throat. The Czechs and Bohemians in the towns around Abbott drank beer like water, old and young alike. When I played music in their clubs, whole families drank and danced and had a big time. The first time I got totally shit-faced, I was drinking beer in a Bohemian social club with my daddy at the age of nine. Dad drove me back to my grandmother's house and made me sleep it off in the car before I could go inside. Mama Nelson would have kicked the shit out of both of us.

The honky-tonk environment is definitely to be avoided if you intend to make a living while staying away from beer and whiskey and dope. Don Cherry has supported himself and all his wives in style for forty years by singing in nightclubs and has never smoked a cigarette, tasted whiskey, or touched dope—but this is rarer than a singing turtle.

The toughest cowboys in the world come to honky-tonks to cry in their beer. They'll request "Please Release Me, Let Me Go" or "Your Cheatin' Heart." They sit and they listen, and their emotions are very visible. They may not admit their feelings to their wives or girlfriends, but they will pay money to hear a band play these songs. If there's not a band onstage, they shove quarters in the jukebox all night long to hear the same songs the women are listening to and sympathizing with. Women have the same emotions as men when they hear those songs. Chances are if you're listening to a love song in a saloon and you catch eyes with a woman and think you'd like to take her to bed, she is thinking the same thing about you.

Drunks like sad songs, heartbreak songs, cheating songs. I love those songs myself. I've written hundreds of them. The trouble with them is they can put you into a self-perpetuating mood of negative thinking. The sadder the song, the sadder you feel. The sadder you feel, and the more you want to buy another round and stick another quarter in the jukebox, the sadder you become in a downward spiral.

It can really get to a musician performing sad songs night after night. You sing those heartbroken, look-what-a-fool-I-am lyrics over and over, year after year, you can find yourself believing life is truly like that and always will be.

A lot of people aren't happy unless they're miserable. I went though that. I thought misery was the way life was supposed to be. I thought we were all supposed to sit down and write how terribly sad and rejected we were.

In my twenties and thirties I started getting deeply into self-destruction. I was taking myself to the bottom. What changed me first was, I realized I just flat wasn't ready to die.

If I was going to die, I wanted to blame somebody else. But there was nobody to blame. It was pretty obvious that I was the culprit. Once I saw it in black and white, a bell went off deep inside. It was the lowest period in my life, I think, but once I realized I had nobody to blame but me, I found myself enjoying sitting there and smiling about it all, knowing that eventually it was all going to be okay. It was sort of funny that I could sit there, believing I had just learned that however you want things to be, create them in your mind and they'll be that way. I started laughing at the situation, knowing how bad it was now, and how good it was going to be later. It became funny that I had let it get so fucked up.

But it wasn't that easy, and it's still not that easy to live positively around people who think negative. I had to turn myself around, and then I didn't want to be around anybody negative. That rubbed off on the people near me, so they knew that if they were going to hang out with me, they had to be positive. I'd made up my mind that I would refuse to have anything negative going on anywhere in my sight. If there's a fight over there, I'll go break it up, regardless of the consequences, because I don't want to see it. Pretty soon the word got around—don't be negative or don't be spreading any negative thoughts around Willie, he don't like them. There's a lot of people, I'm sure, who shied away from me, because they were and still are negative thinkers.

I became aware that I wasn't meant to go out of this life drunk and rejected. I started thinking, well, maybe a guy don't have to die, he don't have to be a miserable son of a bitch all the time to write good songs.

For whatever reason—my spiritual growth or outlook or God or whatever you want to call it—my attitude changed. I haven't written that many songs since the change, but the ones I have written are of better quality. More positive. If I get an idea for a negative song now, I reject it. I don't want to go through what it would require of me to write a sad, negative song. I just don't want to re-live it in my heart and mind. To move into a positive future, you must let go of negative things of the past.

My change in attitude is also partly due to the fact that when I started smoking marijuana, I quit drinking so much. When I quit drinking so much, I felt better physically and mentally. Remember what Coach Bear Bryant said after he quit drinking? He said, "For thirty-five years I walked around pissed off all day, and now I find out it was a hangover."

I started smoking weed regularly as a substitute for smoking cigarettes. Tobacco was a horrible habit. I smoked three to five packs a day. When I was really enjoying smoking, there was nothing like having a cup of coffee and a cigarette in the morning after a meal. Then I started smoking so much I couldn't enjoy a cigarette with my meal because I'd already smoked a pack beforehand. My throat burned and my lungs were sore. I smoked for years after I had stopped enjoying it. I quit smoking a hundred times before the day I finally took a deep inhale and it hurt my lungs so bad I knew at that instant I would never smoke a cigarette again.

I couldn't stand the pain in my lungs. I had been deteriorating daily, and I could feel it. I had no energy. I was trying to sing, but I had no lung power. Deep inside of me this little voice said, *Willie, you've got to stop this right now this instant. You're supposed to be a singer and all you're doing is fucking up. Why are you putting all this shit in your lungs? Don't you understand you're cauterizing your lungs and throat with whiskey so you won't feel what the cigarettes are doing to you? The whistling sound coming from your lungs sounds like shit in harmony.*

Once I finally listened to this inner voice, I stopped cigarettes forever.

Instead of having a cigarette in my hand, I started carrying a rolled-up joint in my hat or someplace. Maybe I'd just smoke a toke of it when I got the craving to smoke. Of course, a person can get to where he smokes forty joints a day instead of forty cigarettes. But if you do that, you will get nothing much done except a lot of gazing. Too much marijuana destroys your motivation to get up and go on with important things in life. That's one reason I am not in favor of kids smoking marijuana when they're still in school. You learn how much is enough for you. It's different for everybody. Children are healthy, growing tissue. They will find out about marijuana later if they need it.

I would be in favor of legalizing marijuana entirely, but I don't like to think of a government having the power to legalize something like an herb. An herb belongs to us people to use as we need, and it is no government's business.

If it came to me standing up in a case like that, I would come out in favor of de-legalizing cigarettes.

My mother and my dad and my stepmother and my stepdad have all died of cancer and emphysema from heavy smoking. I don't need a truck to hit me to know those fucking cigarettes will kill you. Why do we sell them? Why can a kid go in a store and buy them? Why do they send people to prison for smoking marijuana when they are legally selling shit that is a proven killer.

After I quit smoking cigarettes I took up running and working with weights and playing a lot more golf. I was getting healthy again, I thought. But the cigarettes had done serious damage to my lungs.

My left lung was like a balloon that had some weak places in it. I made this discovery in Hawaii in the summer of 1981. I had just got through running and I was real hot and sweaty. The surf was pounding, the ocean looked good and cold. I went plunging into the waves. I was about 200 yards out in the ocean when a sudden terrible pain hit me. I knew something bad had happened. I thought it was a heart attack, but then I somehow knew that it was my left lung that had collapsed. The pain was a sharp, sick feeling, like I had partly caved in. Holding my left side together, the waves knocking me down and just about washing me under, I made it back to the shore and fell down in the sand. They came and got me in an ambulance. I remember the sound of the siren as we sped past the palm trees.

In the hospital they stuck a tube through my back, up through my rib cage and into my lung. This was to drain the fluid out so the lung would inflate itself again. They don't give you anything for the pain. The doctors have got it figured out that when you scream at a certain pitch they've hit the right place. The next morning they had to do it again.

The lung will heal itself quicker than any other part of the body, but still I was laid up for three or four weeks in the hospital, resting and thinking. I was straight and I found my mind standing naked staring at itself. It was time to write something. Laying in the hospital, I wrote the *Tougher than Leather* album. It's a story album about a reincarnated cowboy. He was a gunfighter in the 1800s, killed several people. He died in the electric chair.

Was it something I did, Lord, a lifetime ago?
Am I just now repaying a debt that I owe?
Justice, sweet justice, you travel so slow.
But you can't change my love for the rose.

I think it's my fate to go in and out of these scrapes and then write about them. It's almost like I can't wait to get out of one to get into another.

Half a dozen years before my lung collapsed, after I had moved to Austin back in the early seventies, I got into a nightmare that I haven't wanted to write a song about, much less an album.

Ever since the purely honky-tonk nights, there have been a few shows when I've accidentally gotten a little too wrecked from weed and tequila to know exactly what town I was in when I hit the stage and couldn't have told you in advance what all was about to happen. I don't make a regular practice of it, naturally, and it is nothing to worry about. There is a tape recorder in my mind that I can turn on. It starts with "Whiskey River" and plays for two hours and twenty minutes. Somewhere before the tape runs out, my brain will catch up with what is going on and join my spirit that has been doing the singing and playing.

Except once it didn't work.

Back in Austin in the seventies, a bunch of us got into hallucinogenics. I'm an experimental sort of fellow. I ate peyote, swallowed mescaline, had some fairly astounding adventures and revelations. There was plenty of acid around in those days. Pure Sunshine acid that was easy to get from a chemist in San Francisco. Another good brand was called Purple Jesus. It made you radiate. I understand why acid and the psychedelics were popular in the sixties and seventies. It was a step in awakening our consciousness to prepare people for the spiritual evolution of the Age of Aquarius. The young hippies who were high on acid, some of them are in important places today with their understanding expanded by their acid experiences.

In the fairly short period of time that I used it, acid taught me several profound things. One was that I must not take acid and try to play a show. I knew better than to do it, but I'd had a few drinks, and when somebody handed me a tab of Sunshine I thought, well, why not? Without asking how big a dose it was, I washed the Sunshine down with a beer.

It was still a couple of hours before I was due on stage.

"This ought to be a real interesting show," I said.

"Yeah, man, far fucking out," my friend said."Wow, you took 1500 mikes."

A dose of 500 micrograms of good LSD is enough to put you into a state where people look like walking skeletons, and the road can turn into chocolate pudding. I had taken three times that.

Acid comes on in about an hour with a golden rush of euphoria and energy. This will last about an hour. Then it starts getting tricky. You can go on a spiritual trip and feel a blissful oneness with the universe. Or you can become a terrified, raving nut. Much of it has to do with your surroundings. You have a cleaner shot at bliss if you are sitting on a rock by a creek alone in the woods than you do if you are climbing onto the stage in a honky-tonk packed with thousands of screaming people.

I opened my mouth and sang, but all I heard was some distant voice imitating mine. Great roars came from the crowd, unlike any human sound I'd ever heard. The lights glowed like fiery embers. The whole room started pulsing with a low, ominous jungle beat. I seemed to be standing in chocolate pudding.

"Please, Lord, get me out of this, and I promise I'll never do it again," I tried to say.

But the secret to a successful acid trip is not to try to control the things that are happening to you. Don't try to be in charge. How do you totally surrender your ego, and sing at the same time? The more you try to put your ego first, the more fucked up and paranoid you get. An indisputable fact about acid is once you swallow that tab, it will be about eighteen hours before the experience is over. Acid doesn't quit fucking with you just because you get tired of fucking with it. My fingers began turning into claws on the guitar. I felt like I looked like a werewolf.

My fingers and my throat performed the songs, but I was out of control up there on a stage in front of a big wild crowd turning bright colors and growing giant mouths with huge lips. My hand came off the guitar and flew out into the crowd, then my arm stretched out like a gauzy hose to connect again with my hand. What an ordeal!

Somehow I got through the set and was driven away where I could finish freaking out in relative peace. I decided then and there that I didn't need to do acid ever again. I went as far as I could go with it that night.

I'm in better shape now than I've ever been in my life. I can do a lot of things physically and mentally that I couldn't when I was twenty years old. I can run ten miles. I couldn't run a hundred yards when I was twenty because I was smoking cigarettes and drinking booze. A young professional athlete may think his body is his temple. For me as a young man my temple was the Nite Owl or Big G's, where I spent years neglecting my body. But now I would challenge any ex-professional football player anywhere near my age to a foot race.

A few months ago, I decided to give my lungs a real rest and clear my head. I made a deal with a guy who runs a rehab clinic in California. This guy is an ex-junkie who does an excellent job of rehabilitating people. But he chain-smokes cigarettes.

I made a bargain with him. If he'd stop smoking cigarettes for thirty days, I would stay at his clinic and stop smoking weed for the same period. I said I might look like Cheech and Chong driving a diesel the day I left the clinic, but I would lay off the weed until then.

So what do you think was provided all the new arrivals at our orientation? Cartons of cigarettes. I stuck it out with people blowing cigarette smoke all over the place—including the guy who ran the clinic—until I couldn't stand it.

About the fourth day, I was exploding with energy. I sat down one afternoon and wrote the treatment for a TV movie. Two days later the cigarette smoke finally drove me out the door. I took my TV movie treatment and went to L.A. and made a deal with CBS to hire a producer and a couple of screenwriters.

Once again the writer in me had gone into a situation and come out of it with a story, and songs and album and movie to follow. It's a tip for how to survive—try to look at every obstacle as an opportunity.

CHAPTER FIFTEEN

Things had started going crazy around our ranch on Fitzhugh Road after the first Picnic in 1973. I was getting a lot of national exposure, and my albums had started selling in big numbers. People from everywhere started swarming around, and Connie couldn't stand it. I don't blame her at all. She would get phone calls all night long that were usually drunks looking for me. We made a deal with the phone company to change our unlisted home number once every month, but still it got out sometimes before I even learned it. This wasn't a good way for Connie to live, and it wasn't good for Paula and Amy. Amy had been born on July 6, 1973, so she was starting right off in the middle of all this new attention, but it must have seemed weird to Paula, who was four years old.

I mean by 1975 when my *Red Headed Stranger* album came out there were people showing up at the ranch who thought I could lay hands on them and heal their crippled limbs.

We built a six-foot-high wall with stones three feet thick around the ranch house property. We strung electrified wire along the top of the wall and stuck up signs that said NO TRESSPASSING, NO ADMITTANCE, NO HUNTING, NO KIDDING. Out at the main gate about a half mile from the house we put a closed-circuit television system and a call button with instructions that said, "Press the button but please do not hold the button down."

Me and Connie got to wondering if we were building ourselves a jail to live in.

She led the move to Colorado. Connie bought a three-story Swiss chalet on sixty acres in Morrison in the Denver area and said she already knew too many people and didn't want to meet anyone else. Connie would never really mean something like that, of course. In Colorado she found a new group of friends who were not bowled over by the fact that she was married to me. She fell in love with snow skiing. Then she found us an even more remote place near Evergreen, close to where we had visited my nephew Freddy a few times. Paula and Amy both started to school in Colorado.

The deal was supposed to be that I would live 50–50 between Texas and Colorado when I was not on the road. When I really wanted to get away, truly needed privacy, Colorado was certainly the place to go. I could step outside the door in Colorado and I was in the forest with the mountains all around and the flowers growing and no sound but maybe the wind in the pine trees. I enjoy that and I need it occasionally. It was sanctuary. There were practically zero visitors in Colorado.

We had the Pedernales Country Club twenty-six miles outside of Austin, and one of the houses we owned there was kept as a home for me and Connie and the girls when we came in from Colorado. But the country club was a hot spot, as far as constant people.

In Colorado I talked on the phone a lot, but that was about it for doing business. My business was in Austin. Out at the country club, I had a first-class recording studio and was set up with an office eventually where I could sit at my desk and look through a big plate-glass window at the hills and at Lake Travis.

And I must admit, my office was a wedge shot from the first tee.

So, one midnight in the Christmas season of 1977 I was sitting at the Backstage Bar across the street from the Austin Opera House, swapping bullshit with my old friend Bud Shrake while we passed a bottle of tequila back and forth.

Bud had just quit a great job at *Sports Illustrated* magazine, where he worked for fourteen years after leaving the newspapers in Fort Worth and Dallas. Bud had written half a dozen novels by then and two or three movies, including *Kid Blue*, starring our amigo Dennis Hopper.

We talked and drank far into the night and came up with an idea for a movie. He would write the script and I would star in it. We would be 50–50 partners. The story involved a country songwriter getting fucked by Nashville who moves home to Texas and figures out how to fuck Nashville back and come out on top. The movie was going to be about greed and power and loyalty and love. A musical.

We dreamed up our star cast: Waylon Jennings, Dolly Parton, Emmylou Harris, Dennis Hopper, and me. By the time we came up with a title—*Songwriter*—it must have been about daylight, and me and Bud hugged each other and bragged about how smart we were. This movie was going to be the simplest thing in the world to put together. Everyone would love it.

I phoned Waylon in Nashville who jumped in as an equal partner. He met us at the suite I used to keep as a hideout in the old Gondolier Hotel on the shore of the river downtown.

The suite had a balcony that looked down on the boats at a dock and across the river to a green slope and then the office buildings of Austin. It was a nifty hotel, not expensive but convenient and with that nice view. Waylon kept getting up and going to the bathroom while we were talking. Once he went into the closet and shut the door. When he came out of the closet he said, "I'll tell you one damn thing. If the law ever puts either of you on the stand and asks if you saw Waylon Jennings do drugs on whatever day this is, you sure as shit don't have to perjure yourself on my behalf."

Dolly and Emmylou liked our idea. We couldn't find Dennis.

That afternoon I played Waylon and Bud a tape of the new album I was going to send CBS. It was *Stardust*. I glanced at them while we listened to the tape. Bud started crying during "September Song." Waylon already had tears streaming down his cheeks.

When the tape ended, Waylon said, "God damn, Willie, I've heard them songs all my life but I never realized they were so beautiful. Where did you find all them songs?"

"There's a big book full of them," I said. "If this album is a success, I can make a living in cocktail lounges the rest of my life."

Bud got a call from Marvin Schwartz, who was now a Buddhist monk and was just stopping through Austin on his way back from India. Marvin Schwartz sort of empitomized the 1970s. His story is like *A Star Is Born* crossed with *The Razor's Edge*. Marvin produced movies starring John Wayne, Kirk Douglas, Burt Reynolds, Dennis Hopper and Rock Hudson. Marvin was literally chased out of Hollywood by the studio and his ex-wives' lawyers. He walked across Africa. He arrived in Nepal and became a Buddhist monk—Brother

Johnathan. Brother Johnathan, who was now destined to produce *Songwriter*, we thought.

I leaped in and made my movie debut with the part of Robert Redford's manager in *Electric Horseman*. I just called Sydney Pollack on the phone and asked to be in the movie.

I had started appearing on national magazine covers and I picked up a good movie reputation on *Electric Horseman*, but our *Songwriter* still wasn't happening. I couldn't find out why. Marvin gave up as producer and went back to India. He said Hollywood was wrecking his tranquillity.

Then one night after a concert I did in Reno, a chunky guy named Mark Rosenberg walked in. He said he was head of production at Warner Brothers. He wanted me to star in a script they had. It was called *Honeysuckle Rose*. The story was about a country musician who is on the road a lot and falls in love with a young girl and nearly loses his marriage.

Mark Rosenberg took a check out of his pocket and gave it to me in Reno. I signed up to do *Honeysuckle Rose* instead of *Songwriter*.

When Bud heard I had signed for *Honeysuckle Rose* on the day still another of our *Songwriter* deals was supposed to come through, he drove out to see me at the ranch on Fitzhugh Road in Dripping Springs. He was hung over and upset, but after I told him they put the money in my hand, he said he didn't blame me for taking it. He said, "We believe in Karma, don't we?" I said, "I don't know if I done right or I done wrong with this, but we will someday find out."

So I made the leap from guitar picker to movie star.

When I was a kid going to the movies, I used to like Roy Rogers' clothes the best but I preferred Gene Autry's horse.

The movie that was closest to my heart all along was *Red Headed Stranger*. I talked to Shrake about writing a script in 1976, but he said he didn't know how to write a story where the hero shoots a woman to death for stealing his horse. An old hang-around buddy tried writing a script, but it didn't feel right. I knew this was going to be a movie, but I didn't know how to make it happen.

One day in 1977 Bud introduced me and Connie to his old friend Bill Wittliff and Bill's wife, Sally. I liked Bill and Sally right off. I had seen a TV movie Bill wrote with Johnny Cash in it, and I knew he and Sally owned and operated Encino Press, a very high-class regional book publishing house, which impressed me.

Bill and I went for a long drive in his pickup truck and played the *Red Headed Stranger* on his tape machine. Bill said he would write the script. We got a development deal with Universal and they gave me a suite of offices in Burbank. Bill turned in his first draft of the script, which followed the story line of the album pretty close. The story is about sin and redemption, set in the West in the 1870s. An idealistic preacher falls all the way to the bottom because he can't control his animal nature, but he finds the power of love draws people around him to perform a heroic act and save themselves from tyranny.

Universal put the pencil to it and came up with a budget of 14 million.

Then they sent the script to Robert Redford to play the *Red Headed Stranger*.

What was going on here, I found out, was Universal wanted me to sign with MCA Records, so in 1978 they set up Willie Nelson Productions on the Universal lot for me to develop the movie *Red Headed Stranger*—but not necessarily for me to star in. Basically, I think, they wanted my music contract a lot more than my classic profile on the screen.

Giving the script to Redford froze the project at Universal. The moguls said our movie would only be made if Redford would do it. Bob and I had become acquainted up in Utah, where I had bought a ranch not far from Redford's place. Bob sent word to me that he liked the script and was thinking it over. He thought it over for the next two years. He wouldn't say yes and go ahead and do the movie, but he wouldn't say no and release us to try it somewhere else.

I had mixed emotions about this. Though I very much wanted the movie *Red Headed Stranger* to be made, deep down I didn't want Redford to do it. This was a movie I felt I was meant to star in.

By the time we finally shot *Red Headed Stranger* in 1986, nearly eight years after Universal first gave the script to Redford, I had already starred in *Honeysuckle Rose* for Warner Brothers, *Barbarosa* (written by Bill Wittliff and co-produced with me and Gary Busey) for Marble Arch, and *Songwriter* (which finally got filmed in 1984, only six years later than the six months we had figured on at our Gondolier meetings) for Tri-Star, and had played smaller roles in *Thief* with Jimmy Caan and in *Electric Horseman*. That's on the big screen. I had co-starred with John Savage in a TV movie, *Coming Out of the Ice*, and had been executive producer and co-star (with Johnny Cash, Kris Kristofferson, and Waylon Jennings as my main pals) in a TV remake of *Stagecoach* that amazed the industry by knocking out its competition and becoming the highest-rated TV movie of the year.

To get *Red Headed Stranger* done independently, we had to pay back Universal the money they had advanced me and the money they'd paid Bill to write the script.

I built an 1870s Western town on the hills across the road from my golf course. It cost about $800,000. We did a new budget and cut Universal's $14 million, which by then, eight years later, would have been up to $25 million, down to $1.8 million.

Then with the help of God and friends and good luck and very hard work, we all pitched in to shoot *Red Headed Stranger* and brought it in on time and under budget. I'm proud of that movie. I think all our years of frustration and all our struggles resulted in making it leaner and stronger. You certainly can't tell when you see it—the beauty of Neil Roach's photography and the authentic costumes and all—that we could have made fifteen movies like *Red Headed Stranger* if we'd had the budget some studio spent on making another so-called Western, *Silverado*, that same year.

The movie business and the music business have interchangeable parts. It's kind of like the phone company and the IRS. I think they all work for each other. They all seem to use the same lawyers. There's good people and bad people in both businesses, and sometimes it takes quite a while to tell them apart.

I think they hired me as executive producer on *Stagecoach* because they thought I could keep Kris in line. But they were wrong. I didn't even try. Kris didn't like the director, he didn't like the script. He didn't like anything about the project except that me and Waylon and Johnny were in it with him. I would send reporters to interview Kris and he would tell them, "Man, what a piece of shit this is. I wouldn't watch this fucking movie if they strapped me in front of a TV set and sewed my eyelids open."

It was not a happy location. I was called upon twice to make decisions as executive producer. Once was when someone brought it to Johnny Cash's attention that the Indians hired for the picture were being treated shabbily. The first group of Indians hired didn't look like warriors. They were too fat. They couldn't ride bareback and shoot at the same time. So the company hired some fine Indian cowboys off the Apache reservation. But when the Apaches arrived at our location around Tucson, the company wouldn't pay them enough to live on. Some had brought their horses and trailers down at their own expense. They were sleeping on blankets in the brush. I was appointed by Johnny Cash to protest to the company, and the treatment of the Indians improved.

But the movie company was still fucked up. They kept bringing us out for shots and changing the scenes. We'd rehearse all night for a big scene, and the next morning we would get to the set and they had changed their minds. I was accustomed to all the sitting around and waiting that goes with acting in a movie, and I knew how things could change unexpectedly, but this was ridiculous. It happened every day, over and over.

I got mad and said, "I'll be back at the motel when you need me." Gator drove me away in my *Honeysuckle Rose* bus. A couple of other buses pulled away behind us; the makeup and wardrobe and production people were breaking for lunch. The director, however, thought everybody was walking off the movie. This kind of shook him up and maybe it helped pull the picture together.

There are a lot of things I'm involved with one way or another, a lot of decisions I have to make—so many that there's no need to start worrying about just one. The more things I get into, the less I worry. There's safety in numbers. Things have a way of working themselves out.

This is not the ideal psychological profile for a movie producer. A movie producer is usually a walking heart attack. The producer and the director are hit with dozens of decisions every day. Robert Mitchum said working in Hollywood was like being nibbled to death by ducks. I know what he meant: the constant changing of minds, rewriting of scripts, changing of people, dueling egos.

I've learned a lot about the movie business since our first *Songwriter* meeting in 1977. I've learned you really can go make a movie with a minimum of problems if you've got good people around you who know their jobs, and you have the production money in the bank. I have also learned this is almost never the case.

Having seen all sides of the movie business now, and learned what everybody is supposed to be doing, I have just about decided that I don't have much interest in producing movies. Having gotten *Red Headed Stranger* off my chest, I don't feel the need to leap out there in Hollywood and ask them to strap my ass full of problems and throw me in the pool to see if I float.

But I do like movie acting and intend to keep doing it. I've learned the secret to movie acting. What is important is to learn your lines and be on time. If you do that, then nobody fucks with you much.

I am tempted to say that in the future I will leave movie-producing problems to people who need them—but if somebody should walk up and hand me the money to make any movie I want to make, play any role I want to play, and produce the picture as well, I'll just say, "Hello problems, welcome home."

CHAPTER SIXTEEN

I t was the sort of Hill Country afternoon that makes the boys out at the club grin and say, "Well, another shitty day in paradise."

We were standing on the fourth tee at the Pedernales, soaking up the sunshine, listening to the whirring of the water sprinklers, smelling the wet grass. I had my shirt off and was playing in shorts and running shoes. The fourth hole is a 520-yard par five that doglegs sharply to the right about 260 yards down the fairway. Past the bend in the fairway a dozen deer, led by an eight-point buck, were watching us from the shade of a grove of oak trees. The deer were poised to bound away in the likely event that somebody in our group would nail a drive that carried beyond the turn in the fairway and rattled the branches where the deer were not so much hiding from us as just staying discreetly out of our way.

We love our deer at the Pedernales. A year or so ago, a golf hustler thought he'd show off with a doe that had paused in the middle of a fairway some 150 yards away. He pulled out a 3-iron and said, "Watch this." He kept his shot low and cracked a line drive that flew straight as a bullet, striking that beautiful doe in the ribs with a thump we could hear back at the tee. The doe hopped up and down, stiff-legged, looking back at us as if asking why nobody had at least yelled a warning. She ran for the trees, biting her wound. It must have hurt like a bitch. The hustler smiled proudly and asked, "What do you think of that?"

I said, "I think your ass is barred from my golf course, starting yesterday."

We don't like people hitting our deer with golf balls. We don't like people messing with the wild ducks and geese that land on our ponds. We don't like people chasing rabbits or throwing rocks at our turtles. We feel we are very lucky to be able to satisfy our golf habits in a game park, and that's how we want to keep it.

But back to the fourth tee. I said it was likely one of our group would pound his tee shot past the 260-yard dogleg, because on this particular day we were playing with old friend Lee Trevino, who has won the U.S. Open and the British Open and can carry the load in any kind of match we talk him into at the Pedernales.

Lee drops by the Pedernales when he's in the Austin area to play golf with us and swap needles in Spanish with his longtime pal, Larry Trader. Lee and Larry both grew up learning golf by working as caddies, and they both talk all the time while they're playing.

Instead of distracting them, the continual chatter helps them draw pictures for their subconscious.

Larry will stand up to his tee ball and chuckle as if he is amused at how good he is compared to the rest of us. "I had a dream," Larry will say. "Oh, I tell you, Will, it was so sweet. I dreamed I just drew the club back and brought it down right through this little slot here" —*whack!* Trader has hammered a drive over the big oak in the middle of the fairway, the ball flying toward the hill that is the right boundary and then turning a bit to the left high in the air and coming down at the spot beyond the corner of the hill where a good bounce will leave him a 2-iron second shot to the green. But Larry has never stopped talking. "Do you call that perfect, or what? Maybe a hair off line? Felt like I caught it on the toe just a touch." When Larry says he felt like he caught his drive on the toe, you know he has really coldcocked it.

While Larry is still grinning and talking and picking up his tee, Lee will stick his own ball on a peg and say, "That wasn't too shabby for an old man, Traloo, but you never had a dream that you could hit it up with me. I believe I'll just take aim on this little darling and throw it over the top of those three trees on the right and bring it to a stop at the far edge of the fairway on that little patch of grass because it's in the shade . . ."

Somewhere toward the end of this speech, you will hear the loud crack of Lee's metal driver and see the ball taking off and heading toward the spot where Lee, a master of the game, had seen the ball landing in his creative imagination. In golf you call it "visualization." It's amazing how often visualization works when you can remember to do it. The really good players never forget it.

But the rest of us are liable to get so wrapped up in how we grip the club and how we hold our feet and what to turn first—our hips or our shoulders—that we neglect the vital aspect of creating a mental picture of our ball hitting its target. It's a funny thing about golf. I use visualization in playing music. My creative imagination prints a picture in my mind of where a tune is going, and it goes there. But I can walk onto a golf course intending to visualize a 300-yard drive down the middle, and so many things go through my head—*Keep your eyes on the back of the ball and don't move your head until the ball is gone, and keep your grip real light, like you're holding a tube of toothpaste with the cap off. Make a full shoulder turn but don't forget to turn your hips and get that left knee behind the ball and that left heel off the ground. On the way back down, don't grab the club with your right hand and throw your right shoulder and arm at the ball or you'll come over the top and hit something ugly. Start your downswing with your left knee, plant that left heel and turn your hips toward the direction of the shot and keep your head still. Don't let your shoulders pass your chin until the ball is gone past your left ear. Make a good swing, inside out, full extension of the arms, a big arc, don't try to bash the ball, just swing and the club will do the work. And don't forget to fucking relax!*

All this mental instruction has probably taken about twenty seconds, by which time the swing takes place and there's nothing you can do about it. You've also probably lost sight of your target if you ever had one. But every now and then all this action comes together just right and you hit a golf shot that is so beautiful and so graceful that you wouldn't trade it for an orgasm. With a really good swing, something magical happens. It gives you a high unlike anything else. Then one good swing will follow another until you start believing *this game is easy.* That's when you remember that you haven't been thinking about all your tips, so you review your style to see you're still doing everything right—then it all falls apart. What had been so fluid and easy a few minutes ago has once again become almost impossible. Where your club had felt like a feather a minute ago, it now feels like a shovel. And then, in a sudden revelation, you will see the line unfold before you like a golden path and one-hand a putt thirty feet into the cup to win the Pedernales Scramble match with your pardner, and golf has dug the hook deeper into you.

Golf is not only a game, it is an addiction. You cannot explain the addiction of golf to someone who does not play golf. I have tried, but they simply cannot understand. These are wonderful people I am talking about, too, excellent people in all other ways. People like my wife Connie. It is, in fact, fair to say golf has caused me a great amount of marital discord. Oh yes, that is certainly true.

Since getting my own golf course, I have had a hard time finding an excuse why I can't play golf every day when I am in Austin. I look upon it as going to the dogs with dignity.

Let's return again to the fourth hole, where I started telling this story.

By now the rest of us—this day it was a movie director named Doug Holloway and Reverend Gerald Mann, pastor of the River Bend Baptist Church, and I think the Coach and Bud Shrake might have been a team that day—go down to where Trader has decided to hit a 3-iron for his second shot to the par five. Trader says, "Well, I don't know what to tell you boys except I been practicing this shot for thirty-seven years. Look at what I lay on this little fucker." He knocks it on the green. To me Larry says, "Sorry, pardner, I left it about ten feet above the hole. Must of caught it thin."

We move on up to Trevino's ball. He has hit it twenty yards past Larry.

"How long until you turn fifty?" Larry says to Lee, admiring the drive.

"One year, eight months, two weeks, one day, and twenty minutes," Lee grins. "Man, I can't wait. I'll be like Jesse James."

"You mean crooked and dead?" I say.

It was a joke, of course. We were talking about Lee joining the PGA Seniors Tour when he turns fifty. But the word "dead" sets him off.

"Hey, dead ain't bad, let me tell you," Lee says seriously. "I mean, I believe in reincarnation, anyway. But when I got killed by lightning I realized the passage from this life is a tremendous pleasure." Lee was struck by lightning at a tournament a few years ago. "I was sitting under a tree when the lightning hit. It bolted my arms and legs out stiff, jerked me off the ground, and killed me. I knew I was dead. There was no pain. Everything turned a warm gentle orange color. I saw my mama, who had been dead for years. I saw other people from my life. It was a newsreel like you've read about—my life passing before my eyes. But it was so pleasant, so wonderful, I felt great. I thought, boy, this dying is really fun. It's when I woke up in the hospital badly burned and in pain that I knew I had come back to life again for some reason."

"Sounds like you kind of enjoyed being dead," said Preacher Mann.

"Enjoyed it! Preacher, it was great. There's no reason to fear death. Shit, I wish I was dead right this minute."

There's really nothing funny about the game of golf itself, but the guys who play it make it the funniest game in the world. The more seriously we take it, the funnier it becomes.

Guys are always talking to themselves on the golf course. It should be to give themselves positive reinforcement, but usually it is to remind themselves how stupid they are. A negative thought will destroy a golf shot before you ever take your clubs out of the bag.

I've noticed two types of regulars at the Pedernales—those who talk to themselves, and those who talk to their golf ball.

Steve Fromholz keeps up a running monologue to himself all the way around. Steve is liable to hit a great shot and follow it with a horrible shot. He will be saying, "Steve, you ought to take this ball out of service for disreputable appearance, but give it one more chance to stay on the playing squad. Just put a smooth swing on it . . . There, you see how easy it is? Steve, you're great, you're a natural . . ." Then he tops one. "You moron! You fool! You idiot! How the hell could you make such a grotesque swing? You're the worst fucking player I ever played with, you asshole!"

Johnny Gimble, on the other hand, talks mostly to his golf ball.

Johnny will tee up the ball and then get down on his knees and stare at it. "All right, ball," he will say, "now get legs, go, get up there and turn over, and then hit and stop and back up. Whoa! You got it? I'd better not have to tell you again."

Gimble never seems to be as hard on himself as he is on the ball when the shot doesn't turn out right. His swing, Johnny says, is past worrying about. "Some people say their golf game comes and goes," he says. "Mine went and stayed."

I'll always remember one piece of advice Johnny gave me about my golf swing.

"Willie," he said, "I believe your problem is that you lunge just before you lurch."

There is a false story that has been widely printed about golf at the

Pedernales. I am supposed to have said, "Par at my golf course is whatever I say it is. Today I made a fourteen on the first hole and it turned out to be a birdie."

Maybe I did say that someplace, but it was a joke. For one thing, anybody who has played golf with me knows I have never made a 14 on a hole. My golf ball is in my pocket long before my score would add up that high. And we do take the game seriously at the Pedernales. One of the great things about golf is excuses don't count, but foul balls do. It don't matter how you make the par, it goes on the card as a par. And it don't matter if the other guy hit better-looking shots but made a bogey, it still goes on the card as a bogey. In other words, it's not how but how many. You never know what might happen. When you add up the strokes, a 4-foot putt counts the same as a 300-yard drive.

A lot of people who've heard about our golf at the Pedernales think we kick our balls out from behind trees—the famous Pedernales Stroll—and violate all kinds of rules of the game, but this is a large exaggeration.

Maybe the false stories started with what we printed on our Pedernales Country Club scorecard:

LOCAL RULES AND ETIQUETTE

- When another is shooting, no player should talk, whistle, hum, clink coins, or pass gas.
- Don't play until group in front is out of way.
- Excessive displays of affection are discouraged. Violators must replace divots and will be penalized five strokes.
- Replace divots, smooth fingerprints in bunkers, brush backtrail with branches, park car under brush, and have the office tell your spouse you're in conference.
- Let faster groups play through.
- On the putting green, don't step on another's line.
- "Freebies" are not recommended for players with short putts.
- No more than twelve in your foursome.
- Gambling is forbidden of course unless you're stuck or you need a legal deduction for charitable or educational expenses.
- All carts are not allowed within 20 feet of traps or aprons surrounding greens.

- No bikinis, mini-skirts, skimpy see-throughs, or sexually exploit-ative attire allowed. Except on women.
- Please leave course in the condition in which you'd like to be found.

Also the telephone never rings out on the golf course.

The Chorus

DON CHERRY

I've played golf with Willie for years. During a game in Vegas, I had to leave the group at the ninth hole for an appointment with my psychiatrist. Golf will make you nuts, but so will women. I was romancing a lady and we weren't getting along and she thought this psychiatrist could make me understand her line of thinking. Instead, it made me really hot.

I rushed back to the game as they approached the fourteenth tee. I was steaming. I placed my ball on a peg, glared at it, gritted my teeth and said, "You see this ball? I wish it was her head."

Then I nailed one of the longest drives I ever hit in my life.

Willie teed up his ball, took a mighty swing, and hit it dead solid perfect, right on the sweet spot, bashed it way down the middle.

He grinned at me and said, "I never liked the bitch, either."

Don Cherry is a nightclub singer, recording artist, and noted golfer.

TIM O'CONNOR

In 1971 I was working the register at my club, Castle Creek, in Austin, when this fellow walked up and said, "I understand your name is Tim O'Connor."

I said it was. He said, "I'm Willie Nelson." I recognized him. He said, "I'd like to play your joint."

I grabbed a bottle of whiskey and we went to my office and got drunk and became friends. Willie played Castle Creek for seven nights.

Several months later I went on a tour with Willie. My job was chief cook and bottle washer. I drove the Bronco that hauled our gear. It's hard to believe now, but all the band stuff would fit in one Bronco. I took the responsibility for getting a good sound system and buying Bobbie her own piano and hiring somebody to advance the gigs, which amounted mostly to calling ahead to make sure we had more than one microphone waiting.

We had our share of hairy gigs. One night at Gilley's, for example, the audience literally stole our show. There were 3,000 cowboys in Gilley's that night, and they got so rowdy they swarmed all over the stage. They were kicking and punching each other and crashing into us. The most I could do was grab Willie's guitar and run. Willie and I escaped out the back door, into the pouring rain, and jumped into his old red Mercedes. On our way to the Holiday Inn I was cussing and raising hell.

I said, "What the hell do you want me to be? God damn it, I can't do my job. This is ridiculous."

Just a smartass twenty-seven-year-old kid mouthing off. But Willie stopped the car and we got out in the pelting rain. I was steaming mad, ready to fight. As Willie looked at me his eyes went from a real chestnut brown to very dark black. I was hoping he'd hit me with a beer bottle, anything to set me off, because I was a violent type in those days.

Willie looked at me hard and said, "There's three things I never want you to be."

I said, "What the hell is that?"

Willie said, "I never want you to be cold, wet, or hungry."

He turned and walked through the rain into the hotel. Shit, I thought, I'll follow this guy anyplace.

Tim O'Connor is Willie's longtime business partner in the Austin Opera House and other ventures.

Our third annual July 4th Picnic at College Station, Texas, in 1974. It attracted over 150,000 people through the weekend.

I love looking out at the audience during a concert. This crowd was in Austin in 1975.

With Robert Redford on the set of The Electric Horseman, *my first movie role. I had the best line in the whole movie.*

Director Jerry Schatzberg, me, and Amy Irving, going over a scene from Honeysuckle Rose.

Billy, Martha, and me when Billy got married in 1983.

The band gets ready to record another album. Jody Payne, Paul English, Mickey Raphael, Grady Martin, Bee Spears, and Larry Greenhill.

My home on the range. This is a picture of the main room at my cabin in Austin.

Shortly later, Willie fired me. "I don't think you fit in with us right now," he said. "You want to do things your own way, and that's not how we're going to do them at this time."

I was heartbroken. But it was only Willie saying, "Goodbye for a while. We don't need what you do, but we'll figure out something else."

The next major project I worked on for him was the 1976 three-day Fourth of July Picnic at College Station, Bryan, Texas, where we had to confront one of the promoters with guns in our hands to collect the $10,000 he owed Leon Russell. I worked three months on the picnic, and at the end the promoter gave me fifty $1 bills and said, "I hope your Thunderbird car burns regular gas. Take this fifty dollars and get your ass out of Brazos County and never come back." Since the promoter was also an elected official, I took him seriously and moved to Houston and worked as a bouncer at Liberty Hall.

I drifted back to Austin and was running a club when Willie signed a new recording deal with CBS records. One night CBS had a sound truck parked in front of my club, taping a live album. Three guys got into a beef on the sidewalk. One of them had pulled a knife. I went outside with my pistol to smooth them down. The guy with the knife was very belligerent and menacing. I thought I'd pop a cap over his head, maybe put a crease in his skull to remind him to show better manners. *Bam!* I shot at him, but the guy leaped aside.

The bullet went through the side of the sound truck and hit the CBS record representative in the leg.

It was a couple of weeks before I saw Willie. He said, "Well, Tim, you want to talk about it?"

I told Willie exactly what had happened.

He listened and grinned and said, "Tim, I want you to negotiate all my contracts with CBS from now on."

Later that year I got a message: "Willie wants you to come to Austin and find a big warehouse that he and Leon Russell can turn into a club." Willie got on the line and said, "I think we can get the Terrace Motor Inn, with the Opera House and convention hall." We bought 14½ acres of ground, 218 apartments, the motel office (which I converted into the Backstage Bar), two swimming pools, three restaurants, and the Austin Opera House complex, a 54,000-square-foot building that had been a convention center. We paid $10,000 cash-with a note for $1,600,000.

We founded a company called Southern Commotion—we used to say we were just in it for the commotion—and I asked Willie how he wanted to structure the organization.

Willie tore off a piece of paper from a notepad and wrote "Southern Commotion . . . Tim O'Connor, President . . . Paul English, Vice . . . Willie Nelson, Secretary-Treasurer."

Then he scratched out the line with his name on it and said, "We don't need one of them."

I didn't feel I had the right to be a 50–50 partner. I wasn't bringing much to the table except desire and unproven worth, whereas Willie was already famous and making big money. But Willie graciously insisted we be full partners.

It was our understanding that I wouldn't use his name negotiating with the bank to buy the Terrace unless absolutely necessary. Everything Willie was getting into—like buying the country club—when the seller would hear the buyer was Willie Nelson, the price would go from $400 an acre to $3,000.

But the bank people got suspicious that I was just an imaginary character who just imagined Willie was a friend of his and just imagined Willie wanted to be involved.

The head guy at the loan office said, "I need tangible proof that you've ever dealt with Willie Nelson."

So I threw that little piece of notepaper on his desk. My lawyer, Terry Bray, almost had a stroke. He kicked me under the table and tried to snatch the paper before the banker could see it.

But that piece of paper got us the $1,600,000 loan.

The paper is now in my safe in Montana, along with two wadded-up stock certificates.

In 1978 we sold half our Terrace property and paid off three-quarters of the note. Then Willie had a changing of the guard and his new management decided to restructure our deal. They offered me stock that made Willie and me 75–25 owners.

I took the stock certificates to Willie and said, "How do you want it to be?"

He picked up the stock certificates, wadded them, twisted them, tried to tear them in half. You ever tried to rip twisted stock certificates in half? It's like tearing the phone book.

Willie hurled the certificates on the floor and said, "I don't want to discuss this. We're fifty–fifty partners. I signed a piece of paper and that's all there is to it."

In 1978 I was in the hospital with cancer, could hardly stand up after the operation, when Willie came and said, "Get out of here. I've got a new project for you out at the Pedernales." It's been like that with one project or another, ever since.

Willie poured millions of dollars into restoring the clubhouse and golf course, building the finest recording studio, repairing the condos, buying another 750 acres across the road where he built his cabin and his Western town. He'd say, "Well, this golf course is my *Stardust* album. The other 750 acres is my *Red Headed Stranger* album." That's a nice way to look at it.

His cabin—I have to chuckle at that word, considering the artistic masterpiece it turned into—started as a one-room place with no electricity, no air conditioning, and no telephone. The phone company wanted $10,000 to run him a line, but he said, hell, he was hiding out up there, he didn't need a phone. But the builders kept adding things, like a fireplace, running water, bathroom—and finally a telephone. Now the cabin has 3,500 square feet of deck alone, plus electricity and a satellite dish and a stable for his horses. It's a monument to the builder's handcrafted art—a 5,400-square-foot cabin. The panoramic view across the Hill Country is the most beautiful I've seen anywhere in the Southwest, maybe even in the whole world. Willie has lived in some beautiful places—his house on Maui, his house in the Rockies in Colorado—but his cabin at the Pedernales might be the greatest of all. He's locked away from the world by fences, way up on top of the hill at a place even his close friends know not to phone him unless it's an emergency—and if he gets cabin fever he can be at his country club in five minutes or in downtown Austin in half an hour. We all respect his desire for privacy when he goes to his cabin.

Like Willie says, "If you need me, I'll call you."

In the ten years we've been partners, Willie has never once given me a direct order. Never once has he told me, "Damn it, I want this done now." He gave me the opportunity to make a lot of mistakes but to keep working on getting things right. So I constantly think: how would Willie want it? I observe his actions as my guidelines. I know, well, Willie wouldn't want me to do this or this because he doesn't treat people this way.

He's never lost his temper with me, and I've given him a lot of opportunities to do so. When he does get mad his eyes go steely cold black, his face tenses, his body tenses, his wording becomes short and direct—a slow burn, ready to explode and strike out. He doesn't like himself this way, doesn't like to be put in situations that inspire anger. He feels he should be more in control than to use anger to express his emotions. Willie is the deepest bunch of water I've ever known.

Quite honestly, he gives me chills constantly with his insight. He can be in a room with sixty of his best friends, and each one feels Willie is really with him above all. He's always introduced me to everybody wherever we went, even when I was in no condition to be introduced. With Willie, friendship is for life and he trusts his friends completely. It can be a heavy weight to carry that much trust, but if you do it's very rewarding.

He's not just a songwriter, a singer, a musician. He's on the National Council of Theologians. He's read everything important by every important writer. He's a statesman of sorts. If he wanted to be an evangelist of the Jim Bakker approach, he could raise so much money you could cover Texas eight feet deep with it. But that is the opposite of Willie's kind of message. I love to hear him talk about Christ or the universe, the big things in life. I guess it's like listening to the pope, except the pope is boring.

You know how in the sixties we all wanted to go to the mountaintop to search for the meaning of existence? Willie is sitting on that mountain. I don't think his music is as important to him as it used to be. I know the road and the stage are not as big in his life now. He's in the act of finding himself, and we all may be very surprised what he does in the next few years.

Sometimes I wish his name wasn't Willie Nelson. It's probably selfish on my part, but it would really be neat to know him without him being a superstar. I wish his name was just Willie Jones.

Of course, then he'd probably be a blues singer.

TOMPALL GLASER

When I first met Willie at the Grand Ole Opry in the early sixties, it was a very frustrating period in our business. I would see Willie passing backstage, or jamming with Buddy Emmons and Hank Cochran and the boys over at Tootsie's. Nearly everybody realized how good Willie was, but the people who ran the music industry in Nashville would just keep saying, "Well, I don't know if Willie is country or not. Is Willie country? Because if he ain't country, then this stuff he sings won't get played on the country music stations. If he don't get played on the country music stations, he won't make money for us. And if he don't make money for us, the hell with Willie Nelson. Who needs him?"

It was such a major concern—are you country enough for Nashville? If you didn't fit in, if you didn't do their idea of country material

---

Tompall Glaser is a songwriter, performer, producer, and a leader of the Nashville "outlaws."

whether it suited your sound or not, then you weren't worth a dime. That's how it was.

Willie finally took off and went back home to Texas for good. Waylon and I would fly down to Texas to catch a Willie show and just be amazed at the enthusiastic crowds he was drawing. But still the record company bosses couldn't make up their minds about him.

When I heard Atlantic Records was closing their Nashville office, I realized that since Willie had a contract with Nashville Atlantic, he would be out of a label. I thought that was the biggest mistake Atlantic could make, pulling out, because Atlantic had looked like the only door that was open to our kind of music. So I went to New York and got an appointment with the head of the label to talk to him about the Nashville office and mainly about Willie.

I'm sitting in this guy's office in New York, pleading our case. He pushes a button. A well-known producer sticks his head in the office. This guy says, "Tompall thinks we ought to keep Willie Nelson on our label. What do you think?"

The producer shook his head. No.

But Willie went right on making music, cutting tracks all over the place, music just flooding out. It was called outlaw music: music that didn't get played on country stations because it didn't fit the format.

Hazel Smith worked for me at the time, doing promotion and publicity, and she picked up on this "outlaw" angle and really started hitting it hard. The publicity was pushed to extremes that I found a little embarrassing, but at least it got recognition for our kind of music.

Jerry Bradley got the idea to put us "outlaws" together on an album. We chased Willie down and got him in on the project. Waylon was much easier to find. Waylon's idea of being low-key is to drive an orange Cadillac convertible with a white top and a Continental kit on the back. We always say, if you want to find Waylon, hire a helicopter and go up and fly around, and you'll see him.

Waylon wouldn't do it unless Jessi Colter, his wife, was on the album. I don't think Jessi was really an "outlaw" but there was an awful lot of talk about Waylon and Willie and me being outlaws. They made it sound like we were the Three Musketeers.

We took a bunch of old tracks and combined them with some new songs written for the album, added a guitar here, some harmony there—and suddenly we had an album called *Wanted: The Outlaws*. It was released by RCA in 1976 and immediately went platinum— sold more than a million albums.

It was named Album of the Year by the Country Music Association. "Good Hearted Woman" won best single record, and Waylon and Willie were selected for the Vocal Duo of the Year Award. "Mammas Don't Let Your Babies Grow Up to Be Cowboys" was on that album.

Everybody rushed to buy the *Outlaws* album: rock and rollers, kids, lockjaw types from the East, people who'd never bought a country album in their whole lives bought that album. All of a sudden we were a big hit and we had to deal with it. So we put together the Outlaw Tour. We did eighteen dates in California, Texas, Oklahoma. We didn't go East.

Waylon and I traded off nights closing. The nights Willie would close, me and my boys would go back to the hotel early, change our clothes, change our attitudes—and on our way out of town we could hear Willie still on stage picking. They'd have to pull the plug on him if they wanted him to stop. He'd just keep playing and playing until his fingers would bleed. He really loves to play, and the crowds love him for it.

People came out to hear our outlaw shows like they were rock concerts. All at once we were in coliseums and stadiums, we had tractor-trailer trucks and a huge overhead.

Ultimately, I think the outlaw movement or publicity or gimmick or whatever you want to call it did a great thing for country music as a whole, because it opened the way for different styles. There are much broader opportunities now than there were ten or twelve years ago. I hope people remember that it all started with Willie, who always insisted on doing his own kind of music regardless of what the record companies wanted and regardless of the popular styles. All he ever wanted was to do his music and do it right.

BILL WITTLIFF

When I was hired to do a rewrite of the *Honeysuckle Rose* script, I phoned Willie and said I'd love to come out to his ranch on Fitzhugh Road in Dripping Springs and jawbone with him about life on the road. I knew Willie pretty well by then because we had already been working on making the *Red Headed Stranger* album into a movie—which was to take another six or seven years to happen, though we didn't imagine it would be so long at the time.

Bill Wittliff is a movie producer, writer, and director—who worked with Willie on Honeysuckle Rose, Barbarosa, *and* Red Headed Stranger—*as well as old friend and co-director of* Farm Aid.

Reading the script of *Honeysuckle Rose,* I thought it lacked a sense of what it meant to be a country musician on the road. I asked Willie, "Do you ever get vulnerable when you're on the road?"

Willie looked at me like I was from Mars.

I said, "When the concert is over and the parties are over, don't you get lonely?"

Willie said, "There's always a woman."

"Don't you need more than a woman? Don't you ever pick up the phone and call Connie and say, 'Why don't you fly down and join me for a couple of days'?"

Willie looked at me funny, like my questions weren't registering.

"Do you know where wives come from?" he said. "Wives come from the fourth row. You see, when you're on the stage singing, you make eye contact about the fourth row. There'll be some pretty lady there and you sing to her. After the show you have somebody invite her backstage. All the guys are enormously friendly to her, light her cigarettes, open the doors for her, say yes ma'am.

"So you invite her on the bus and she thinks this is the most romantic thing in her whole life. This goes on for about three months —or until you marry her, whichever comes first. Suddenly nobody lights her cigarette or opens her door or pays her the slightest damn bit of attention any more.

"She starts thinking, God, I've got to get off the road, this is horrible, I want a house and a place to sit. You buy her a house and a chair. She's so damn happy to have a roof over her head and a place to sit that for a while she doesn't care what you do. You're gone on the bus, but it's okay with her.

"This lasts about three more months. Then it all turns to shit. She's sitting there thinking, isn't this wonderful, I've got this lovely roof over my head, this comfortable chair to sit in. It would be really perfect if that sorry no-good son of a bitch out on the road was sitting here with me."

We stayed up all night talking.

I had a date with Willie for the next morning. When I called, Billy Cooper told me, "Willie ain't here. What the hell did you all talk about last night? The minute you left, he grabbed his bag and took off for Colorado to see Connie."

I got fired from *Honeysuckle Rose* because the producer and director had different notions from mine about what a musician's life was like.

Willie phoned and said, "Do you have any other scripts in your trunk?"

I took him the script of *Barbarosa.* I told him it was about a blood feud between this old cowboy and a family of Mexicans who cut his ears off. Willie opened the script and read two pages.

He shut it and said, "I want to be this guy."

Honeysuckle Rose hadn't come out yet and Willie was a hot actor. We made a deal to co-produce *Barbarosa*. I could see that Willie wanted desperately to learn to be a movie actor, but he wasn't getting much constructive help from his directors so far. They mainly told him where to stand and where to walk and left the emotional content and the techniques up to him.

When we finally decided to do *Red Headed Stranger* as a low-budget independent film—after years of chasing around with the studios who claimed we needed Robert Redford and a $14 million budget (about seven times more than we eventually shot it for)—I signed on as the director, and Willie and I went to work.

It was exciting. We learned together. I had a TV camera in my office, and Willie and I would read scenes, record them, and study them. I found if you told Willie what you wanted in a scene, by God he'd give it to you and illuminate it.

Willie has always had a fixation with *Red Headed Stranger*. The album turned him into a national figure. It is a very religious tract. Take Willie's history with wives and women. If one believes in reincarnation, there was probably a lifetime where he killed a wife. Willie's relationships with women don't work out well. He has a fear that to be a husband is to be owned—and Willie certainly does not want to be owned. I think this is why Willie has such a fascination for outlaws—this determination to go ahead with his own ideas despite advice to the contrary by people who are supposed to be experts.

It would not at all surprise me if Willie becomes a more private person in the near future, in the sense that he'll actually spend time by himself writing songs again. For the last ten years or so, his need has been to be a singer and an actor more than a writer. But Willie is primarily a poet. When he reaches deep into the well of his soul, he comes up with a bucket of pure water.

JIM WIATT

At three o'clock on a Thursday afternoon in February 1978, I found myself walking along the deck toward Willie Nelson's condo

Jim Wiatt, president of ICM, is Willie's first and only movie agent.

on the water in Malibu. I didn't know Willie. I didn't know what the hell I was doing. After managing John Tunney's Senate campaign and losing a tough one, I had gotten out of politics and gone into show business as an agent. I had been an agent for exactly two years and three months, didn't know shit about the movies. But I had been bugging Jan Michael Vincent and Gary Busey to introduce me to Willie, because I loved the *Red Headed Stranger* album and thought it would make a terrific film.

I remember realizing I was wearing a white three-piece suit as I walked toward Willie's door. Well, maybe the color was closer to beige, but it was definitely a three-piece suit. I could imagine Willie with his beard and earring squinting at me and saying, "Who the fuck is this guy in the ice cream suit?"

When I was in college at USC, I had long hair and wore beads and they called me Indian Jim.

But now I was a guy in a three-piece suit on his way to meet Willie Nelson, and I had no idea what to expect. I was nervous.

Jan and Gary opened the door and ushered me inside the condo. The place was a cloud of smoke. I saw Willie sitting in a chair at the dining table near the windows with a view of the ocean. He was looking me over.

"Hello, Willie, I'm the man from Prudential," I said. "How are you fixed for life insurance?"

Willie laughed. He said, "I hear you want to talk to me about *Red Headed Stranger.*"

"Yeah, I love it. I think I can put it together as a movie," I said.

He said, "Fine. Consider yourself my agent."

We shook hands. I had my first major client.

This was at a time when Willie's career was starting to explode. A lot of people in Hollywood didn't know who he was yet, but they were just about to find out. From a professional standpoint, for Willie to let me represent him was monumental to me. It certainly got me instant attention. Very soon people were saying, "Who is this guy Wiatt to be able to represent this Willie Nelson who is turning up on all the magazine covers?" So for me from our first handshake—an agreement that still holds good ten years later—Willie has been a pillar of strength and a friend.

Willie hired me during a transition period. He was breaking up with his manager, Neil Reshen. I became a focal point for his activities for a few months while he was without a manager. My own boundaries with Willie were never formally set. We never sat down and had a business conversation where he said, "Okay, Jim, this is what I want you to do." I just felt my way along.

I was certainly walking on eggshells in my early dealings with Willie's band. Most of them looked at me like, "Who is this guy?" I remember setting up a deal for Willie to play for a private party given by HBO. They were paying him $70,000 for one night, just to play a party for like 800 people.

I certainly did not yet have a relationship with Paul English. In fact I actually stayed away from him, because Paul is a very scary guy if you aren't his friend, and I hadn't reached that place with Paul. But the HBO party concert was about to start, and Willie hadn't showed up. I was waiting around, not knowing what to do. The HBO people were getting very anxious and kept asking me where is Willie, and I was looking for answers but I wouldn't ask Paul.

Finally Willie arrived. The anxious HBO people said, "Great. You go on in fifteen minutes."

Paul stepped out and said, "No, we ain't playing. We don't play until we get paid."

I said, "Paul, they've got a check right here."

I tried to hand Paul the check.

"We don't take checks," Paul said.

"Paul! This is HBO! Time-Life! A billion dollar company. And it's eight o'clock at night in Anaheim!"

"I don't give a shit. We don't play unless we are paid cash up front."

Willie and Paul were used to the old days, when they couldn't take anybody's word or their checks.

The HBO guys ran out and scrambled around and somehow came up with a bag filled with $70,000 cash. The show went on.

The same thing happened later when Willie did a Showtime special up in Tahoe. The band was about to go on, the cameras were ready to roll—and suddenly Paul and Willie insisted they have the money in cash. But by that time they trusted me to tell them the check was good.

Another night in Tahoe, I gave Willie a check for $50,000. He was wearing jeans and a T-shirt, and he kind of rolled up the check and put it in his pocket. Years later Price Waterhouse—his accountants at the time—called me and said there was $50,000 unaccounted for. Obviously, Willie put his jeans in the laundry, or even washed them himself, with the check still in the pocket. We never found the check. That's pure Willie.

We made a deal at Universal for *Red Headed Stranger*. Willie was given a suite of offices as co-producer. I don't know if Willie ever even visited his offices. He put a Hell's Angel biker friend, Peter

Sheridan, into Universal as his representative. We called him King Peter—big, powerful guy with a deep voice and overwhelming, intimidating vibes but really down deep a sweet person who wanted to write songs. Most people never thought of "sweet" when they encountered Peter. They were terrified of him at Universal. When Peter came to see me at ICM, he rode his Harley up the curb on Wilshire Boulevard and then up the ramp and right on through the double glass doors into the lobby of the ICM building. He had long hair, a scarf around his neck, his gloves on. He put down his kick stand and told the receptionist, "Say, bitch, take good care of this Harley. I'm going up to see my man."

Willie is incredibly easy to work with, except that he has the propensity to say yes to everybody that walks through the door with something. Then when the calls come to me, I have to investigate, finding out what it's about, asking questions like, "Where is the money in escrow?" Or Willie will just tell me to get him out of something that he has second thoughts about, and it's up to me to do the dirty work. Willie has a very difficult time saying no to anybody. A big part of my job is cleaning up these situations. Sometimes I hang up the phone after an unpleasant discussion with Willie—about stuff that is negative or isn't going the way Willie thinks it should go— and am literally sick at my stomach because I am trying so hard to please him but also to protect him.

Willie has been on top for a long time now. He's got a very large core group—unlike the rock and roll business, which is very fickle, based on young kids screaming and yelling and all of a sudden they grow up. Willie's audience grows up but still goes to see him. Although he is considered country and southern, it's interesting that he has a huge market in Detroit, San Francisco, Seattle, Chicago, Boston, New York, Los Angeles. Big urban cities full of working men, the real blue-collar guys. Willie's got a great voice for the working man. His songs are stories that never go out of date.

Willie doesn't have any fear. He says he was happy riding around Nashville in the back of Roger Miller's station wagon without a nickel in his pocket. He loves the life-style of having toys like his bus and his Learjet and his golf course, but I have the feeling that if everything was lost tomorrow and Willie was left with his guitar and a pickup truck, he'd be fine. Not that he's about to lose anything. Even though he protests about getting tired and being on the road too long, if he sits still for more than three or four days, he wants to be out on the road again. As long as he can play his guitar and sing his songs, he's basically a happy guy.

MARK ROTHBAUM

I had been a student at the University of Cincinnati and worked in nightclubs four or five years, helping musicians and club managers. When I went back to New York after college, I sought out a job on a little record label. I started in the mailroom.

My job was menial, but soon I was working in management. They had hired a guy who was supposed to be this super addition to the firm. My desk was next to his. This guy would roll into the office about eleven in the morning, looking sleepy-eyed, he hadn't shaved or showered, his hair was mussed, he was slow on the phone. Watching him, I just snapped to the notion that anything this guy could do, I could do better.

It was like a sudden awakening for me at the age of twenty-three. The business started making sense to me—touring, records, television, everything. I figured out the role of a manager: to coordinate all aspects of an artist's career in addition to the artist's personal life. A manager has to be part of the ongoing enterprise and interpret for the artist what is happening in the clearinghouse, if you know what I mean. I became determined to become a force to be reckoned with.

I started working on tours. In September of 1978—God, that's ten years ago, an eternity in this business—Willie asked if I would start handling his bookings. I opened a little shop. Responsibility started falling on my shoulders. Gradually I became his manager.

I have many functions, but one of them is to field the information and suggestions and advice that come from Willie's accountants and lawyers and agents. Because of his itinerant life, it's very hard to reach Willie. But he will call me three or four times a day and I can put him in touch with all the things that are happening in his business and personal life.

People ask me if Willie is difficult to work with. And I have to say, "Compared to what?" I haven't worked with that many other clients. Willie, Kris Kristofferson, Roger Miller and Emmylou Harris are my main list. Willie may get hot at me but he compensates with a whole lot of love at other times.

Love, in fact, is really the key to Willie and his whole way of doing things. Take Paul English, for example. Paul is a very moral guy. He's honest. He'll tell you where it's at, and he tells the truth. Paul is really the band's leader. He gets the show from place to place, keeps the band happy, is everyone's sounding board. Paul shares respon-

Mark Rothbaum has been Willie's manager for ten years.

sibility for money on the road and accounts to Willie's business manager for it. Paul does the payroll taxes on the road. He is Willie's closest friend. Personally, I would rather die than hurt Paul. He deserves nothing but good things. Paul has done so much good in his life, never asked for a lot of money. He's with Willie because they love each other. As I said, love is the key.

One story I have to tell is when Willie and I were at a hotel in Baton Rouge on the evening of a concert. We were on the twenty-third floor, and we could see the coliseum in a straight line from our windows. Looked like it was just right over there. So we decided we would run to the concert.

Willie and I took off running through Baton Rouge after dark. We ran and kept on running through the neighborhoods, and we still weren't arriving at the concert. After we had run ten miles, we decided we were totally lost. The gig was starting, and we had no idea where we were.

Willie said, "I'll just go up to that house and knock on the door and ask for help."

I said, "You can't knock on some stranger's door."

He said, "I ain't a stranger, I'm Willie Nelson."

A mother and her teenage kids invited us in, gave us a beer, and drove us to the concert. They came on in with us to see the show. Usually when Willie brings in guests, he says, "They're with me." This time he said, "I'm with them."

I can remember the first time I met Willie and Connie. I was absolutely taken aback by these people. To be honest, I really didn't know much about Willie before then. I was given a copy of the *Willie Nelson and Family* album. It just floored me. So much love surrounding these people, a genuine feeling of family with Paul English and Willie and Bobbie and of course all the wives and husbands and children and everything. I was very impressed. I knew I wanted to have an ongoing relationship with them. I loved them and their music, and I just wanted to be around. And I still feel the same way, happy to be around.

JOEL KATZ

I have in ten years only seen Willie get mad at me one time. Real mad. I went to see him and brought an estate plan to show him

---

Joel Katz is Willie's deal-making lawyer in Atlanta.

how he could earn and keep more money for himself and for his family. Willie erupted. "Why are you doing this and it was really none of your business and I didn't really ask you to do this!" He got really very angry and then just stomped out of the room. I was dumbfounded. How did this happen? What did I do wrong? Oh, my God, I'm about to be fired from my biggest client and my whole career has just evaporated.

Willie came back after fifteen minutes. He was quite different. He was very calm. He put his arm around me and looked at me and said, "I know you're really trying to help, so I apologize. I did not mean to be so cross with you because your motives are certainly good. You were trying to do what you thought was right for me. But you've got to understand my philosophy of life, Joel. I want the people around me to be happy, but I look at life as a roller coaster. When I'm up, I'm up, and when I'm down, I'm down, and I hope when it's all over, the money runs out just about the same time that I'm through with my life."

I looked at Willie and I said, "Well, we can plan so that it happens just that way." He laughed and said, "No, let's not plan. It's a lot more fun if we don't." I said, "Well, I'll never mention this to you again, sir." And he said that's fine, and he gave me a little wink, that little Willie wink, and that was the end of the conversation.

SYDNEY POLLACK

I had never listened to country music. My idea of country music was the hillbilly music that I heard in the army, and I remember I used to throw ration cans at the guys who played the stuff.

In 1979 an agent asked if I would do him a favor and meet a guy named Waylon Jennings that he thought would be terrific as an actor. I didn't have any particular part for him, but I said sure. Waylon came to my office in Burbank. I was fascinated by him. What an interesting-looking guy. We talked for about an hour, a real good meeting, and Waylon left me a stack of records.

I started playing the records and I thought, gee, this stuff is pretty good. I heard this one voice that really touched me somehow, and I kept looking to see who it was. On the album I saw this picture of Willie in bib overalls with no shirt. God, this guy was good. I went

Sydney Pollack is a producer-director who got Willie *into the movies with* Electric Horseman. *He also produced* Honeysuckle Rose *and* Songwriter.

out and bought a couple more Willie albums. I was learning how musical country music can be.

I was with Redford in Nashville, scouting locations for a film. Waylon was at the RCA studios cutting some tracks and asked if we wanted to come watch. Bob and I went, and there was this guy Willie, crazy looking with long hair. I mean, he was really something. I loved Waylon, but I became just totally fascinated with Willie. They had the instrumental tracks laid down and were laying the vocals in, and Willie had this sort of relaxed manner and this terrific voice that got to me in some way that's hard to explain.

Willie, Waylon, Redford, and I went to dinner afterward. Willie told me he had sold a couple of concept albums to Universal and was real interested in trying to do a little bit of acting to get ready for some sort of movie work he thought he was going to do with *Red Headed Stranger.* I didn't think much about it at the time, but I did think Willie was such an intriguing person, a captivating-looking guy.

When it came time to start *Electric Horseman,* I got a phone call from Willie. He said, "I'd sure like to be in that picture with Robert." Willie sounded as if he just assumed that he would be in it. I said, "Well, Willie, it's not quite that easy. I don't think I have a part for you."

"I'll be right over," he said.

He showed up at my office. I sat looking at him, this great face and demeanor, and I thought, well, there is this one small part of the manager. I thought, oh what the hell, I'll take a chance on this. I called the wardrobe designer in and said, "This is the guy that's playing Leroy. Suit him up and get him going."

I didn't bother to read Willie for the part because he simply wasn't practiced at that. I decided to sort of tailor the part to Willie rather than try to make Willie play the part, because there was something so right and interesting and colorful about him. I was probably way behind the times in figuring out who Willie was. He was already very popular by then. He was really crossing over and hitting mainstream America about that time. Willie came onto the *Electric Horseman* set and he just blew everybody away. He was relaxed, he was right on the money all the time, he knew what he had to do. I tried to help him improvise the part a little. He came up with one line in that picture that knocked me and the whole crew on our ass. I had told him, hey, Willie, you know what the attitude is, you know what the character is, just tell this actor here whatever you want. So the actor asked Willie what he was going to do and Willie said, "I'm gonna get myself a bottle of tequila and one of those waitresses who can suck the chrome off a trailer hitch and just kick back." The cameraman blew apart laughing so hard he nearly fell in the pool at Caesar's Palace.

Willie could do no wrong for me after that.

We became closer friends. I listened to more and more country music and ended up producing Willie's next picture, *Honeysuckle Rose.* Then I produced *Songwriter,* my third movie with Willie. There's something about Willie that makes you want to do things for him. First of all, you know he'd do them for you. He is so authentic. He just doesn't have a false bone in his body and the camera reads that honesty. He's incapable of telling a lie, which I think is the mark of a great actor.

I directed Streisand early on in her career, and listening to the way she sang a song with all that juice in it you just knew she could get the juice disciplined in another art form, too. I think that is how Willie is. I can certainly see Willie becoming as big a movie actor as Barbra Streisand.

CHERYL MCCALL

I went to Colorado on an assignment for *Life* to write about Willie, Connie, and their daughters Paula Carlene and Amy in their mountain hideaway. My story made the cover of *Life* in August 1983. You see Willie, Connie, and the girls looking beautiful and happy, like some utopian hippie clan, in the photo on the cover. He had just bought her a bright candy red Ferrari 308 GTS for Christmas. I don't think Willie was so crazy about living in the mountains near Evergreen, but Connie loved it. She could go skiing, which she was addicted to like he is to golf. Paula and Amy were in school. Connie's mother and father had a house close by and practically lived at Connie's house. They would run to the store for groceries, do a lot of errands.

Connie had friends in Colorado who knew her as Connie—not as Mrs. Willie Nelson. She had her own group, and the daughters had their own group, all quite apart from Willie. Some days Connie would take the girls to school and then ski all day until it was time to pick them up.

They had quite a compound on the mountain. There was the big house Connie and Willie and the girls lived in. Connie and Willie

---

Cheryl McCall is a former writer for People *and for* Life, *a movie producer, and now a law student at Yale.*

slept on a king-size mattress on the floor of their upstairs bedroom with a United Airlines moving carton as the bedside table. They had a redwood private deck with a view of the pasture and mountains, a master bath with a tile Jacuzzi and earth-colored Spanish tiles on the floor.

There was a very nice guest house, a caretaker's cottage, and a fourth house that they used for an office. Up the hill was a barn with the horses. Willie had a teepee up in the woods where he'd go and sit around and . . . muse, I guess.

Connie and the girls did all the cleaning and laundry for the household. Connie cooked most of the meals. Willie liked to fix his own scrambled eggs and sausage for breakfast. The girls papered their walls with posters of their heroes—Tom Selleck, the Who, the Rolling Stones with special emphasis on Mick Jagger. If Willie wasn't home, the girls constantly played MTV on the giant screen television and listened to their favorite records—not country artists but Billy Squier's "Emotion in Motion," Prince's "1999," and Michael Jackson's "Billie Jean."

Both girls went to public schools, usually on the school bus. Paula's junior high was thirty miles away. Amy played the flute, Paula played the piano. Paula was a cheerleader and a member of the volleyball team. They were unspoiled, decent kids who squabbled with each other and were totally irreverent toward the national monument in the family. They played with Willie's braids and would tack them up on his head and call him "Princess Leia."

Inside the main house a wooden plaque said "He who lives by the song shall die by the road"—a saying of Roger Miller's. Above the sink Connie had hung a sign: "An equal opportunity kitchen." Willie was quick to wipe the table, fix his own breakfast, soak his dirty dishes, whip up a pot of English tea.

I have to give Connie a lot of credit. She did everything to make the Colorado place somewhere Willie would want to come to. It had every toy Willie wanted, like that huge computerized chess game with a robot player. It had the teepee. Where the dining table would be in most houses, Connie put a pool table there for Willie.

The Colorado compound should have been heaven for Willie, except it wasn't in Texas.

DENNIS HOPPER

I haven't got a clue how Willie knew I was in jail in Taos. At the time I couldn't imagine how Willie Nelson even knew who I was. This was during the middle seventies. To me everything that happened in the seventies was moment-to-moment reality. "Anything that is not a mystery is guesswork," my fellow Mad Dogs used to say in Austin.

In Taos I had gotten real drunk and proceeded to win a lot of acid in a poker game, so I swallowed the acid and saw weird dangerous shit going on, and I pulled my pistol out of my boot and shot up the plaza. I was ranting and raving in the jail, people were out to get me, man, and here came the sheriff saying Willie Nelson had come and paid my bill and was waiting outside. I was free to go with him.

I freaked fucking out. Willie Nelson? Come on, man, who do you think you're kidding? You're gonna lure me out and yell jailbreak and blow my ass away! But I thought, hey, be cool, you are after all hallucinating all this.

So I walked out of the jail and got into Willie's Mercedes with him and his wife Connie and his golf pro, Larry Trader. We drove off across the desert toward Las Vegas.

Later I remembered I had met Willie and Connie a few years earlier when a couple of fellow Mad Dogs took me backstage at the Austin Opera House and introduced us. Willie and I stayed up and partied together for three or four days. Sure, I knew Willie Nelson. This was no hallucination. These were my friends!

Willie and Trader and I nearly drove Connie nuts with our laughing and shouting. Connie is an angel, but we were too much. At one point Connie said, "I'm going to stop the car. Either you guys get out, or I'll get out. Who do you think has the best chance of hitching a ride in the middle of the desert?"

It was the first time Willie played the Golden Nugget downtown in Vegas. We didn't sleep for a week. Sam Peckinpah got us barred from the casinos for throwing pesos against the walls. One night it was to be Elvis Presley's final show on the strip. I had a front-row table, but Willie didn't want to go. I took Mickey Raphael. Elvis canceled at the last minute. Jesus, did I get paranoid!

I've stayed friends with Willie over the years. After I cleaned booze and drugs out of my life, I went to Austin in 1985 and started learning to play golf at Willie's Pedernales Country Club. Playing with Willie

Dennis Hopper is a movie director and star.

and the boys out in the hills among the deer and the rabbits is a great way to take up golf. You don't get too self-conscious about your golf swing. It's too laid back to worry about that.

Life is good at the Pedernales, man. Playing golf there one day just at sunset, we gathered on the seventh tee to witness Larry and Linda Trader's wedding ceremony. I cried like a baby.

Someday the Movie God will let Willie and me make a movie together. It's got to happen.

PART SIX

It's Not Supposed to Be That Way

It's Not Supposed to Be That Way

It's not supposed to be that way;
You're supposed to know that I love you.
But it don't matter anyway,
If I can't be there to control you.
And, like the other little children,
You're gonna dream a dream or two;
But be careful what you're dreamin',
Or soon your dreams'll be dreamin' you.

It's not supposed to be that way;
You're supposed to know that I love you.
But it don't matter anway
If I can't be there to console you.
And when you go out to play this
evenin',
Play with fireflies 'til they're gone;
And then rush to meet your lover,
And play with real fire 'til the dawn.

It's not supposed to be that way;
You're supposed to know that I love you.
But it don't matter anyway
If I can't be there to console you.

CHAPTER SEVENTEEN

Y ou may have noticed that I haven't said much about my kids so far. After fathering five children in the past thirty-five years, you'd think I should be some kind of expert on the subject of fatherhood. So I have been trying real hard to figure out what I have learned about fatherhood, and I have come up with one important lesson. I learned that my own father was doing the best he could. You probably have to reach middle age and experience all the problems and joys of fatherhood before you can understand the truth in such a simple statement. I was, before I realized it.

It's certainly tough for a kid to understand that the guy they call Father who is out there screwing up right and left is really just doing the best he can.

The guy you call Father is just a kid himself in his own mind. Maybe he's got some gray hairs and his face is wrinkled like a road map, but inside he is wondering how it can be that the mirror tells him he ain't young any more. The face he sees in the mirror changes from being a little kid or a teenager into being a grown-up and then an elderly person so fast it seems impossible.

I wake up feeling eighteen years old physically and somewhere in my thirties mentally, and then half a dozen children come to the door and say, "Good morning, Granddad." It's kind of a shock, really. I love being a grandfather, but how could I possibly be old enough to be one? When I was in my twenties, I was pretty sure I'd be dead by age forty. John Derek said a line in a movie we thought was romantic—"live fast, die young, and have a good-looking corpse." I remember turning thirty seemed like a big deal at the time. We were raised to regard thirty as some kind of watermark. By thirty you were supposed to be full grown and in command. You were either an up-and-comer, or you weren't going to make it in life. Forty was the dreaded beginning of middle age and fifty was when you finally got it all together just in time to turn sixty and die.

I think the Indians had the best way of talking about age. An Indian was a baby, then young, then prime, then old. They never referred to years. When a guy was prime, he was expected to be out doing the hunting and the fighting. It was not his job to sit and dispense wisdom to the young, because he was still out there learning what life was about. He sat around the campfire and bragged about how much meat or loot he had brought to the family, and how many enemies he'd knocked in the head. The Indians had big families around them, all moving together from place to place, with a lot of wives to tell the kids what to do. An Indian child looked upon all the mothers and grandmothers in the family as the child's own mother or grandmother. The child's real mother's sisters were just naturally considered as close to the child as his real mother. The old people sat around the fire and told long stories about their lives and what they had learned, passing on the knowledge of the tribe to the following generations.

The "Willie Nelson and Family" that grew together over the years was not consciously modeled after the Indian family concept, but, as you can see, it has a number of similarities.

My daughter Susie had a hard time adjusting to our constant moving around and our financial ups and downs. When she was in high school in Nashville, a cheerleader and in love, we jerked her out and stuck her in Travis High in Austin. Susie dropped out of school and took a job at Mr. Gatti's pizza parlor. I asked her why she had done it.

"To pay for my car," she said.

We both knew she wasn't responsible for car payments.

I asked Susie to go for a drive with me. I told her to take the wheel. "Just head west," I said.

Susie drove us through the Hill Country, past the peach orchards and the old stone farmhouses with tin roofs, and the sheep and goats in the meadows with the creeks running through and the hills rearing up higher as we went farther west. I wasn't saying much, just listening to Susie and picking at my guitar.

"Why don't we go see Freddie?" I said after a while. Freddie lived near Evergreen, Colorado. I sang all the way—songs I was writing for my *Phases and Stages* album. This is the story album that tells about divorce and discovering how to love again. One song I had written directly for Susie: "It's Not Supposed to Be That Way." The song is a father talking to his daughter, saying to her what I was now singing to Susie. Instead of trying to give people advice, I am better at putting my feelings into a song.

By the time I finished singing "It's Not Supposed to Be That Way," Susie and I were both crying.

I wasn't really trying to talk Susie into or out of anything. I just wanted her to know I loved her and was thinking about her.

A man likes to believe his wife is his best friend.

But when children come along, your wife doesn't have time to be your best friend. She has babies that must be taken care of. They may be very small people, but they are real, and they require a lot of attention.

When Martha and I started having children, all of a sudden she had to stay home and change the diapers. She couldn't go out with me as much as she had before. And she had to work because we needed the money to support our family. I'll admit that I was jealous of the kids because they were stealing time away from Martha and me. I'd come home off the road and have two days I wanted to spend with Martha, and with the kids too, but there was very little time. People used to tell you that two kids were no more trouble than one. We rapidly found out that two kids are ten times more trouble than one. With three kids, you can triple it. You could pack up one kid in ten minutes to go to Grandma's house or the babysitter, but three kids took an hour and a half. We spent some good times as a family. But the little things that Martha used to do for me, like wash my hair or scratch my back, she didn't have time for anymore. I'm sure my jealousy had a lot to do with some of the asshole stunts I pulled.

I think under different circumstances, somewhere in another time, Martha and I would have made it together. But me being a picker, and Martha loving to party, it was just an impossible situation. If Martha and I couldn't understand it, how could we expect Lana, Susie, and Billy to understand it?

You know you fall in love and you go together a while and you decide this is it, this is the perfect deal, it can't get no better than this, and you get married, and you're no longer lovers any more, you're husband and wife. Then from wherever you come from, whatever raising you've had, you start drawing on that knowledge of how you're supposed to act as a spouse. What do I expect my husband or my wife to do? That's where all the problems come in.

I've been married nearly my whole life, and I've been a road musician nearly my whole life. And I know those two are incompatible.

I'm fifty-five years old. I've been married to three women. Maybe it's not supposed to work for me.

My marriages weren't really failures. I've got a whole gang of great kids. No matter what, I'll always have a big family around me. Someday I'll hear them saying, "Here comes Great-Granddaddy Willie again. That old son of a bitch must have just finished his new TV show." I mean, my family ain't going to forget me, and I ain't going to forget them.

Back when Lana, Susie, and Billy were little, and I was with Shirley and Martha was getting a divorce, I wasn't allowed to talk to my kids. About four or five months before Martha's divorce was granted in Las Vegas, I wrote my kids a letter trying to explain myself to them.

It has been a different story with Paula and Amy in that they grew up without ever knowing what it is like to be broke.

When Lana, Susie, and Billy were little, I'd go in to buy a pack of cigarettes and they'd have these toy racks where you could buy little, cheap toys. I bought a lot of that stuff. It was all junk, but the kids liked it anyway.

With Paula and Amy growing up, the price of toys shot through the roof. Not their toys, necessarily. My toys, too. We were surrounded by the trappings of success and by mobs of people we sometimes didn't even know.

Once Paula and Amy came along, Connie couldn't travel with me anymore because she had to be a mother. We started spending time away from each other. Absence does not make the heart grow fonder, regardless of what people say. Maybe it will for a few days or a few weeks. But if you start spending too many hours or days or weeks away from each other, things start happening.

Probably everybody around me feels that some of the people around them are using them to get to me. Some of it's true and some of it isn't. Still, you have that paranoia. You never know whether someone likes you for you or for another reason. I think Susie felt that and all the kids felt that, and maybe still do to some degree, but they've toughened up some and come to realize that it's not that serious. People just react differently around celebrities, that's all. But

Connie wanted to spare Paula and Amy all of that and raise them like normal kids, whatever *normal* means.

Normal is just a word our society uses to describe kids who fit the pattern the authorities have laid down at the moment. Kids are people, and people are different in different ways for different reasons that have to do with working out their Karma. You can't tell a kid to be good and expect it to work automatically just because Father said so.

I've watched kids raised in all sorts of ways, following every theory ever invented by parents. I've seen kids who were poor and neglected and abused turn out to be outstanding people. On the other side of the coin, some of the worst people I ever met have had what seemed like ideal childhoods—loving, undivorced parents, plenty of money, a good education.

I guess having money and nice homes made it even worse for me to be at the golf course when I should have been at home. But I couldn't really convince Connie and the kids to move out to the golf course and stay with me. It was just a matter of where do you want to live? You may say it's not important but it damned sure is. When you've got time off you want to spend it with the people you love, but you also want to spend it at home, a place that feels like home to everybody. That seemed to be our problem. We were all too scattered and what was home to one of us wasn't to the other. What I had wanted everybody to do was to move back to Abbott and all the kids go to school there where I'd gone to school. But that wasn't necessarily what they wanted. You force your ideas on everybody, it doesn't work. Yet me being stubborn as I am and was, I tried and tried and then I would get upset because I couldn't make it happen the way I wanted it to be.

One thing I do know. In a few more years—a lot sooner than they realize—my kids will look in the mirror one morning and realize that while they may still feel like kids inside, they are in fact grandmothers or grandfathers.

I trust when that morning comes they will understand—if they don't understand already—that I did the best I could.

Go hug your daddy. It ain't too late to save him.

The Chorus

LANA NELSON

In 1962 I was nine years old and we were in Nashville right when Daddy and Mama were fixing to break up. "Mr. Record Man" had been recorded by Billy Walker. "Hello Walls" had already been a hit and we had gotten to move into a pretty nice house on the outskirts of Nashville.

I kind of wished Mama and Daddy would get a divorce because they fought so much. I always figured if they could get away from each other and not be together, maybe that was the answer. In order to get divorced, Mama took us to Las Vegas. She had to be a legal resident for six months in order to be able to get the divorce. It was kind of exciting. I wasn't very happy or anything, but it was something different. Mama was trying to make it, and she wasn't doing a very good job of it. Where before it was her and Daddy fighting, now it was her being really depressed over them being broke up, so it didn't solve anything, them breaking up, like I thought it would.

Daddy was on the road and he had met Shirley and they were living together and Mama was really pissed at that and she wouldn't let Daddy come around or bring Shirley or have anything to do with us for quite a long time. Shirley had supposedly been a friend. She

---

Lana is Willie's oldest daughter and longtime business associate.

and her husband socialized with Mama and Daddy. Mama hated Shirley more than if it had been anybody else, I think.

Mama had a way of driving Daddy really to the edge. He was driven to the edge quite a lot. Mama had such a bad temper. She was always instigating the physicalness of the fight and putting him on the defense. With Shirley, I noticed later, it was the opposite. He'd get mad at her to the point of wanting to hit the walls and throw things and stuff, and she'd be on the defense.

He wrote us a letter about life when he was with Shirley. That was during the time when Mama wouldn't let us kids see him. Letters and Candygrams were basically our communication, other than his songs. The first song I remember him singing to me was "Red Headed Stranger." I was about two, I guess. I can remember being in a crib and him singing that song. That's my earliest memory of him.

I'll take you back to being in Nashville. About the time that Patsy Cline recorded "Crazy." Soon after that, she was killed. I can remember the morning she was killed. I guess Mama and Daddy had already split up, because we were staying at a babysitter's and Mama would come pick us up in the morning when she got through with work. And we watched the news that morning about Patsy Cline's plane crash and Mama goes, you know if there's one woman in the world I hated, it's that Patsy Cline. So I can just remember that. That's my memory of Patsy Cline, Mama saying if there's one woman I hate, it's Patsy Cline. I thought it was kind of cruel since she just died that day, but . . .

I remember when we were in Houston and when Daddy was gonna sell "Family Bible." I think it was when I must have been about four. Daddy came home and told me he had sold "Family Bible." I just cried and cried and cried. You remember when you heard there was no Santa Claus? I felt like that. I wanted everybody to know that he wrote it, that it was his song. He told me it doesn't matter whose name is on it, he wrote it, and he will always have wrote it, so not to worry. Some day he was gonna buy me so much stuff and some day we were gonna have as much land as far as we could see, and don't worry about a thing, that this was just one song. So that was when I decided, well, ya know, he's gonna be this big star. So that was when I started planning on being his secretary, when I was four years old. I groomed myself for years, to grow up and be his secretary. Worked out real well, too.

I've seen him through many happy times. I remember when I had my son Nelson, I was sixteen and I woke up and Daddy was there in the room and Pop, his daddy, was there and Steve, my husband, was there. It was pretty nice. Daddy was beaming pretty good then. His first grandbaby. Who looked like this little bitty Indian papoose with a bunch of black hair and everything.

Steve and I had started having fights. He beat me up. We had to go pick up the kids at Daddy's house one night. He heard that I had been hurt. I had told Susie the truth, she told Daddy, Daddy and Connie came into our house. I'll never forget Connie had on this white fur coat, it's like this white full-length mink coat, and her white hair was striking and Daddy was flinging through the house in the fur coat that Shirley had bought him that made him look like a brown standard French poodle. Steve had broken out the plate-glass window and the door and the screen and the glass and all the crystal and everything, and it looked like a bomb exploded inside our house. Daddy comes in and he and Steve have a big fight. Daddy said to me, "Are you gonna stay with this son of a bitch or are you coming with me?"

Steve was laying on the floor bleeding and crying, and Daddy, it seemed like he was doing pretty good. Steve had kept yelling, oh, don't hit me, Willie, don't hit me, Willie, I got anxiety, I got anxiety. In a way I felt sorry for him and I figured well, ya know, he's all right tonight, and well, I'm gonna make this work. I had two kids and was just eighteen.

By now, Mama and Daddy had become friends again. Mama had married after she and Daddy got the divorce. She had two more little boys during the time that I lived with her. We traveled around, we went to California and New Mexico. Gradually, she let Daddy call and then she let Billy live with Daddy, and then she let Susie and me visit him in the summertime and eventually one summer we just stayed with him in Nashville.

Shirley was the lady of the house at the ranch at Ridgetop. We had chickens and pigs, it was a fun time. Shirley was doing a lot of writing with Daddy. At the time of the shootout, Mother was living with us in Ridgetop. She was working as a waitress in a truckstop where Steve's mother was the cook and she had rode to work with Steve's mother, who had to bring Mama home only she couldn't bring Mama home to our house because it was all trashed out and Daddy'd just shot up Steve's car in the front yard. So we had to have Mama come to Daddy and Connie's house. Steve's mother had to drive up in that territory and let Mama off and all the way over there she's saying if they've hurt my Stevie, I'll just kill somebody. And Mama says fuck your Stevie, and they get in a fight on the way over. So here's Mama, she's mad, she comes in, and there's Connie, and there's just a whole house full of people, and Steve drives by, and he's shooting up the house. Mama's running through the house screaming we're gonna get killed, we're gonna get killed. Connie tackles her in the hall and says get down, Martha, you're gonna get killed. Bullets were flying everywhere. After everything was over and years passed, that was one of the funniest things I ever saw— crawling on my knees to see Connie tackling Mama who was running wildly through the hallways, yelling, we're gonna get killed, we're gonna get killed.

Looking at the lights shining in the windows of Daddy's cabin, I just remembered Mama getting me, about two or three years old, and pulling me in the light to look at shirts that Daddy had worn the night before to see if I could see the lipstick traces. Because she was saying lipstick was there and Daddy would say, Martha you're crazy, there's nothing there. She would get me in front of the window and say, Lana, do you see that lipstick? I'd always say no, Mama, I don't see a thing. She'd get so mad.

She used to send me to sit on his lap and ask him for more money when they were getting a divorce. She'd say tell your daddy that you need, that we need, that Mama needs more money. And I'd go say Daddy, Mama wanted me to tell you she needed more money.

Listening to "Mr. Record Man," I can remember when Mama and Daddy were getting a divorce, and this song was on his very first album. I remember playing the single over and over and over. When she was getting a divorce, Mama would play Ray Charles, all those really sad, sad songs—"Your Cheatin' Heart," "I Can't Stop Loving You"—and she'd just cry and be depressed. She loved Daddy. I think she loved him maybe more than anybody else I've ever known him to be with. They really got along the worst of anybody I've ever seen him with. Mama heard Daddy singing "Mr. Record Man" on the radio. She knew the songs because they were written when they were together and were just now getting recorded as they were breaking up. He bought her a Cadillac in Nashville right before they got the divorce.

The saddest I ever saw my dad was when his mother died.

We tried to get to the funeral. Daddy had his Lear and Mount St. Helens had just erupted. His mother lived close to Mount Rainier, in Yakima, Washington, where the funeral was. We had to fly over Mount St. Helens. Weather forced us to land four hours away from the funeral. We radioed for a limousine to meet us. When we landed, the limo was two hours late.

We missed the funeral oration, but they waited to bury her body until we got there. In a way it worked out just perfect for such a sad thing. There had been so many people, so much press earlier. When we got there nobody was in the whole funeral home except for us. It was about midnight. We had traveled for twenty-four hours. We had our own private ceremony, and that was the saddest I ever saw him, but then he started feeling a little better. He started feeling at peace, thinking about her, because she had been in terrible pain from cancer, so she was much better off. And we started laughing about her looking at us and watching us and we could hear her laughing at what we were doing and what we had on. We started back, two or three hours over the mountain, to the airport. The limousine catches on fire. We can't go any further.

In the limousine it's me and Daddy and Connie and Aunt Bobbie and Jack and Mark and the limo driver. There was snow everywhere, and we saw a golden light way off in the distance and Mark said well, I'm gonna go for that light. He walked through the snow, through fields, over fences, having no idea where he was going. He finally got there and called the police. We had a police escort into the town where the airport was. We stopped and had breakfast with the officer in the patrol car and he had already called several of his friends to come meet him at the Denny's and so it was like this big party in the town as we were leaving the airport. And we had a good laugh about how Grandma Harvey had probably staged the whole thing and how funny she thought it was for us to get stranded in the middle of the mountains in Washington in a snowstorm on the day of her funeral.

PART SEVEN

On the Road Again

On the Road Again

On the road again
I just can't wait to get on the road again
The life I love is makin' music with my friends
And I can't wait to get on the road again.

On the road again
Goin' places that I've never been
Seein' things that I may never see again
I can't wait to get on the road again.

On the road again
Like a band of gypsies
We go down the highway
We're the best of friends
Insisting that the world keep turnin' our way
And our way

Is on the road again
I just can't wait to get on the road again
The life I love is makin' music with my friends
And I can't wait to get on the road again.

CHAPTER EIGHTEEN

W e were rolling along the highway on *Honeysuckle Rose* aiming for Salt Lake City in the very early morning for a show at the Salt Palace. Out the window I could see patches of blue snow in the fields. Crowns of snow on the mountains looked like starched white nurse caps—like most musicians, I owe my life to nurses and waitresses—and the jagged rocks turned purple in the rising sun, like you might see in a Zane Grey novel or a good Western movie.

From my mound of coats and blankets on the floor at the foot of my king-size bed in the rear of the bus, I could see Gator Moore sitting up straight at the wheel. Gator had been driving all night, since we left our last show at the Universal Amphitheater in Los Angeles. It would be another six hours before we reached the Holiday Inn on the outskirts of Salt Lake City. I pulled the blankets closer around me in the cold. I could hear Kimo Alo, the Kahuna I had met in Maui, breathing in a deep sleep in my bed. My back was hurting. I had been to Kimo's people in the mountains in Maui to treat my chronic ailing back, and what they did to me worked for a while. But on the road, my back started hurting again. I couldn't get comfortable in my bed, so the Kahuna medicine man slept in my bed and I shifted around on the floor, as usual, aching and sore. It might sound like some kind of metaphor for show business that the doctor was in the bed and the patient was on the floor. But I had suggested Kimo sleep on the bed, told him I'd be happier on the floor. Hell, maybe it *is* a metaphor for show business.

I had been up half the night prowling around *Honeysuckle Rose*, listening to a tape of our last show, playing computer golf, cleaning up. I was tired, but I was pumped up from the show. We had played our music with a lot of power and the crowd gave us their energy and love in return. That feeling really jacks me up. Friends like Dennis Hopper—so clean and straight these days he looks like a mad scientist preppie—joined us onstage for "Amazing Grace." When Larry Gorham hustled me to the bus, I found out he and Gator had hidden it to avoid the after-show visitors. I didn't really want to avoid anybody, but L. G. and Gator must have seen I was tired and hurting.

My old friend Jan-Michael Vincent found me, anyhow, and we sat at the table on the bus and talked movie bullshit for a while. Jan and I are always just about to make a movie together, and I guess one day we will. Meanwhile, we swap a lot of good bullshit, and in honor of Jan's visit and my aching back, we drank a few swigs out of a brown bottle of rare Sauza tequila and burned a joint that smelled like a cave where skunks went to die.

So I was feeling mellow by the time Jan bailed out in his dark glasses and his limo, and our convoy got loaded—five buses of people and two semi-trucks of equipment. Gator drove *Honeysuckle Rose* down the winding hill through the lights of Burbank, and all seven vehicles took off rolling toward Salt Lake City.

In the early morning now, after maybe two hours of sleep, I could hear the tires humming on the highway and feel *Honeysuckle Rose* singing with energy. I went up front to drink a cup of coffee and watch miles and miles of Utah roll past the window.

It makes me feel good to gaze out the windows of the bus at the towns and signs and landscape going past. It's like the other side of the feeling I got when I was a little kid and heard a railroad train whistling and rumbling into the distance in the middle of the night. This is what might have happened if you had ever really caught that mysterious midnight train.

Most people have that fantasy of catching the train that whistles in the night. It's a hunger for freedom, I guess, that holds in the heart. The last time I was on David Letterman's TV show, the first thing he said was, "Willie, can I ride on your bus?" I told him sure he could, and I meant it, but he wouldn't really do it, which probably is why he brought it up so fast.

A couple of days ago, taping the Johnny Carson show in Burbank, we'd parked our bus convoy in the middle of the NBC lot at Universal, causing much comment. Johnny Carson had to work his way through the buses to slip his sports car into his own parking spot, which is right by the front door to the NBC studio.

So on the show, the first thing Johnny talked about was the buses. The day before, one of his producers had phoned me at L'Ermitage in Beverly Hills and drilled me on the questions Johnny would ask. I remember one question was how did I handle female groupies. The producer said, "I guess you just get rid of them, huh?"

I said, "Sure. I can do that."

But on the show, Johnny kept talking about the buses being the center of attention in Burbank that day, and how he could barely squeeze his car into the lot, and what a wild, free, glamorous kind of life it must be out there on the road rolling on the bus.

He said, "How do you handle the groupies?"

I said, "Well, I try to give them whatever I can."

That broke up Johnny, because he was expecting the answer about getting rid of them. It got a real big laugh everywhere, in fact. But, shit, it's the answer I was going to give the producer, because it's the truth.

Whatever I can don't mean what it used to.

As I stood in the aisle, pouring a cup of coffee, my sister Bobbie was in the lower berth with her curtains shut. *Honeysuckle Rose* has two Pullman-type berths, except they're big enough for a guy like Ray Benson, who's 6'6", to stretch out in. There are color TVs at the foot of the mattresses and reading lights at the head. It is the bunk you should have had on the old midnight mystery train, for sure.

With her curtains shut, I couldn't tell if Bobbie was asleep. She might be looking out the window at miles and miles of Utah. Or possibly she was fingering chords on a practice keyboard she carries, working on a piece by Beethoven or Mozart, hearing it in her mind while her fingers touched the board. Bobbie is pure music. In her soul she is a spiritual Indian who vibrates music. My sister has put in about as many miles on the road as I have, playing her music.

Traveling was always one of the things I was supposed to do in conjunction with music. The fact that my family sort of disintegrated when I was a youngster made it easy to become a gypsy whose home is wherever he finds his hat. The home that was Abbott faded away in my teens. I had a home wherever my mother was, or wherever my dad was, but they were the traveling kind, too. All of us in the family were constantly moving up and down the highway. Even my great-grandfather, Mama Nelson's daddy, was a circuit preacher who rode the hills of Arkansas in a buggy and horse.

I think everybody is looking for a home. It's one of the strongest motivations in life. The movie *Songwriter* was about artists struggling for freedom against bankers and greed and the sometimes crooked rules of the music business establishment. But at bottom the character of Doc Jenkins that I played was looking for a home. Bud Shrake used to say he thought of Doc Jenkins as a boll weevil. Remember the *Boll Weevil* song? It was a big hit for Tex Ritter.

"First time I see de boll weevil
he's settin' on de chair;
Next time I see de boll weevil
he's got alla his family dere . . .
Jus' lookin' for a home, Boss,
Jus' lookin' for a home."

This is a universal truth. It's just as true for the old as the young. Chinese, Russians, Republicans, Mexicans, cowboys, university presidents, preachers, you name it, under the skin they're all just like us country singers on the road—their hearts break, they know loneliness, they want love, they're looking for a home.

One of my homes is *Honeysuckle Rose*, my bus.

Could be that's the fascination people feel about life on the bus—you've got a home, but you don't have to stay too long in one place.

If you get tired of Texas or California, you can move your home to Florida or Maine with no problem.

My bus is like a cocoon, too, that I can seal myself up in if I need to be alone.

I've always enjoyed being alone. I've never had a problem with talking to myself, because some of my best conversations are between me and just my own self cruising down the highway. There are plenty of times I like to have people around me. But if I need privacy, my bus gives it to me. I can be close enough to the so-called real world that I could reach out and touch it from inside *Honeysuckle Rose*, yet I can be as quiet and alone as I wish.

There is a telephone on the wall beside my seat at the booth on the bus to use when I need to check in with Mark Rothbaum or somebody, and we put a TV satellite dish on the bus so I can watch Cable News Network no matter where I am.

Despite how people fantasize what is going on inside *Honeysuckle Rose* on the road, most of the time these days it is like this run from

Los Angeles to Salt Lake City—just Gator and me and Bobbie and probably somebody I might never have dreamed would be there, like Kimo the Kahuna.

Kimo woke up in my bed and came down the aisle rubbing the sleep out of his eyes, wearing jeans and sandals. He's a tall, ropy-thin young fellow who took me into the mountains on Maui and got his Kahuna relatives to work on my back and my sinuses. I believe in the Kahunas. Then Kimo followed me to the country club in Austin and later got on my bus for this tour. The crew and the guys in the band were still checking Kimo out. A newcomer doesn't just walk into our gypsy family without arousing distrust and suspicion. We're too close for a secret agent to penetrate our circle. It's not like the old days of the Outlaw Tour when we had roadies out the ass and every third guy wearing a Waylon or Willie T-shirt was a narc.

There was a lot of well-deserved paranoia on our buses in those days. I remember when one of Waylon's guys proudly told him he had rigged a trap to catch the narcs on Waylon's bus.

Waylon asked what did he use for narc bait?

"Simple," the guy said. "I planted transmitters all over the bus— under the table, in the bunks, in the bathroom—everywhere but your bedroom. Now you can go in your room alone, shut the door, and tune in to any conversation on the bus. You can hear what everybody is saying."

Waylon shouted, "You're fired, you dumb son of a bitch."

"Fired? I did this for your own good."

Waylon said, "Don't you understand one fucking thing? If I heard what the guys in the band are saying about me, I'd have to fight every one of them assholes every day. I don't want to know all that shit. Get your ass out of my sight."

But now the paranoia level has justifiably gone way down, and so have the numbers on my bus. Once I hit Austin or Los Angeles or some other big town where I know a lot of people, the bus gets crowded before and after the shows. I see folks I'm glad I got to see. But when we reach Salt Lake City, it's a totally different scene. Fans will gather around the bus, but there's not a lot of old friends to come on board.

I went through a period of leasing a Learjet in 1983 and flying to a lot of my shows to meet the buses. It was not economically a sound practice to be spending $400,000 a year leasing a jet, but it made sense to me to shell out $1,700,000 to buy one. So I did. Paul said, "Same old Willie. Spends more money than he makes."

Marty Morris had been my pilot while I was leasing the Lear 25—

a seven-passenger model built in 1979—and Marty stayed at the controls when I bought the plane. Our most frequent trip in the Lear was from Austin to Denver. Marty was bringing us into the lights of Denver one night when our co-pilot, Ken Miller, handed me a set of earphones and said, "You've gotta hear this."

Marty had just finished telling the tower we were ready to land. An air traffic controller was talking on the radio. "You other guys shut up. This is my big chance," he said.

Over the earphones I heard the air traffic controller sing *On the Road Again*. He sang it all the way through. He wasn't half bad.

The Lear has a small refrigerator and a good sound system and those big soft, sweet-smelling leather seats like you used to get in a good Cadillac in the 50's. Connie had notepads and matchbooks printed up with the logo *Air Willie* and a cartoon of me sitting in a running shoe with wings on it.

I've sold the Lear back to the company again—somewhere I heard the chorus of voices that kept telling me I had no business buying a jet—but I still lease it all the time.

Here's an example of the way I use the jet now. In September of 1987 I was in Los Angeles playing in a CBS-TV Western movie called *The Last Texas Train*. The director worked us all day until after dark shooting a dancing scene in the ballroom at the Wilshire Temple. The company finally wrapped—and the next shot was to be the following afternoon at the Old Tucson movie town outside Tucson, Arizona.

Gator drove me overnight to Tucson in *Honeysuckle Rose*, which was my home during the filming. We shot until late Thursday night at Old Tucson.

On Friday at noon Gator drove me to the location at Mezcal, about forty miles on the other side of Tucson. Mezcal is where Steve McQueen shot his last Western, *Tom Horn*. The scenery there is so big, the distances so vast with the mountains rising close around but also very far away, that it makes you want to sit around a campfire and be close to people.

I like Burt Kennedy's style of directing. He knows what he wants, works fast, and shoots with two or three cameras at the same time for coverage. Burt is an old pro, so he didn't panic when Gator cranked up *Honeysuckle Rose* at 9:30 Friday night and drove me to the Tucson airport.

The Lear was waiting for me at midnight. We took off and flew from Tucson to Lincoln, Nebraska.

At the airport in Lincoln, Johnny Sizemore picked me up in one of our tour buses. Johnny drove the bus to the University of Nebraska football stadium, underneath the stands. It was about 5 A.M. by now. I slept on the floor a couple of hours.

Out the windows I could see people already walking around in large numbers. In about three more hours, there would be 75,000 people in the Nebraska stadium for one of the strongest concerts I've ever taken part in, both musically and in response from the audience and the whole state.

You might have seen it on television. It was Farm Aid III. Although this was the final Farm Aid concert—I think—I'm happy that we have been able to raise the national consciousness to confront an intolerable farm situation. Everybody from the White House through Congress should have been in the Nebraska stadium for Farm Aid III to feel the heartbeat of the country.

The minute the concert ended, Johnny Sizemore drove the *On the Road Again* bus back to the Lincoln airport. At about 1 A.M.— roughly twenty-four hours since we had set out for Lincoln—I was again in Tucson, ready to go back to work on *The Last Texas Train* again.

I lived on *Honeysuckle Rose*, when I wasn't in my motel suite, for the next seven days while the movie was shooting. On Saturday afternoon the movie company broke the Tucson location to return to Los Angeles and resume shooting the following Monday.

But I had gigs to play Saturday night in Waterloo, Iowa, and Sunday night in Grand Forks, North Dakota.

Gator dropped me at the Tucson airport and headed *Honeysuckle Rose* toward Los Angeles. Marty Morris, my longtime pilot, picked me up in the Lear and flew me to Waterloo, where the band and crew were waiting. After the Waterloo show I rode in Paul's bus to Grand Forks. We rang down the flag at midnight in Grand Forks, and Marty picked me up in the Lear again and flew me to Los Angeles in time to be on the movie set Monday morning.

And that's just a routine schedule. I really couldn't make it without the Lear. It's practical. But I do admit that when I owned the jet, it was like a new toy I wanted to show off. Roger Miller had a jet years before I did and used to fly me around in it some. Now it was my turn. Roger was living in Santa Fe, and we flew in to pick him up just to run him to Los Angeles. We took off and circled the Sangre de Christo Mountains and headed west.

Roger tapped me on the shoulder.

"Willie, I got to piss."

"I believe we can arrange that," I said.

"Listen, I ain't gonna piss in one of these Lears. I know all about these sons of bitches. I want to piss on the ground."

"Would a regular size bathroom do?"

"Yeah. But I don't see one up here."

I told Marty to put the jet down at the next opportunity. Turned out, it was Palm Springs. Marty landed and Roger got out and went to the bathroom.

That was about a $2,000 piss.

But how can you put a price on a good piss?

Another time we landed at the strip in Santa Fe to pick up Roger, and he wasn't there. I went walking along the road toward town, hoping Roger would show up and I could jump his ass about making me wait.

Here came what looked like a taxi with a driver in the front seat wearing a cabbie's cap. Roger was slumped in the back. I jumped in bedside Roger and said something like, "Airport, buddy, step on it."

We roared off in the taxi, showering sand and rocks. I grabbed for something to hang on to and was about to shout at the driver when I noticed he looked sort of familiar under that cap. He turned around to me and said, "How about all them royalties you owe me for making you famous? I'm here to collect."

Then I got a good look at his face and realized it was Don Meredith.

For several seasons, at the peak of the show's popularity, Meredith had been singing "turn out the lights . . . the party's over . . ." on ABC-TV Monday Night Football as his way of telling the viewers the game was about wrapped up. Meredith, Frank Gifford, and Howard Cosell were the hottest thing on sports TV with their Monday Night Football for a decade or so. I had known Don since back in the sixties when he was a great quarterback for the Dallas Cowboys. Most people don't realize he came within four feet of winning two National Football League Championships in a row, and he retired from the game at age twenty-eight. I used to watch Don play football, and he'd come to my shows and get onstage. Don had career ideas as a country singer—he cut a couple of records, in fact.

As I recall, I had sent Don a bouquet of roses the first night he sang "turn out the lights . . ." on Monday Night Football. Then as he kept using the song, year after year, I was thoroughly enjoying it, of course, but I thought I would kid him about it. I had my office put together a thick stack of royalty statements and sent them to him with a letter that said, "Look, Don, I know how badly you need material, but my family has got to eat."

A couple of weeks later, Meredith sent me an accounting of the royalty statements I had unloaded on him. "Turn Out the Lights" had shown a sharp increase in sales in the years Meredith had been singing it on Monday Night Football, he said, and by rights, I owed him a percentage.

This was the first time I had seen him since.

Don said, "No shit, now, Willie, I want my royalties. I've made you so famous you've got a jet plane, and I'm reduced to driving bums around in a taxi. Give me my money."

I said, "Well, first I'll have my people take lunch with your people. I think the truth is, you owe *me* money."

Don was kidding, of course, about him needing money. He got richer than a honeybee cave from TV commercials and endorsements and speaking engagements. He lives back and forth between Santa Fe and a huge apartment that overlooks Central Park in Manhattan. He can sink down in a giant bathtub full of bubble bath and look through a plate-glass window at the kids playing touch football in the park. Don needs money about as bad as I need fleas.

Maybe if he turns his apartment over to me on demand, I will call my mean lawyer off his case.

In my early frequent-flier period on the jet, I used to figure I might as well use the plane all I could before somebody took it away from me. Any of my old beer joint fans who might resent the thought of me flying around in a Learjet wouldn't be upset for long, is the way I looked at it, because the plane was bound to be repossessed.

But the money was stacking up so fast for a while it was hard to get rid of. We tried our best though. I do believe money is not to be hoarded—it is to be spread around. That is what true capitalism is about, using money for energy instead of fat. Look at all the people whose lives were made better by the fact that I didn't care how fast I spent money.

When I was in my twenties I used to say I hoped I owed $50,000 at my funeral. Twenty years later, I changed the number to $1,000,000. Now even $10,000,000 don't look like half enough to have seeded the planet with by the time I shuck off this body and start the process of choosing a new one.

With the jet I could wake up in the morning in my own bed in Austin, play golf at my country club, leave the last hole about four or five in the afternoon, and fly to Kansas City for a show that night. After the gig, I'd fly back to Austin, sleep in my own bed again, play some more golf at my club, then fly to a show that night in Omaha or someplace.

It was definitely a luxury. I was high rolling. At first I told myself I'd get some writing done in the quiet hours on the plane cuddled in those soft leather seats, but instead I got more sleep than I had counted on.

Having your own jet is a stage you reach if you are successful enough in show business—exactly like getting your own bus is your symbol of success when you put together a band. If you were still riding in a station wagon with the fiddle sticking in your ear, you needed a bus. So you bought the first bus that came along that you could get into financially.

However they'd let you have it, wherever you could sign your name, you took the deal. The first bus I bought was Marty Robbins's old bus that Hollywood people had used in a movie. I made the deal in front of a motel in San Antonio. I told the guy, "Okay, I'll take it." Ten minutes later we started up the motor and the bus died right there in the driveway. We named it the *Open Road*.

The *Open Road* broke down in Louisiana, in Arkansas, in a lot of strange places. Johnny Bush or Paul or me, whoever was sober enough to climb behind the wheel, was the driver. But we needed a mechanic as often as a driver, and none of us could put together a Christmas toy.

The last time I spent the night on the *Open Road* bus, the wood had rotted through above my bunk and I could see the stars and feel the wind and rain blowing on my face.

The next bus I bought was Porter Waggoner's when Dolly Parton was working with him. You could smell her perfume inside. I used to sort of fantasize about it.

The *Honeysuckle Rose* bus that was taking me toward Salt Lake City was built by the Florida Coach Company. My bus must have cost $500,000 to put together, with all the hand-carved woodwork and a bedroom bigger than some of the joints I've played in. There's a plaque on the wall inside that says, "This coach built for Willie Nelson and family, Connie, Paula and Amy by Florida Coach Company." But Connie and the girls never rode *Honeysuckle Rose* much.

Kimo poured a cup of Gator's power coffee, lit a cigarette and slid into the booth. I don't like to see a healer or a doctor smoke cigarettes. I've had guys walk up to me in bars with a martini in one hand and a cigarette in the other and say, "Willie, I am Dr. so-and-so, the eminent brain surgeon." It makes me shudder.

But Kimo is an important step in the evolution of things. He's a very logical, bottom-line thinker. The bottom line is *love thy neighbor* and *do unto others as you would have them do unto you.*

I put a can of chili into the microwave and ate it with soda crackers and skim milk for breakfast. From my table I could see the broken land that led off toward the Bonneville Salt Flats.

Consistency is the main requirement for a performer on the road to keep in mind. I have always been dependable. If I am supposed to be there, I show up. In my own mind, I'm still playing for the gate.

It's kind of like everywhere I go on *Honeysuckle Rose*, whatever town I wake up in, I'm in my old hometown. I go out and walk the streets, drop in for coffee at some cafe. People say hi to me. It's very flattering to be recognized.

I personally think the more security you have, the more problems you are going to have. Larry Gorham's job is to watch out for me on the road—always from a discreet distance—but if I'm not on tour, there's no entourage marching around me to clear a path. People have asked, "Aren't you worried about being kidnapped?" Who the hell would want to kidnap a guy like me? Of course, it might happen tonight. But the point is, if anybody has a mind to kidnap you or blow you away, you could be surrounded by security guards and they'd still get you. If somebody drove up with a car full of machine guns and started shooting, the security guards next to me would keel over at the same time I did. I ain't learned how to stop bullets in midair yet.

A few years ago in Dallas, a girl climbed halfway up on stage to kiss me. So I leaned over to kiss her, and her husband took a swing at me. He was boozed up and probably pissed at her for something else, anyway. That didn't make me mad. It was some guy in Phoenix who reminded me I was still an animal with a long way to progress up the spiritual ladder.

I was in the dressing room in Phoenix and this guy came back and said he was looking for Willie Nelson. He said he wanted some autographs for folks who were waiting in a car behind the club.

I walked out the back door with him into the parking lot. It was dark and I was looking for the folks in the car when—*wham!* The guy slugged me in the head with a crescent wrench. My head poured blood.

I picked up a two-by-four about four feet long. Every time the guy swung at me with the crescent wrench, I dodged and whaled him with the board. We fought for twenty minutes, breathing hard and drenched with blood and sweat. I kept whacking the poor bastard with the board, and he kept coming after me with the crescent wrench. We hardly said a word except for cussing. It was like *Bad Day at Black Rock*.

Finally somebody broke up the fight. It turned out that the last time I'd played Phoenix a few months earlier, the band had been out with this guy's wife. She went home and told him she'd been with me.

Barroom brawls are something I try to avoid. I know my temper has always been a problem, whether I inherited it or developed it. Having a hot temper is like being an alcoholic, you always know it's there. I don't like to get mad. It makes me feel terrible. I am not pleasant to be around when I get mad. People actually get up and leave the room. Anger and anguish are basic emotions everybody feels. I'm sure I'll always feel them, but I hope it's for more important reasons than just to get pissed off. I guess life is a continual process of trying to wise up.

Honeysuckle Rose and our caravan rolled into the outskirts of Salt Lake City early in the afternoon. The buses parked in the alley and around the corner. The Holiday Inn had a swimming pool indoors, so the lobby and the bar were kind of warm and humid.

Darrell Wayne English, Paul's son and our tour coordinator, had already checked me and Bobbie in under an alias. She went to her room. The guys in the band drifted to the bar beside the swimming pool inside the hotel. We had the night off. The pleasures of Salt Lake City beckoned to the band and the crew—fellows with imagination.

In my room, I switched on CNN on the TV and ordered a cheeseburger and a glass of tea from room service. I checked through a dozen phone messages. All of them were from people who knew enough to find me, and most of them I should call back.

The room service kid took the lid off my cheeseburger and unpeeled the plastic wrapper off my glass of tea. He acted pretty suave.

Day after tomorrow the band would be at Caesar's Palace in Las Vegas. I would be in a suite as big as a house. I knew the Caesar's Palace suite well—I like washing my jeans in the bathtub there and hanging them out the window to dry in the desert wind.

The toughest spot to work up a frenzied exchange of energy with the crowd is Las Vegas. Most of the people who come to the big dinner shows when I work on the Strip are just glad to be sitting down. They've been standing at the slot machines all night, or losing at the tables. What they want is a couple of hours of rest and relaxation. If they get to eat something and hear some music, so much the better. Mainly, though, they're trying to get off their damn feet.

A Las Vegas dinner-show crowd is not a rock and roll crowd, that's for sure. In his heyday, when he was really hot, there was an explosion of energy between Elvis and his audience. I wasn't a wild fan of Elvis's, but put the man onstage doing his music, and you got something more powerful than the sum of its parts. You got magnetism in action. Maybe it was sexual, I don't know, but if ever a performer could get up onstage and turn a crowd into crashing waves of energy, it was Elvis.

Yet Elvis couldn't really whip up a Las Vegas dinner-show crowd on a regular basis. I went to see Elvis one night on the Strip and I slipped in at the back of the room and listened a minute and thought: what is going on here? There was Elvis up there working his ass off, and the crowd was just kind of politely exhausted. They clapped and whistled, but you couldn't feel them giving anything back. I felt like jumping on top of a table and yelling, "Hey, everybody, that's Elvis Presley up there! You should be jumping up screaming."

But the crowds in Las Vegas are normally not screaming crowds. Las Vegas is the place where you make more money than you do anywhere else, but it's not the place where a performer is the most appreciated.

When I finished my cheeseburger and tea and made a few of my phone calls in the room at the Holiday Inn, I sneaked back out to *Honeysuckle Rose* and put some ballads on the tape machine and drank a couple of beers to make me sleepy and burned one down and crawled into Bobbie's bunk and shut the curtains. It was cold, so I pulled the blankets around me and snuggled up. I felt like a kid camping out, real cozy and nice. Maybe my back wouldn't start hurting.

For all you fellow pilgrims, here is my list of statements to watch out for on your journey:

THE 60 GREAT LIES ON THE ROAD

1. The booking is definite.
2. Your check is in the mail.
3. I promise not to come in your mouth.
4. We can fix it in the mix.
5. This is the best dope you've ever had.
6. The show starts at eight.
7. My agent will take care of it.
8. I'm sure it will work.
9. Your tickets are at the door.

10. It sounds in tune to me.
11. Sure, it sounds fine at the back of the hall.
12. I know your mike is on.
13. I checked it myself.
14. The roadie took care of it.
15. She'll be backstage after the show.
16. Yes, the spotlights will be on you during your solos.
17. The stage mix sounds just like the program mix.
18. It's the hottest pickup I could get.
19. The club will provide the P.A. and the lights.
20. I really love the band.
21. We'll have lunch sometime.
22. We'll have it ready before tonight.
23. If it breaks, we'll fix it free.
34. We'll let you know.
25. I had nothing to do with your marriage breaking up. Your marriage was on the rocks long before I ever met you.
26. The place was packed.
27. We'll have you back next week.
28. Don't worry, you'll be the headliner.
29. It's on the truck.
30. This coke hasn't been cut.
31. My last band had a record deal, but we broke up before recording the album.
32. Someone will be there early to let you in.
33. I've only been playing for a year.
34. I've been playing for twenty years.
35. We'll have the flyers made tomorrow.
36. I'm with the band.
37. The band gets free drinks.
38. You'll get your cut tonight, no problem.
39. He'll work the door tonight for us.
40. You'll have no problem fitting that speaker cabinet in your trunk.
41. There will be lots of roadies when you get there.
42. I know we'll get some applause after the next tune.
43. We'll have more than enough time for a sound check.
44. This is one of Jimi's old Strats.
45. We'll definitely come see you play tonight.
46. You can depend on me.
47. You won't have to play any requests.
48. We have this great gig in Vegas next month.

49. The other band will be glad to let you use their P.A.
50. I am singing on key, the P.A.'s screwing up.
51. Sounds good to me.
52. You won't have any trouble finding the place.
53. I've played there before.
54. We can turn the volume down if it's too loud.
55. I just use this little amp for small gigs. I've got a Marshall stack at home.
56. This tour itinerary you can count on being correct.
57. You only have to do two sets.
58. The laundromat is just around the corner.
59. Best party club in town. Go check it out.
60. The guy with the dope will be here in twenty minutes.

The Chorus

DUDLEY (BUDROCK) PREWITT

When I first went on Willie's payroll, the production crew rode in a station wagon. Now we have our own bus.

My job is to do all the advance work and scheduling of the trucks and my crew. I negotiate the sound and light packages. By that I mean I communicate with Mark Rothbaum's office in Connecticut and find out what the dates are in advance so I can get a fair deal for the sound and light equipment we need to rent. I'll design a lighting plot, for example, and Fed-X it to four different lighting companies and then take bids on the telephone to get the best price. I keep in touch with Paul about it, but he pretty much leaves it up to me.

That is before the tour starts. The real fun part of the job is doing the lights during the shows.

I use seven or eight colors and there are seven or eight people onstage I have to cover with lights. I can do general washes and throw special colors on one person, change to different looks. I call it accenting the mood.

Take a simple number like "Georgia." It starts with Jody Payne doing a little guitar intro, and I highlight him with a flesh pink which comes up when the rest of the stage is dark. It's very quick and

---

Budrock is production manager and lighting director for the band.

subtle. Then, boom, spotlights hit Willie as he sings. Then I change the color scheme again, directing the attention, helping create the mood. We may have lavender lights on stage right and stage left, maybe light blue on the sides, and a different color—an amber spot —on Willie to make him stand out.

Willie sings along and I add subtle bumps and looks, then Willie fades out. Boom, hit Mickey for his harmonica solo. I go to a straight red on Mickey, but his next solo I don't use red on him again. Don't want to identify Mickey with nothing but red. At the end of Mickey's solo, Mike Garvey hits the echo on his sound board. I bounce a different color, bop it, pop it to white, and then I add Willie in there, and Mickey gets his applause and slowly fades out. Then it's back to Willie. And you give a soft highlight to Mickey as the song ends.

That's a simple one, four cues. We use fourteen cues on some numbers. A couple of songs are just one cue—the opening cue on Willie and let him do it. But there we are, maybe 200 feet from the stage directing the attention of the crowd to the musicians. The average person who goes to the show wouldn't have any idea from a distance which one was playing the guitar unless he's accented by the lights.

Every night Willie comes out onstage, he's going to have the exact same sound, the exact same microphone, the exact same monitors, the exact same lights. We put a carpet down, and it's just like a living room. The only thing that might change from night to night is the way Willie enters the stage.

He comes off his bus and he may have to go up the center back, center of the stage, or right side of the stage. We got a place called the "Grady Gap," which is between Bobbie on the piano and where Grady Martin stands with his guitar. Willie comes through the Grady Gap, or maybe around the side of Mickey Raphael. Once Willie hits the stage, he could be like Ray Charles. He could be blind and still know he's got eight feet between the end of his microphone and his amps. He can keep his eyes on the crowd, take two steps and hit a knob on his amp and never miss it. Unless Jody Payne sees him coming and hits it for him first. It pays off in satisfied audiences. At a Willie show the band is not irritated by a bad sound system that makes them lose their timing or their feeling. It makes everybody real comfortable to know what to expect.

RANDY (POODIE) LOCKE

We were a beer joint band in the beginning, and we're still a beer joint band—because in a heartbeat we'd go back to the beer joints and be just as happy.

We were doing a tour of the South fifteen years ago, alternating opening the show with Poco. We'd play our gig and drink all night and chase women and shit and get up at noon and roll six hours and show up at the next gig at eight. Poco would have done two sound checks and lifted their three split-level risers into place and be wondering where we were—and here would come thirteen Texas yahoos piling out of buses and trucks at the last minute. Willie and the band would walk onstage and just blow Poco away. It killed those Poco guys. After Atlanta, they quit the tour. Their road manager told us, "Hey, we like you guys, but we can't work with you because you ain't professional. You guys are never gonna make it in this business."

We do things a lot different now. We're organized, calmer, saner, use tons more equipment, try to arrive at the gig with plenty of time to set up. But the spirit is the same. We're still a bunch of Texas yahoos.

People would get on our bus in the old days and change their lives. They'd come back speaking strange languages. We were crazy then. We're crazy now, but back then we had no regard for anything. We didn't hurt anybody, we were just wild. Our only rule was, we had no rules. And if there's no rules, there ain't no penalties. Now we do have rules and penalties—a sign of progress, I suppose. Country bands didn't have large road crews in the old days. We'd run in and play the show, check the money, and rumble. We can't really do that any more, because things have gotten too big. But if the time should come when we cut way back and start playing the beer joint circuit again, we're ready.

We're not like a lot of music people who get greedy because they've got a good living coming in. That's what's so fucked about the show-business industry. Greed just kills people. One of the things I regret about this whole business is meeting certain stars that I've looked up to and finding out most of them are just turds in a punchbowl. They'll try to screw you just to keep in practice. They'll quibble over $50 so hard they lose a $100,000 contract.

I was never in business on Wall Street, but the fucking entertain-

---

Poodie is Willie's stage manager.

ment business is the nastiest I ever heard of. I think the movies are nastier than records. It's hard to say. But if anybody ever walked through a fucking war zone without a scratch, it's Willie. He cruises through it, smiling and unscathed. Paul walks a little in front in the jungle to keep the branches from snapping back and hitting Willie in the face, and the rest of us work our asses off to be sure when Willie reaches the stage he's as safe and comfortable as in his own living room.

If Willie could see all the shit that goes on behind him, he might get upset. But he has created the situation where he goes onstage and performs, and it's up to us to make sure he ain't bothered. We have to do the miraculous pretty often, but that's what Willie has come to expect and that's what he gets.

The first few years I worked for Willie, I hardly talked to him. Because when I was a kid in Waco, he was to me the greatest, an immortal, a guy that don't shit between his shoes. It was like working for John Wayne. I was scared to approach him. I had worked for some big acts before, and some of them were just total assholes. They'd blow their money on drugs and whores and let their crews rot. But Willie has always taken good care of his crew and expects the same in return. Our guys get their own rooms at hotels, where some stars put four to a room. We all play golf together on the road. So we draw the crème de la crème, the best engineers, the guys who do the Rolling Stones and the Who and the Beach Boys, they want to work for Willie.

It's like a big machine when we hit the road. You got to keep everything moving, don't throw the rhythm off. People who don't do it right don't last long. We have worn out a lot of people. The strong survive, and the weak fall by the way. We travel now with five buses and two trucks, plus a motor home for Bo and Scooter Franks who sell the T-shirts and caps and such as that. One bus is for Willie and Bobbie. The next is the business bus—that's the one with Paul English, who is the business head of the operation and either number one or number two in command of the whole caravan, depending on how you want to look at it. I ride on that bus with Paul and Paul's son Darrell Wayne, the tour coordinator, and Larry Gorham, who's in charge of security. Larry—we call him L.G.—is a Hell's Angel from San Jose. The stage crew rides on Paul's bus, where the important decisions are made about the tour.

The third bus is the band bus—Bee Spears, Jody Payne, Grady Martin, Mickey Raphael, and Billy English, Paul's brother, who plays percussion. Bee is third in command of our outfit. The fourth bus is the Animal House. That's where Buddy Prewitt, our production manager, is in charge of the sound and lighting guys like Mike Garvey and David Selk and Tommy the Tuner (Tom Hawkins)—who tunes Bobbie's piano and the guitars—and others. The wild, rowdy shit that most people think happens on every bus mostly happens only in the Animal House. The fifth bus is for the Wrangler folks and their guests. The two forty-eight-foot semi-trucks are crammed with equipment. We all roll together, partly for safety's sake. Trucks rolling alone full of expensive equipment have been known to get hijacked. Waylon has lost a truck, Alabama has lost two trucks. It can get dangerous out there.

When the caravan pulls into town to do a gig, the first thing we have is the rigging call. A rigger is a guy who crawls up the beams to the stress points of the building and connects the cables to hang our sound system and lights over the stage. They can drop a chain down 90 feet from the ceiling—250 feet at the Superdome—and hit an X on the floor. Our big amps weigh 1,000 pounds each, so you don't want them crashing down. A rigger can kill you. Buddy likes to have the rigging call at 10 A.M. Buddy and Mike Garvey oversee this part of it. Buddy is lights, Mike is sound. The lights go in an hour after the rigger because lights take longer to put up than sound. Two hours later they fly the amps and put the monitors onstage. They lay carpet on the stage and hang our big Texas and U.S.A. flags. By then it's about 3 P.M. That's when me and the stage crew—Paul's bus—come in. We set the amp lines and the band gear. First up is Bobbie's grand piano, which Tommy proceeds to tune. We polish and tune the guitars, set up the drums. If all goes well, we're ready by 5:30 P.M. We eat at six. The band gets there at seven for an eight o'clock show. And Willie comes in right as the show starts. Boom, boom, he's singing "Whiskey River."

After the show if we're running to another town, we do it all in reverse, but we do it in a couple of hours. The two forty-eight-foot semi-trucks are loaded, the buses rendezvous—and we roll.

Before we got so big we'd travel in station wagons. I had a battery TV that I'd put in my lap and the guys would crowd around to watch the football game or whatever. I guess that's one way we really became like a family, as far as I'm concerned.

Mickey was real skinny then and didn't take much room. Mickey the kid. Mickey Meskowich, we called him. Half Mexican and half Jewish. A great harmonica player, but he'd drive you crazy asking questions constantly. One day we thought we figured out a way to shut him up for a while. Me and Bee and some others each threw

$100 on the table, maybe $500 in all. We told him, "Meskowich this jackpot belongs to the one who can go the longest without asking a question."

Mickey said, "Hey, that's great. When do we start?"

We bought an old bus from Dolly Parton and Porter Waggoner. Bee's daddy—he called him O.M., for Old Man Spears—and Baby Earl, who's a carpenter, remodeled the bus. They gutted the thing, tore out the front two bedrooms to make a lounge, ripped the bathroom out. Suddenly we had to run back on the road and had no bathroom. What we did was find a big red funnel and attached a coat hanger to it. You'd hook the coat hanger on your belt loop because it was so rough in the back of the bus you had to use both hands to hang on to the wall while you was pissing in the funnel. One night Bee sneaked into the room where the funnel was and nailed the door shut behind him and went to sleep. Willie got a knife and cut the door open, pissed in the funnel, and took the hammer and nailed the door shut again with a two-by-four. Bee never woke up.

O. M. got a good deal on a bunch of ugly-ass blue shag carpet. He covered the floor and padded the walls of the lounge with it, and that became our Blue Room. We had a driver named Maynard Lutz. We called him Homer Bounds—you know, homeward bound?

Paul designed a new bus for us. It was covered with quarter-inch steel, half-inch steel plate by the door, two drop safes, bulletproof glass, like a fucking armored car. Named it *Pauletta*. Paul ordered it to sleep seven, but before it was finished we had nine. We'd carry our gear in the back and strap the rest of it on top. It was red and black velvet inside, like a rolling whorehouse. By the time it was ready to roll, fucking *Pauletta* was too heavy to drive on most roads. We just parked it at the Austin Opera House and it sat there forever.

One of our old buses was called the *Tube*. It got bizarre on the *Tube*. We had as many as thirty-two people riding on the *Tube* at times—our guys, Waylon's guys, Tompall Glaser's guys, Hell's Angels, Hank Cochran, Bonnie Bramlett. You talk about a bunch of gypsies. When we did the Outlaw Tour, we expanded to two buses because Bobbie needed her own space to escape from all the shit on the *Tube*. You'd get on the *Tube* and there'd be ten people in the front lounge, people sleeping sideways in the aisles. Mickey and Bee and I would go scratch on the door of Bobbie's bus, and ask if she could find us a place to sleep. On the *Tube*, Bee made a rule that the last person still awake would get the best place to sleep—so Bee usually tried to stay up the longest.

We finally sold the old gold-and-black *Tube* to Beast, who Willie hired as our traveling chef. Beast tricked up the *Tube* like a big kitchen. He was a good cook, but he was a Yankee and none of us is Yankees. I love veal parmigiana and I love pasta, but Beast baked everything. I swear to God, he even baked black-eyed peas in aluminum tins. Everybody knows you got to eat grease to make a turd. The whole band was plugged up from eating baked food. I almost went to blows with Beast over iced tea. I mean, how hard is it to make iced tea? Even after I showed him how, he couldn't do it. Beast was a good guy, but he never fit in.

In the beginning nobody's job had a title or an official salary that went with it. Nobody was hired, you just kind of came along at the proper time. The organization wasn't conceived, it happened. Willie would reach in his pocket and hand you a wad of walking-around cash. Willie has no respect for money, see. That's why his cash is always wadded up.

I guess you'd call me the stage manager. My job is like a combination of a foreman, a referee, a cutting horse, a body guard, and a psychiatrist.

We used to play a lot of dumps like the Palomino and the Troubadour in L.A., the Boarding House in San Francisco, Gilley's in Houston, the Rio Pall Mall in Longview, Big G's in Round Rock, Panther Hall in Fort Worth, the Longhorn Ballroom and the Sportatorium in Dallas. The only thing you could expect was the unexpected. We played Panther Hall one night in summer when it was hot as shit and the promoter wouldn't spend the money to turn on the air conditioning. It was so fucking hot the guitars warped. Everybody in the band —except Bobbie, of course—played stripped to the waist. At the Sportatorium the promoter, Gino McCoslin, used to oversell the place every time. To solve that problem Gino hung signs that said MEN'S ROOM over the exit doors. Guy would go in to take a piss, and *bam*, he's locked outside. He'd hammer on the door and yell, "Let me in, my wife's in there!" And Gino would say, "Fuck you, buddy, we're sold out."

Gilley's was the all-time worst. I hate that fucking place. On the stage, your back is to the wall with no exit. You've got to go down the side and out the corner. The stage is only a few feet off the floor. We've played plenty of rough fucking beer joints, but we'd do a gig at Gilley's and come out with bruises and cuts and our shirts torn. People would be fist fighting in the crowd. Gilley's is a fucking skull orchard. You look out there at the crowd in that dim light and it's like a melon patch. People throwing shit. They could shoot each other without us even knowing.

One night in the midseventies at Gilley's this big-titted, cotton candy blond with red shoes and a little waist and big arms with the sleeves rolled up on her cowboy shirt—I think she was a fucking off-shore welder from Pasadena—grabbed the rail and came right on-stage, eye to eye with me, just a few feet from Willie. I said, "Lady, you got to get down, you know. This place is crazy enough already."

She says, "Eat my shit, you asshole."

I poked her in the solar plexus. Boom. She kind of buckled. But she jumped right up, and I thought: Oh my God, this bitch is gonna whip my ass right here in front of everybody I know. I hit her another good shot, and she backed down.

Another night in San Diego, Willie invited the Jazzercise class to come up and dance onstage. It was 150 girls. Well, 150 girls onstage is dangerous enough, but get them dancing in step and you got an earthquake.

In Vegas the stage is about table high. People leap onstage and you got to deal with their shit. You can't be violent with them, be-cause Willie don't like it, but sometimes it's hard to restrain a person without being physical. I looked around at one show, and here was some drunk bitch on the stage heading for Willie. I stepped in front of her and she said, "Get out of my fucking way. I'm gonna touch Willie."

I said, "No, you ain't."

She said, "Have you ever touched Willie?"

I said, "No ma'am, but I jacked him off once in Kansas City. Does that count?"

She looked startled, and it gave me a chance to ease her away as gently as possible.

Westbury, in New York, is a theater in the round that is a night-mare because the stage is so accessible. This goofy motherfucker jumped over somebody's shoulder at Westbury and landed onstage and walked right over and looked at Bee, then walked behind Willie and looked at Paul. They're still playing, right? So he goes over and sits down on Bobbie's piano seat and puts his arms around her and tries to kiss her. We got hold of that fellow and took him off in the darkness. I wanted to kill the son of a bitch, but you can't really do that.

We played with the Grateful Dead in Arrowhead Stadium in Kan-sas City in 1977 to a crowd of 80,000. Us and Waylon. The Dead played three and a half hours while we watched clouds building up. This big fucking storm blew in and it was pouring rain when Waylon took the stage. Waylon freaked out. Lightning ain't the best thing to have happen when you got all this electrical equipment around you. Waylon hadn't been to sleep in about a year—he just ate Hershey's

Kisses and snorted cocaine. Waylon started hyperventilating. He froze. So Willie walked onstage, took Waylon's guitar, and kept on picking.

I says, "Willie, it's dangerous out here."

Willie says, "If you got to go, you got to go."

We changed bands in the rainstorm, moved Waylon's stuff off and ours on. Willie never missed a lick with rain pouring on him. I told the Grateful Dead guys, "You fuckers played so long you made it rain." They said, "Yeah, so why don't your old man make it stop?"

Soon as we got our band set up, the rain stopped.

But one of the strangest happenings was in Birmingham, Alabama. We had done a show at the coliseum downtown. The Franks brothers had a Suburban then to carry their T-shirts, and we were loading our gear on the old *Tube* parked at a six-deck parking garage. We all carried two or three guns and plenty of ammo back then. Half the band was already on the *Tube*. Mickey was off chasing the monkey someplace.

All of a sudden we hear *Kaboom! Kaboom!*

It's the sound of a .357 magnum going off in the parking garage. *Kaboom! Kaboom!* The echoes sound like howitzer shells exploding. It's kind of semi-dark, and this guy comes blowing through this parking deck and jumps in the Franks brothers' Suburban. Now here comes this bitch with a fucking pistol. *Kaboom!* She's chasing this motherfucker. It sounds like a fucking war.

People are piling out of the show and they start scattering. Here come cops from every direction. They're flying out of their cars, hitting that parking deck, spread-eagling the whole crowd—"On the deck, motherfuckers!"—because the cops don't know who is shooting at who.

We cut the lights, and slip around to the back of the bus. All you can see are police headlights in a big semi-circle and hundreds of people lying flat on the ground all stretched out. It looks like Guyana.

All these cops are squatted down in the doorjambs, turning people over, frisking them, aiming guns at everybody, just waiting for the next shot to be fired.

And here comes Willie. He walks off the bus wearing cutoffs and tennis shoes, and he's got two huge Colt .45 revolvers stuck in his waist. The barrels are so long they stick out the bottom of his cutoffs. Two shining motherfucking pistols in plain sight of a bunch of cops nervous as shit.

Wilie just walks right over and says, "What's the trouble?" Well, he's got some kind of aura to him that just cools everything out. The cops put up their guns, the people climb off the concrete, and pretty soon Willie is signing autographs. He's got those eyes, that smile, it's magic. It he's singing to one girl or fifteen people in a hotel room or 200 people in a club or 50,000 people at a football stadium, these piercing eyes find the people, and he sings straight to each one of them. The men who don't like him are stuff-in-the-muds, bureaucratic assholes and chicken dicks. Women all love him. Everybody relates to him. Everybody has heartbreaks and problems with their families and their sweethearts. Willie plays to them. He's got this low wave of the hand that covers the first fifty rows and this high wave that covers the second deck, and everybody feels like he's waving at *them*. And he really is.

Our crowds have changed over the years. It used to be the hard core, then the older people started coming, and eventually the kids joined the crowd. Now everybody's there, from generation to generation. People are going to buy Willie Nelson records for the rest of their lives, and so will their children.

But if we ever do go back to playing nothing but honky-tonks, it's all right with me. At heart we'll always be a pile of wild Texas yahoos.

GATES (GATOR) MOORE

Most nights on the road, Willie sleeps on his bus instead of in a hotel. When he plays Atlantic City, for example, they provide a big suite. But he wants to sleep in his own bedroom on the bus—on the beach in Atlantic City. So I found a parking lot on the beach about ten miles out of town, and that's where we head when the show is over unless we're running to a new gig in another town.

There was a hurricane blowing in one night a couple of years ago as we drove to the beach. I kept checking the weather reports. They sounded grim. The cops told us we weren't safe in the parking lot— the hurricane was a big one and was coming straight at us. I suggested to Willie we might ought to move, but he said, "Don't worry about it, Gator. We'll get some fresh air tonight."

Willie was tired and went to bed listening to the rain pounding on the roof. All night long I sat nervously in the driver's seat, ready to pull out. The waves started showering the bus, the sand piled up

Gates Moore has driven Willie's bus for the last eight years.

over the wheels, the whole bus rocked back and forth, the wind howled. I thought: God, I guess we've had it this time.

But in the wee hours the hurricane split in half and the two forces veered away from us. In the morning I was outside looking at the sand banked up against the bus. I was still shaking. Willie opened the door and got out, yawning and stretching.

"I love the sound of rain," he said.

I came by my love of traveling naturally, I guess, because I was born on a navy base in Maryland. My dad, a test pilot, was killed in a jet crash when I was little. My stepfather was also a navy test pilot. I grew up all over the country and drifted into driving station wagons and trucks for bands like the Rolling Stones, the Beach Boys, the Kinks. In 1978 I got a job driving Willie's equipment truck. I moved to driving the crew bus and finally to driving Willie's bus—the one we call *Honeysuckle Rose.*

It's funny. This used to be a real young business. All the roadies for all the bands were in their early twenties. Now it seems the population bubble has just moved up. We all got older, and no young people are coming in as roadies. It's going to be real strange in a few years—a bunch of ragged, geriatric roadies.

You don't have to be a Teamster to drive a band bus. This is like a motor home. All you need is an operator's license. If we had to fill out Teamster logs—drive ten hours and take eight hours off—we couldn't get creative enough to do the paperwork. For us a twenty-six hour run is routine. You'd have to sit for three days to let your paperwork catch up.

My personal record is ninety-six hours straight. Four solid days and nights behind the wheel with no sleep. It's only my personal record, but I don't care ever to break it.

We used to pull into the parking lot of the big hotel near our gig, and the word would have gotten out that Willie was coming. There'd be thousands of people thronged around the place, waiting. We might turn off the motors, turn off the lights, get off the buses, and lock the doors—leaving Willie inside in the dark. Maybe the people would go away. But usually they'd stand there all night long and watch Willie's bus. Willie would be asleep inside. Not that he'd be avoiding his fans, but even Willie has to sleep now and then. Sometimes the crowd would pound on the bus until Willie woke up and came out.

Now we stay at hotels that aren't so obvious, maybe twenty-five to thirty miles from the gig. But people still manage to find us. Willie won't let us escort him through the crowd. He'll stop and talk to every one of them. If they're too nervous to ask for his autograph or ask him for a picture, he'll say, "Hey, why don't you pose for a picture with me?" or "Hey, did you want an autograph?"

It's been kind of rough on Willie after the show. He's soaking wet from being on the stage. We have used 100 subterfuges to sneak Willie onto his bus to change his shirt, at least, before he goes back outside to sign his name a few thousand times.

Every kind of star and politician you can think of has been on Willie's bus. But maybe the most peculiar visitor was Richard Pryor.

It was Willie's birthday, about three or four years ago. We had a huge ornate birthday cake in the back room of the bus parked behind the Holiday Inn in Las Vegas. Richard Pryor showed up with his monster bodyguard. Pryor walks in and says, "Nice cake, Will. It's beautiful."

Willie says, "Why, thank you."

Pryor says, "Happy Birthday.'

And Pryor went *whap!* Hurled his whole face and chest headlong into the cake. Buried himself in it.

So Willie picks up a double armload of cake and mashes it all over Pryor's bodyguard.

"A happy birthday to all," Willie says.

The wildest bus is the crew bus. They're still wanting to live the legend or enhance it in their own way. Paul cracks down on them the most.

But when the guys were drinking real heavy, the buses inside would look like a baseball stadium after a big game—ankle deep in bottles and rubbish. They used to play poker for maybe thirty straight hours until Bee Spears got mad and slammed his fist on the poker table so hard it exploded the thick glass top into a million pieces, glass flying all over the guys. I haven't seen a card game on a bus since then. Now it's dominoes or chess or computer golf. I've seen some terrible, red-faced, screaming arguments on the bus—never with Willie, mind you—but it's an unspoken rule that fist fighting is forbidden. Nobody ever swings on anybody. They might scream in each other's face all night long, but deep underneath they know they're going to be buddies again tomorrow.

It's my job to go grocery shopping and stock Willie's bus with food and drink. He wants raw vegetables and fruit—like carrots, apples, celery, radishes, oranges, bananas—on board all the time. I buy fifteen cases of Mountain Valley water for a trip, and plenty of Budweiser. And skim milk. Willie won't drink milk if it ain't skim. He gets into diets, takes a lot of vitamins and bee pollen. Willie doesn't eat much, but he does like cans of Beanie Weenies and pork and beans—pops 'em in the microwave for a quick meal—and he loves potted-meat sandwiches. Potted meat is probably his favorite thing.

With the big four-cylinder diesel generator that runs the central air and stereos and TVs and VCRs, one of our buses gets about six miles a gallon. We'll run a bus about five years before we replace it or get a new motor—and five years is about as long as drivers last. I've seen seventeen changes of drivers since I came to work for Willie. It's a hard grind. You have a high burnout rate. I keep myself going by playing mental arithmetic games: How far to the next town? How fast are we going? What are we averaging? What is the fuel consumption? I don't know why I do it, but I can tell you within two minutes what time we'll arrive.

Willie likes looking out the window and seeing all our buses and trucks in convoy. If anybody screws with one us, suddenly they've got all of us to screw with. It's a real feeling of camaraderie, being on the road.

KIMO ALO

Willie is one of the first outsiders who has ever been worked on with our medicine. He has been coming to Maui for twenty years, and we have been watching him. We saw that he loves our islands and our people, so finally the old Kahunas—I am what you might call an apprentice, waiting and learning to take my place with the old Kahunas—agreed to use their powers to heal Willie's recurring back injury and his problems with his sinuses and his lungs.

I received permission to take Willie into a secret place in the mountains to see Uncle Harry. Uncle Harry has the knowledge of the *Kala*, the cleansing process that comes through the use of herbal medicines.

First Willie was given the seed of the candlenut tree. It is a round seed that you peel and find a nut inside. You crack open the nut and eat it. For a person Willie's size, four nuts are the perfect amount. In the beginning it made him very sick. The reason for this is the cleansing—bringing the poison out of him from his mouth and elsewhere. This is the basic level from where the healing can start. After he got over being sick from eating the nuts, he felt much better than

Kimo Alo is a Kahuna—one of the magician-priests of Hawaii.

before he ate them but still not strong enough for us to do the healing of the bones in his back.

Kahunas can heal compound fractures in five days through prayer and special medicines. Licensed physicians may call us heathens and say we cannot heal, but they do not understand our ways. Our knowledge of the divine laws of nature is much older and deeper than theirs. The white man covers up this knowledge because he thinks of us as heathens. The missionaries were strongly against Kahuna magic, afraid of our power. They forced the Kahunas into seclusion. But the knowledge has passed down through generations of Kahunas who know the strength of sunlight and natural elements.

After we cleaned Willie out, we let him rest a couple of days. He had been drinking alcohol for many years and had much bile that had to be drained from his stomach and intestines. When he was rested we took him to a woman who does the Kahuna way of massage. She examined him and found everything out of proportion. His stomach was resting on his bladder, his intestines were turned improperly. She realigned his internal organs through massage and removed much of the pressure from his back. Soon Willie was riding his horse bareback through the high mountain valleys. You could see the joy in his face.

I was in the army during the war in Vietnam, was shot down in a helicopter and spent eighteen months in a prison camp in Laos. In my younger days maybe I didn't listen to the wisdom of my Kahuna ancestors, but in the camp I had plenty of time to think and evaluate. When I was freed, I went to my people in the mountains and became a "gatherer." It is my job to gather people for the great coming-together of the native races, like the American Indians, the Eskimos, the Hawaiians.

I kept an eye on Willie for eleven years, after I met him in Charlie's Bar in Piai near his house on Maui. Willie has an Indian bloodline. He is one of us. He will be very important in drawing the native races together.

There are Vietnam veterans living in caves in the mountains of Hawaii, guys who are fed up with society, who have turned their backs on the world, guys who are very violent toward intruders. But I have seen Willie go and talk to these veterans and coax them down from the mountains to take their place in peace once again. Willie has all the tools to accomplish great things, to cause the ancient mysteries to be revealed for healing and peace and power.

That is why he came to Maui in the first place. So we keep watch over him, because he is in fact an Old King.

PART EIGHT

The Healing Hands of Time

The Healing Hands Of Time

They're working while I'm missing you,
Those healing hands of time.
Soon they'll be dismissing you
From this heart of mine.
They'll lead me safely through the night,
And I'll follow as though blind;
My future tightly clutched within those healing hands of time.

They let me close my eyes just then,
Those healing hands of time.
Soon they'll let me sleep again,
Those healing hands of time.
So already I've reached mountain peaks,
And I've just begun to climb;
I'll get over you by clinging to those healing hands of time.

CHAPTER NINETEEN

In the winter of 1980, Connie and I slipped off for a vacation to the Kauai Surf, a beach hotel in the town of Lahaina on the island of Kauai, Hawaii. We'd been there about two days when Bud Shrake phoned me from Hanalei on the north end of the island. He had big news. Our three-year-old movie project, *Songwriter*, was a cinch deal again, for at least the fourth time in the past eight months. Yet another agreement with a studio was set in wet concrete. "No bullshit," Bud told me. "No way any assholes will back out on us this time. The concrete is drying around their knees even as I speak."

He said why didn't Connie and me come up to Hanalei and celebrate? Red Johnson, who owns Mariposa Air in Princeville, would fly down and pick us up in a helicopter.

Red planted his helicopter on the lawn of the Kauai Surf. Connie and me got aboard with the rotor blades whipping the leaves in the palm trees and fanning sand out of the grass. Red is a Korean War chopper vet who came to the islands and stayed. He has a red beard and sly, mischievous eyes and smile, like he's only giving you about half the clues but you must trust he knows what's he's doing. We flew north to Hanalei over maybe the most dramatic and sensual scenery on this earth. Kauai is called the garden island. Green mountains rise straight up from the jungle behind the beaches and disappear into the clouds. Waterfalls come down the mountains in constant torrents from the forests in the clouds where it rains sixty feet a year. From Red's helicopter we could see brown lava peaks poking through the breaks in the clouds above the timberline.

We fluttered down in a field near Dan and June Jenkins' house, where Bud was staying. They had mountains and waterfalls out their back door, white beach and the surf in front beyond a stand of ironwood trees.

Dan and Bud ran out, ducking under the rotor blades, and climbed into the helicopter. Red shot us into the sky again.

Some of us—not Red Johnson, I hope to this day—lit up cigars rolled out of Kauai supernatural weed. Red instructed us to put on the big, padded earphones at each seat. He was playing one of my albums. I settled back in the seat, next to Connie and Dan, dragging deeply off the local herb, listening to a familiar voice in the stereo earphones, and I was totally at one with the universe, like an eagle, when—*Whoa! What the fuck was this?*

The earphones became silent. We were flying straight into the side of a huge green mountain. We were going fast, and I could see the treetops just below us, and the vast green wall looming straight ahead. I glanced at Red. He was leaning back, his hand on the stick, grinning like a maniac. I realized I was utterly stoned. Heading directly and rapidly into certain death against the green wall of the mountain with a madman at the wheel. Connie squeezed my arm. She understood. We loved each other. The big moment of transition was at hand.

Suddenly the stereo earphones boomed in "Zarathustra" by Strauss—the *2001* movie music. It was a shattering, soul-shaking sound: the enormous horns and strings, zinging electrically through our entire bodies as Red shot the copter absolutely straight up. The green foliage was only a few feet in front of our eyes. Overwhelmed by Strauss pouring through the stereo earphones, I was ready to experience death—and here we went, up and up and impossibly up, zooming straight up the green wall of the mountain. And now we popped over the peak into the glorious light of a setting sun in the Pacific—just as the music struck a heart-stunning crescendo and our spirits flew off into the universe.

You talk about a rush! It was a mystical experience. By mystical I do not mean mysterious, weird, inexplicable, or unreal. Mysticism is all about the self and knowledge of the universe.

Have you ever wondered how it is possible for music to give you the rush I am talking about? The feeling is like the power of the stars exploding inside your body. As a matter of fact, that's exactly what it really is.

The purely physical impact of music works this way: the nerves of your body feel the vibrations of the music. The vibrations of your nervous system pick up the tempo with the vibrations of the music until you feel pumped up mentally, physically, and emotionally. What is it that passes through the air from the piano or the violin or the orchestra that sets your nerves into spontaneous arousal? You can't see it. A great law is at work here.

After the Strauss rush, we were still tingling when Red set down the copter on another peak. There was just enough room for the machine and the five of us to stand on it without a foot to spare. We looked out at the fire of the sunset rolling on the ocean waves, and down at the green fields and blue rivers of Hanalei far below. It was like standing on the roof of Eden. My heart was full with the thrill and beauty of it. I don't fear death, because there is no death. I am afraid of a root canal or a barium enema but I am not at all afraid of what we call death.

The next time I saw Dan and June Jenkins was at Elaine's saloon in Manhattan. It was a year after our soul flight with Red Johnson. My lung had collapsed in Maui. I had written the *Tougher than Leather* album in the hospital. We were crowded around a table in the front room.

Dan said, "What's your new album?"

It was very noisy. Elaine was hugging the writers and the stars who came in, directing them to tables, confronting the corporate biggies with their ladies in high-heeled shoes waiting in line at the register.

"Reincarnation," I said.

Dan squinted at me over the top of his glasses and lit another Winston with his gold Dunhill. Pepi, the waiter, put down another J&B and water—Dan calls them "young scotches."

"Red Carnations?" Dan said. "Great title."

I leaned forward through the noise.

"It's about reincarnation," I said.

"About what?" Dan said, bending toward me and cocking an ear.

"Reincarnation," I yelled.

Dan sat up. He pondered a moment and sipped his young scotch.

"No," he said. "Red Carnations is a much better title."

June, who is a beautiful black-haired woman with Cherokee blood, shifted over to me and said, "What's he talking about?"

I said, "Dan don't think I know what reincarnation means."

Even as a child, I believed I had been born for a purpose. I had never heard the words reincarnation or Karma, but I already believed them, and I believed in the spirit world.

I remember walking down the road toward the cotton fields in Abbott when I was six or seven years old, and finding a piece of quartz. I didn't know it was a mineral. I thought it was a rock, a curious shiny purple stone. The more I looked at it in the morning sunlight, the deeper I saw the shapes and colors and intricate intensity in the quartz. It felt very warm in my hand. I glanced down at the ground and saw tiny bits of rock shining up at me from the dirt, and I had a flash of illumination. This piece of quartz was not a separate thing from the shiny bits, or from anything else. Everything was one thing held together by some power.

In school and in church they tried to knock this awareness out of me by teaching other ways of viewing the world, but I never lost it entirely.

Now I know that what I was feeling in the quartz was the energy of the spirit. Glass and metal, flesh and wood, stone and plants—all are formed by the great force that radiates through space as vibrating spirit. It is hard to understand that just because your five senses tell you the chair you are sitting in is solid, your chair is in fact vibrating with energy as the atoms and molecules that form the chair are held together by a force strong enough not to dump you on your ass. Some people can feel these vibrations through their nervous system. But you can't see the vibrations any more than you can see music or see the vibrations that make a magnet work.

I recently saw an interview with one of the hostages who had escaped his kidnappers in Lebanon after a few months of being blindfolded and chained alone in a room. He told the interviewer that during the first week of confinement, he started talking to himself. Then suddenly he realized he wasn't talking only to himself—he was talking to God. "It's true," he said. "I can talk to God, and it's real. Those guys in the Old Testament who said they talked to God, they really did it. I never believed any of this stuff before. I thought anybody who said they talked to God was crazy. But in that room I found out I was talking to God, and God was answering me through my intuition—not a Charlton Heston voice booming through the roof. God was talking to me through my inner being. You can talk to God, too. Try it, you can do it."

The interviewer switched the subject, clearly a little nervous, but you could tell from the look on the ex-hostage's face that he was a changed person. It had taken an extreme circumstance to get his full attention, but when he began to hear his inner voice responding to his cries and his anger, he learned to talk to God.

You can learn to do it.

Sit on top of a mountain in the Hill Country at sunset, looking off at the mountains and ridges poking up as far as you can see to the west, and pretty soon your inner self begins to see the smoke signals put up by the ancient Indians on the distant ridges, one after the other, and you will reach an inner peace that becomes a conversation with God. This is called meditation, and it is a much easier way to reach God than being handcuffed in a bare room in Beirut. But you don't need either a peaceful, meditative situation or a hostile, threatening situation to talk to God. I talk to God all the time.

A little common sense must be used when making statements like this. I wouldn't walk up to you at a cocktail party and say, "Hey, I talk to God, you know." I wouldn't sit down beside you at dinner at Elaine's and say, "So what do you think of the Holy Ghost?" If you go around telling people you talk to God, they might burn you at the stake like they did Joan of Arc, or destroy your reputation one way or another, because people who talk to God are a threat to the authorities of both the state and the church.

Of course there are plenty of evangelists on television who say they talk to God and don't get burned at the stake, because they claim God tells them to take your money and buy real estate with it. This is recognized in high places as just business as usual, nothing dangerous.

A Louis Harris poll a few months ago revealed that ninety-five percent of U.S. citizens say they believe in God. There is a great need for people to emerge into a state of peace. We realize there is something else beyond this reality, something we are supposed to do on this earth. A sort of religious fever is sweeping the country. But attendance figures at churches and synagogues are steadily falling.

This means the churches and synagogues are not giving us what we need—which is to know the truth about the laws that rule the universe, and to be free to think in a new way that is really as old as creation.

Dr. John Wheeler, who won the Nobel Prize for his contribution to the big bang theory of creation, is a neighbor in West Lake Hills in Austin. I was moved by something he said on a TV show about creation: "At the bottom of everything is an ultimately beautiful idea, so simple and beautiful that when we finally discover it we will say, oh, why did we never see that before?"

I know Dr. Wheeler was a protégé of Einstein's. Einstein believed that the sensation of the mystical is the closest we can come to knowing the truth and that the source of everything is what he called the Old Man. This is the divine force behind the universe. The big bang started with a thought in the mind of God. Everything that has happened since is a continuation of that thought. The greatest star and the smallest cell exist because of the energy of this thought.

Scientists have identified the fundamental forces that govern all matter in the universe: gravity, electromagnetism, nuclear energy, and so on. What they are looking for is an explanation that will bind all of these forces together into one force that controls all the laws of the universe.

This one force is God.

The scientists, not the preachers these days, are investigating the nature of God. Instead of being so busy thinking up ways to convince ten-year-old kids they're going to burn in hell for smoking cedarbark, or ways of sucking up money for business investments, the leaders of the major churches and synagogues should be paying attention to raising the consciousness of humans to know the truth of the divine law. Pretty soon the scientists will prove it as reality.

The law I mean is that all is one, that every atom in your body was once in a star, that life is continuous and nothing dies, and that the law of Karma—what the scientist would call cause and effect—is as real as electromagnetism is real.

The law is love. What puts the law of love into proper operation is the Golden Rule: *do unto others as you would have them do unto you.*

Most people don't really believe in this law, to the whole world's regret. The leaders of world governments, concerned only with holding on to their power, ignore the law of love, and are overthrown as a direct result, and cause wars of terrible destruction. We are only one bad decision away from destroying our planet. We live with famine and disease and violence, and terrible corruption in our big financial institutions—and we claim not to know why these things are happening.

I know why they are happening, and so do you if you're not too cynical to admit it. We are not obeying the divine law. It is as simple as that.

We must realize that there are entities called adepts or Masters or angels or archangels—the heavenly hosts—who surround us. They are attempting to help us by pouring out their energies and their knowledge and their wisdom. An angel is literally a messenger from God, trying to give messages to the human race through energies that we are able to receive into our consciousness by turning a dial on our interior radio set. We can turn the dial merely by thinking correctly.

When human beings can come to this point, the secrets of the universe are open to them. This is what is taught in Masonry— though the Masons are so secretive that my dad, Ira, a high-degree Mason, never mentioned any of this. This is taught in all the mystical orders that have come down from ancient times and given the great knowledge to mankind. Since the organization of the state and the churches, all religions have tried to squelch certain aspects of this knowledge. The knowledge has been lost century after century and comes back over and over again in different forms.

Today this knowledge is being given back to mankind in the form of science and psychology. It is impossible for us to get this knowledge except from the heart, from the Christ, from God, from the Masters. And when the human race can understand this and begin to really live by it, then we will begin to get someplace.

The whole purpose of religious holidays and observances is to convince the human race that the Masters exist and that the great Master of the Masters is the person called the Christ. The Christ, in the person of Jesus, manifested this great truth: that the lame shall be healed, the halt shall be made to walk, the persons who have leprosy can be cured, the persons who are deaf can hear, the persons who do not understand can be given understanding. And everything that needs to be done in order to correct anything whatsoever can be done because of the presence of the Christ in the world today. But the people who want this to happen through them must change their energies and their vibrations and their thought processes, and become one with Him. He cannot force us. We must choose to become one with Him. It has to be on our own initiative. This is the great secret. It is really the key to the kingdom of heaven.

It is a matter of transformation of energy, like the energy that makes leaves green. What we call photosynthesis is really the transformed energy that gives life to the tree that bears fruit of a wonderful color. The human being is kept going by this energy. We call it grace. We inhale this energy with every breath. It flows through the lungs, though the vascular system, though the 100,000 miles of nerve fibers in your brain, through every part of the body. But there is another way the energy must work in human beings: we must become not just living bodies but living souls. Our consciousness needs to let the energy flow into the mind by means of the soul so that it will do for us what it is doing for that tree. It will give the consciousness illumination. It will give the consciousness knowledge and wisdom when it is needed. It will give the consciousness an open door into the kingdom of heaven. Where there is hate there can be love. Where there is ignorance there can be knowledge. Where there is tremendous ill health and weakness there can be great strength and perfect power on a mental and emotional and physical level.

I know why I am here on this earth. I used to tell Ray Price that I owed him hundreds of dollars in education because I could just stand around and watch what he'd do, and then I would know to do the opposite. If people would just do the same with me, they would pick up a lot of shit, save a lot of steps. In *Yesterday's Wine* I wrote that some people were put here to show how perfect a guy could be, but I was put here to show how imperfect a guy could be.

We are all here to progress and learn and have a good time and be happy. I think the higher intelligence, God, intends us to love and be loved and work and sustain ourselves. As I've gotten older, I play music for my own happiness. I do it to keep busy, keep moving.

A song I wrote last year sort of sums up my position on many things I've been talking about, like vibrations and the Holy Ghost.

Still is still moving to me
And I swim like a fish in the sea
All the time.
But if that's what it takes to be free,
I don't mind.
Still is still moving to me.
It's hard to explain how I feel.
It won't go in words, but I know
that it's real.
I can be moving,
Or I can be still.
But still is still moving to me.

My own guardian angels are always talking inside my head, chattering, arguing, carrying on a narration of what's going on around me. Could be I'm just imagining voices talking to me. But it doesn't make them any less real. Creative imagination is the way buildings get built.

Another name for this is intuition. I listen to my intuition every time. The more you trust your intuition, the more you learn to believe the vibes you pick up are true, the sharper your machine becomes.

How many times did your old man or old lady come in from someplace, and your intuition instantly told you they had been at the

Lucky Motel with a lover? But then you would say, naw, they wouldn't have done that, they only went to the dentist, everything is okay, you are paranoid. Months or years later you discover your intuition had been right that day. It happens to everybody.

Intuition is just an attunement of your inner self with the universal mind. The average person ignores these higher vibes if they seem to oppose the distinct and familiar impressions transmitted by the physical sense organs—such as your eyes or ears.

To develop intuition, the moment you ask yourself a question you must give credit to the answer. You must not permit reasoning or argument to take place and change the answer your intuition gives. As soon as you can abandon your willpower and anxiousness and tune your mind to the inner self, you will gain a wonderful bullshit detector. Batteries included.

All right, you are thinking, if everything is so simple, how come the world is in so much trouble?

The answer is we will never stop paying for our sins of the past until we change our thinking about the present and the future.

Now you may be thinking, okay, but what can I do about it?

Be idealistic. That's how to start. Never mind if people call you an idiot. Just because your idealism can't instantly cure all the ills in the world, don't be cynical about it. Be idealistic and take a step forward.

Obviously the three Farm Aids we have done have not cured the problems of the American farmer. Only our government and our major business and social institutions can really do that, and their leaders don't want to cure the farm problems because they might lose their power or their wealth if they do.

But with Farm Aid we at least took a step to say that a lot of people care what is going on. Farm Aid got started when all the musicians got together to do the We Are the World benefit for the starving people in Ethiopia. These people were starving because leaders of the state and big business wanted them to starve, and a bunch of musicians couldn't stop the situation. But we did call the world's attention to it, and what we did was good if we turned even one powerful head around to the right way of thinking.

Ray Charles and I were talking at We Are the World, and I said this was great but wouldn't it be nice if we did something for the people in our own country. Then at the Live Aid benefit, I heard Bob Dylan say part of the money ought to go to farmers. I put two and two together and figured out if we could do Farm Aid as well as we did those others, we would have something.

James Thompson, the governor of Illinois, heard what I was thinking. He phoned me and said, "What can I do to help?" The governor gave us the University of Illinois football stadium for our concert. I talked to John Cougar Mellencamp, Neil Young, Waylon Jennings. We had a nucleus already. Neil's agent, Eliot Roberts, called Bob Dylan. I talked to Kris and Alabama and Kenny Rogers. The next thing you know, we had a show going.

The first Farm Aid mushroomed so quick—quicker than anyone thought it could. We did it in six weeks. So you know it had to be a popular idea. All this time people have been going out of business, getting a raw deal and getting screwed, but the American people were just now finding out about it. When people made $15 and $20 a week, beef was 37¢ a pound. Now it's still 37¢ a pound and people are making $500 a week. It's not right. A bushel of corn was $3.50 when a brand-new Chevrolet was $600. Now a bushel of corn is down to about $2 and it costs $3 to grow it.

The people who determine the price of the grain are the ones who furnish grain to the rest of the world. To compete with the rest of the world, the prices have to stay so low that our farmers can't make it. With all of the embargoes we have, we've got a lot of grain stacked up and people hungry all over the world and hungry here. The Reagan administration hasn't done anything to help it, but the trouble began back in the seventies. With all the excesses, surpluses, and embargoes, the farmer's land value dropped so much that he couldn't pay his bank loans. The banks are now owned by big corporations and not by the small family bankers and so they just said, sorry, pal, get out. The young aggressive farmer went for the loans because he wanted to enlarge and to build and he was encouraged to do it. Then the ones who encouraged him pulled the rug out from under him. There are a lot of good farmers, proud people used to paying their bills, who can't make it. These are family farms owned for generations and now these farmers are losing them and feeling terrible about it. A lot of banks are going under too. Anybody who wants to come in and buy cheap land can get it. There used to be six or eight million family farms early in this century. Now there are only 600,000 left and in the next six months, 200,000 will be going out of business.

I met with a lot of the senators about the farm bill and I tried to focus a lot of attention on it because no matter how much money we raise, it's not going to make a dent in the farmers' debt. It's over $220 billion. If we raised $100 million, it still wouldn't help for long.

The farm bill would raise the price of the farmer's product thirty percent. It would cost the consumers three or four percent. The guy in the middle would pick up the difference, but since he's the one making all the money, he can afford it. It would also call for a moratorium on foreclosures and for restructuring the loans.

After three concerts, Farm Aid is a year-round operation that has spent millions helping farmers with legal aid or direct payments or whatever we can do.

Even though I'm not kidding myself that Farm Aid can bail out all the farmers who are in need, we have proven that a little creative imagination can bring forth dramatic results. Visualization leads to action and accomplishment.

We create our own misery and unhappiness. Our creative imagination tells us to get on the ball and use the higher mind to create positive conditions. The purpose of suffering is to make us understand we are the ones who cause it. The possibilities live within each of us. "Let this mind be in you that was also in Christ Jesus," is how St. Paul put it.

The world won't be changed by treaties or summit meetings. Physical conditions can't change until our minds change. The sum total of the power of all the thoughts of all the people in the world is what will change physical conditions.

After Jesus was baptized as the Christ by John the Baptist, Jesus was faced with three temptations. He could use his power to accumulate wealth, or he could use it to make a show-business circus out of his self-importance, or he could become the emperor of Rome. Instead he lived with his great power on the spiritual level, which is why we feel his power in our hearts today. The rest of us probably would have fallen for all three temptations—starting right away with the first one, worshipping the Golden Calf.

If you have a lot of money, pretty soon you realize it don't mean anything and that's a big step forward. But I really think that I instinctively knew that to begin with. When I was young they called me irresponsible because I didn't know the value of the dollar. Now that I have money and I still don't know the value of the dollar, they call me something else.

Money is energy. That's what true capitalism is all about. Money is energy that should be used for the good. Just think for a moment how much good could be done for our people with the billions our military blows on showing off in places like Grenada or the Persian Gulf. We send five or six destroyers to shoot more than 1,000 high-explosive shells at one Iranian oil platform that is forgotten the next day. For that cost, we could have cared for all the homeless in, say,

Seattle for a year. Instead of wasting all this money energy, why can't we apply it to our real problems.

There are people who have evolved higher than we are. Believe it or not, there are smarter people in the world than us.

They are the Masters, and they're out there walking among us now, going about their business, not interfering. A Master wouldn't necessarily be a holy man wandering down the road with robes and a cane. He could be the guy on the telephone pole fixing the wires, or the guy driving the cab. There are all sorts of Masters. Potentially we are all Masters. Jesus and Elijah and Moses and you and me—we all come from the same source.

Meanwhile I am just a troubadour going down the road, learning my lessons in this life so I will know better next time. In the field of love, some say I have loved too many people at the same time. They get confused and don't understand that love is what I live on.

WILLIE'S HOROSCOPE

Reading by Diane Eichenbaum, 1987

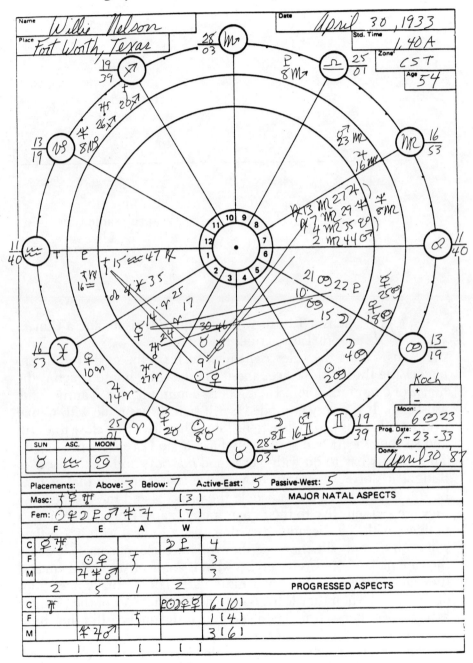

Name: Willie Nelson
Place: Fort Worth, Texas
Date: April 30, 1933
Std. Time: 1.40 A
Zone: CST
Age: 54

SUN	ASC.	MOON
♉	♒	♋

Koch

Moon: 6 ♋ 23
Prog. Date: 6-23-33
Done: April 30, '87

Placements:	Above: 3	Below: 7	Active-East: 5	Passive-West: 5

Masc:	♄ ♀ ♃	[3]	MAJOR NATAL ASPECTS
Fem:	☉ ♀ ☽ ♇ ♂ ♆ ♃	[7]	

	F	E	A	W	
C	♀ ♃			☽ ♇	4
F		☉ ♀	♄		3
M		♃ ♆ ♂			3
	2	5	1	2	PROGRESSED ASPECTS
C	♃			♇ ☉ ♀ ♄	6 [10]
F			♄		1 [4]
M		♆ ♂			3 [6]

[ ] [ ] [ ] [ ]

Willie is a Taurus with an Aquarius rising and a Cancer moon. Taurus rules the throat.

He has Venus the ruler right next to his Sun, so that even enhances the throat, the voice, and it's in the third house which is the house of communication. He is a born communicator. Taurus is the artist sign. It is a very grounded Earth sign. It has to do with primal instincts. Taurus people like to be safe. They like to be close to Earth and so their heart and soul really have a kind of magnetic quality. The Taurus has to do with Texas and cowboys and all that sort of thing. Parts of Texas are ruled by Taurus so it is apropos that he lives here. I always call Taurus people the princess and the pea because they are too sensitive to their environment, and Taurus men have a problem with that because they don't want to deal with it. So they will be in a family situation and they will have a lot of anxiety because they are picking up psychically on what is going on around them and they almost have to close their mind to it. They actually need a lot of space and when they learn how to accept that part of their nature as a positive then it becomes a very nurturing quality. But they have to learn how to take care of themselves.

Willie's chart starts separating a little bit because he has an Aquarian energy, which is a totally different kind. Aquarius is the eleventh house, Taurus is the second house. Willie is a Taurus in the Gemini house, which is the primitive need to communicate through the mouth. Then we go all the way around to the eleventh house for his rising sun. The ascendant has a lot to do with how he projects himself to the world. Taurus is instinctive. Aquarius is abstract thinking, extremely creative and mental.

There are several things in Willie's chart that say that he is very intelligent, learns quickly, has almost a photographic memory. He is a quick study. Aquarius is a sign that is hard to know. They like distance, they like their space, and I would say that Aquarius people sometimes can't say what they mean. So he had to learn ways to get around that. At this period of his life he would be more comfortable with these two signs and they would be blended more comfortably for him, but in his early life there would have been a conflict. Aquarius is eccentric, nonconforming. Taurus is conformed. Taurus is very family minded, say let's be like my family, but Aquarius says I can't be like my family. There is the inner conflict. Aquarius is an energy that has to do with electronics, so there we go with the singing and the guitar and all that.

He has the planet Saturn in his first house. Saturn has to do with responsibility, it makes him more conservative and more private. Actually, psychologically, it could be somewhat repressed and Saturn in his chart squares his Sun and Venus so this says that no one ever helped him, he felt isolated, and that he had to take care of himself always, even as a boy. That pressure made him creative so in his chart there is a real longing to be integrated with friends and people and a real hunger for that. It has been one of his biggest lessons. Also, he doesn't want anyone to tell him what to do.

His moon is in Cancer. The moon rules Cancer. It is very strong in that sign, very intuitive. Cancer is the sign of the mother and when a man has strong Cancerian traits, it says he is extremely psychic and sensitive. So you have got the Cancer, sensitive moon, the Taurus on a primitive, emotional, creative person, and the Aquarius ascendant. That is the conflict of the chart. There would be a strong, emotional tie to the mother, and sometimes that is almost too much, to have your moon in Cancer. Also, he has a real love of women. A moon in Cancer loves women, and looks for a strong woman, who has nurturing, motherly qualities, but it could be a woman who is an authority, and he would have conflict with it. Willie has had a lot to work out with the women in his life. He would have to be married more than once. There is a kind of desire for fuel, something has to be happening all the time. Looking at his chart, we see compulsive energy. Like if you get tired, you can't stop. Now that moon aspect squares his money out so it says that he has conflicts with his money house.

He would be a person who would attract money. Taurus people do. The planet Jupiter, good luck, has moved into his money house this year. He has got a big enterprise and it takes a lot to keep it going. It is something that he likes, and yet it can run him, and he sometimes doesn't know how to get out of that. He loves his home and he wants his home, but it is like he wants to have his cake and eat it too. A lot of Taurus people are like that. It is almost an adolescent attitude.

Willie was born old, he is a very old soul, but his child in his personality is the creative part. It can still run him and get him into trouble. This is something he is learning. How to be adult without being negative, how to combine the adult with the child. He is getting to the age that he is more likely to do that, and actually he will be younger as he gets older.

The chart shows that he would have a large family. He is two people. He is a down-home family man. And then he has got another side of him that comes like an alter ego, it has made his life exciting, but sometimes with a lot of conflict. He is under an aspect today that says he is going through an emotional change, and it is on his fifty-fourth birthday. The planet Pluto takes 250 years to go around the chart. Consequently it only moves about a third of a person's chart, so this aspect has never been here before. Pluto is opposing his sign in Venus and when you get Pluto in contact with your personal planet it causes an emotional deepening. In some ways, it could be like a purge because it forces you to deal with your own feelings and because he is such a deep, emotional person with a Taurus energy, this might not be easy. But he is going to have a major emotional change in the next year and a half. This is very positive. It is changing his attitude about himself and certain areas of his life. It is like an opening up spiritually, and psychologically. He is going to go through a very productive, creative period in his music. He writes all the time, so this is a very profound aspect. He is understanding his place in the universe and not trying to control everything, going with the flow. He attracts some very positive work situations again.

His values change. This is spiritual. He is more willing to be with himself and easier to communicate and explain himself to others on a personal basis. But it comes through as something creative in his work. He is almost religious, a very spiritual person. He probably had a very conservative, religious upbringing. This would have meaning for him now not in the same way he was taught, but in other ways. This has just started this year, and he will be feeling it.

Out of ten planets, he has five in Earth. Earth people are practical. They want to look at things realistically. Actually, it is too much Earth, it is a little negative. When he was younger, he was so secretive and he tried to be so adult and grown, he didn't learn ways to process his information sometimes and he would be too heavy and maybe too profound. A lot of Earth people have to watch out for depression. He doesn't have the aspects that say it would be a chronic, terrible depression, but there is a tendency to be heavy or worry about things. When you have that much Earth and you have out of ten planets, seven of them in feminine signs, you are what is called a magnetic person. Generally, men are dynamic, or they are supposed to be. Dynamic energy being going out into the world and linear thinking, and objective pioneering and all this sort of thing. His best energy is magnetism. He is the type that all he really has to do is know what he wants and set it in motion and it comes to him.

He is a born psychic. He has been psychic since he was a boy. He would know what it is, he understands it. It is more of an instinctive, Earth-type psychic, but he also has the ability to be clairvoyant and see pictures. It really has to do with being able to tap into the universal consciousness, the spiritual aspect, the unconditional love. That psychic, creative aspect is being set off right now. Neptune is in his marriage house so he would not know who he was marrying. He would think he did, but he didn't. He would see them the way he wanted to. With his first wife he married someone he loved, but he didn't know her totally and it wouldn't work.

But he has three planets in his marriage house and he has Jupiter in there, and Jupiter says he will marry until he gets it right. The second marriage would be maybe worse than the first, and there would be no real understanding and no real depth.

The eleventh house, which is the present marriage, is the house of friends. Taurus really likes passionate love affairs, but Aquarius likes relationships that are like buddies. So, whoever was pulled in on this pattern has a more easygoing nature than the person he had married before. She doesn't have to be in control. The other two marriages had control signs.

With his Aquarius rising Willie would be the type of man that always had two relationships. He is two people, he is salt-of-the-earth family man and he is also totally free and always has love lessons, always. Whether this is a divorce aspect or not is hard to tell. It is like his wife's personality changes and moves off into another direction.

If he has another woman in his life his wife may have always thought about not saying anything but she might finally say something. It is like he has a lesson with his love life and what he values. He is going to have that pressure this year and next year. There is a decision about his love life. What does he value? Do the two people get together and make a commitment? He might not be able to. He might not be ready for that sort of thing.

All through 1986, Saturn squared his marriage house so there were definitely problems then. If there is a discussion about their marriage, it would come up again this summer. By September it would be either resolved, or there could be a divorce.

There would be another woman in his life and there would be conflict with his wife and he would have a pressure on him now to make a choice on what he is going to do with his life. There are other pressures on him because of his business. He has to make big decisions about what he is going to do, that he could change his way of working. Basically his best aspects right now are professional. His personal relationships for his love, his family, are stretched. When he was younger he would make a commitment and he would believe it and he would fool himself. As he has gotten older it's like it is harder for him to lie to himself. He is getting more and more honest with what he willl say that really comes from his heart. His earlier upbringing and his behavior start integrating. He always said don't do what I do, do what I say. But he would now be at a place where he would be going to live in peace with himself, where he wouldn't have inner conflict. His Aquarius rising says he is so abstract and eccentric and unusual and doesn't like to be ruled by the rules. He flirts with taboos and wants to be on the edge. The fuel freak side of him runs him a lot. That is the child part of the personality. He has aspects now that he would be able to fit those together.

Jupiter moved in his money house and will stay there through the spring of 1988. A group of people come to him and give him an opportunity to do a business that would make him a lot of money. This could already be going on right now. If it goes into the workaholic personality, he shouldn't do it, the money wouldn't be worth it. Money doesn't mean anything to him in one way and it does in another. But his conflicts with love and money are the same. He is in a place of power where he has many choices and yet he is in a transition period emotionally. It is really hard for him to make some of these decisions. He would be somewhat pulled apart.

Pluto opposes his Sun and brings out the opportunity for purposeful action. It focuses in a place where he has to make an important decision. It would bring up any negative aspects in his personality that he didn't like about himself. Psychologically, he would face his own shadow. He wouldn't have any secrets anyway. Everybody would know them.

By the time it is finished with him, he will have had to let go of old ways of doing things. This is like a subconscious pattern. When Pluto is in aspect to your Sun, you feet it emotionally. It is a purge. This period requires maximum self-evaluation of passions and attachments, goals and personal realities, and your own integrity of direction because if you don't go through and redefine your values and goals in this period, you won't go into the happy period that you can go into. If you hold on to the past, fears and negative patterns, and self-undermining habits, whatever they are, you turn left instead of right, you don't go along with your destiny. This pattern would make him think about his life, about his relationship of himself to himself, his family, to his upbringing. He might have to let go of old family patterns that have limited him. It would be a time when he could leave all that.

He is going to go through a spiritual psychological change of values, of how he lives his life. It is a little bit against his will. He doesn't want these issues to come up and this is not an easy aspect to have. Always when Pluto comes in it is like the IRS or something you can't do anything about. It is also a Mafia. Pluto is anything that is subversive, seemingly, that seems to work against you and you can't do anything about it. There is a chance in the next two years to move into a different stage of his life. It is not going to be easy because he hides in a world of fantasy. You can't be real half the time and in fantasy half the time. That's what leads him into getting in with people that might be dishonest, but it looks like it has already happened. Or he faces something and he has to make a decision that he doesn't want to make.

There will be a lineup of planets in Capricorn. It has to do with being very conservative, whereby people in the arts become more conservative. This is a trend that is going to last about fifteen years. This is going to be very meaningful in Willie's chart. It is a subtle pressure of choice. But after that is over and he moves into a more centered position with himself, then all the major planets are sitting in a beautiful aspect for him. This is one of the most creative periods he has ever had in his life.

It looks like he will have his love life straightened out about 1989.

In 1988, Jupiter goes into his fourth house which is his home. He gets his homes straightened out. This is going to be another aspect of change that is very favorable.

He is going to go through a religious experience. Not the old-fashioned type, but it is pretty close. It is almost like letting go of control, in the areas he can't do anything about, and that's a major initiation step. He is ready for it. It seems like it is working on him now. After this is finished and he lets go, he has more than he has ever had and it isn't the same. It doesn't pressure him all the time. His health, by the way, is good. He had some health aspects back in the early 1980s that slowed him down a little bit.

To look at him just as a soul, he is connected to the universe as far as creativity. He just channels it. But in early life, Taurus wants what they want and they are very self-gratifying. Being spiritual all his life, he would have said I don't want to worry with that. He would go looking for love in all the wrong places. He will start really understanding what love is now. Love is really a vibration and we are all connected and so he is beginning to move into the place where he will live by that spiritual truth. He may have to let go of some things. It has to be his choice. He may not know right now because he has got to go through these pressures. His success was a pressure, and he likes it.

He is very mystical. If Pluto stays in his house of mystery, after it gets off the sign of Venus, which is love, he goes through a love change, and he might go into politics.

But it may just be in spiritual energy that his transformation transforms others. This pattern of deep transformation goes on the rest of his life and he is a man that will live to be very old and he will be creative all of his life. His music grows with him but his music will go to another dimension. It will be more symbolic in deeper meanings so that it will almost be religious.

CHAPTER TWENTY

My life today seems pretty quiet to me, although you might not think a quiet life is playing 150 concerts a year on the road, touring Europe with the band, starring in a movie, cutting a few record albums, and hugging Dolly Parton on national television.

But I feel I am gathering my strength to do something, though I don't know exactly what.

It ain't at all unusual for a guy to start thinking about becoming a hermit when he hits his middle fifties, when he's been hard at work for thirty-five or forty years. He starts to yearn for a little solitude so he can ponder the question of what it has all been about and what it is going to be as he rounds the turn and heads down the home stretch. Geronimo's great-grandson lives outside Tucson in an adobe house with a wire fence around it and a sign that says GERONIMO III LIVES HERE BUT KEEP OUT! Sometimes I think I'd like to live like Geronimo III. But that is not what I am going to do.

I've been hanging out in Abbott a lot with my old friends from childhood. It is important to me to maintain those feelings and sounds and smells that I grew up on.

But two things keep drawing me back to Austin when I come in off the road. One is golf. The other is my recording studio. Don't ask me which is more important. Let me just say that when we're making a record we go into the studio at "golf-thirty." In other words, we play golf until it is too dark to see the ball, and thirty minutes later we start hitting licks in the studio.

My studio, I have to admit, is one of the best in the country. The great producer Chips Moman came over from Nashville and designed it for me in 1981. He brought with him a kid named Larry Greenhill, who is a genius at putting electrical things together. Larry installed every mile of wire in the studio. He runs it for me now. Bobby Arnold is our studio sound technician. Bobby sees sound as colors—red at the high cycles on down to blue at the low cycles—and he thinks of making a record as painting with sound.

When I make a rough cut of a record, I take a tape of it with me in my golf cart and listen to it all day while I keep trying to learn how to play this confounding game. I then give the rough cut back to Larry and Bobby with suggestions for changes in the sound. At our forty-eight-track control board with its state-of-the-art digital equipment, they can take a song recorded in a big dance hall and make it sound like it was cut on a tile floor. Larry and Bobby go into the control room and turn out all the lights, get it totally black in there except for the glow from the board and the meters. They'll listen and mix all night in the darkness. Then they take the tape to Larry's house and listen to it on a sound system like an average person might have. They go listen to the tape in Bobby's car. Finally they put it in their Walkman sets and stroll around the pool listening to it. They go back in the studio and turn off the lights and mix it some more to get the sound exactly right.

The next day I ask them to do it again.

This isn't as uneventful as it sounds. There's always something going on. Not long ago the heavy metal band Aerosmith dropped in to cut a record with me, which is kind of a bizarre collaboration. Ray Charles, who, as you know, is blind, came in to record "Seven Spanish Angels" and astonished us by picking up a computer chip and explaining exactly what it was used for just by feeling it. Ray runs his own board at home, does his own soldering, even drives his car around his farm.

When Julio Iglesias came to the studio to sing "To All the Girls I've Loved Before" with me, he brought five limos and a considerable entourage that included video cameras. The word had got out and thirty or forty people from around the hill came to see Julio. Julio smiled, and the ladies clutched their hearts. Julio told them, "I am a professional love-aire," and a couple of them fainted.

Meanwhile in the control room Larry and Bobby had been working all day with nothing to eat. Julio's manager came in and the boys noticed he was carrying a can of Planters peanuts. They couldn't speak Spanish, but the manager got it across to them that one of his major duties was to have a can of Planters peanuts always ready for Julio. He took out one can of the several in his briefcase and gave it to Larry and Bobby, who ate the peanuts for lunch.

Later in the afternoon, Lana brought in a can of peanuts that when you opened it a rubber snake popped out. Larry and Bobby coiled the spring-snake into their empty Planters can. They sealed the lid back on. Then they sneaked the Planters can back into Julio's manager's briefcase.

He was still carrying the briefcase at Julio's side when we all hugged and waved adios and they got into their limos and the parade went off down the hill, heading toward Julio's private jet.

We got a chuckle out of thinking that somewhere in midair Julio nudged his manager, who reached into his briefcase and opened a fresh can of Planters peanuts.

At one end of the studio is a kitchen where somebody is always cooking big pots of pasta or chili for whoever drops in. Past the kitchen is a big room with a card table and folding chairs. Most everything we do on the hill, we use the verb "play." We play music, play golf, play pool, play poker, play chess, play dominoes. Everybody likes the sound of the word "play." It helps keep us smooth and calm.

Along one wall of the big room is a long bench where Larry and Bobby fix the equipment. It is covered with tools and meters and the necessities of the trade. When the movie *Songwriter* was being shot, there were a lot of scenes around the studio. They built a wall and made the studio look different. The set decorator walked into the big room with Bobby and peered carefully all around.

"I want to see what a real studio sound technician's workshop really looks like," she said.

"Well, this is it," Bobby said.

The set decorator shook her head.

"No. No, this is not at all what it would really look like."

They rebuilt the workbench and changed everything. But it's back as messy as ever today.

We don't operate like most studios. Our records aren't cut by the clock, like they are in the big commercial studios. When I'm doing an album at my studio, I pick ten songs and then record only those ten songs, some of them on the first take. I don't believe in recording forty songs to pick out ten. I also don't believe in overproducing. Some producers will keep saying, "Do it again," until they have gone past the freshness and the peak of the performance. You can chew the juice out of the music if you push it too far.

I can't even conceive of how some of the famous bands can stay in a studio for an entire year and spend two million dollars to cut one album. I think that practice came along about the same time drugs did. If you have plenty of money, time, and drugs, there's a tendency to kick back and say, "We'll cut this sucker all year until we get it right." But if you go in there with a handful of musicians and a good singer, chances are you'll get it right on the first take. I learned to record in a commercial studio atmosphere in Nashville, with musicians working three eight-hour shifts a day, and you had to cut your tunes and get out of the studio to make way for the next bunch. I don't stick to the clock any more, but I like to get the music done while it is ripe.

We cut the *Red Headed Stranger* album at Autumn Sound in Garland, Texas, in three days for $20,000 with Phil York as the engineer. I mean mixed and fixed and ready to release in three days.

We'd go in the studio about dark and stay until three or four in the morning. The first night we laid all the tracks. The second night we overdubbed and fixed the parts where I blew a line. The third day we mixed it. And not long afterward we had a gorilla of a hit and we became famous and lived happily ever after.

In one way we were very lucky with the *Red Headed Stranger* album, because usually the record company big shots will look at the budget before they listen to the music. If they see you only spent $20,000 on your album, you probably get dumped. They'll put out your record, but they won't promote it. The big shots are worried about how to sell the $2,000,000 albums and save their jobs. No telling how many really fine albums went into the garbage just because they were made too cheaply. There's no way a lot of record company people can make money off a $20,000 album. But if they've got a couple million, they can spend half of it on studio time and the rest on musicians and a well-placed number of dollar bills in different guys' pockets, and everybody gets fat off somebody's album.

That doesn't mean the album has ten good songs on it.

I can say the same thing about the movie business.

When I'm out on the hill in Austin, I keep office hours that you might call irregular.

Sometimes I sprawl on the grass under a tree near the practice area beside the seventh tee and have meetings with people who show up from everywhere with propositions they don't see how I can pass up.

If it's cold or raining, or if I need a telephone handy, I go to my office in the clubhouse. It's down a walk beside the golf shop. Jody Fischer, my assistant, has an office upstairs where she and Lana put out the *Pedernales Poo-Poo* newspaper, among their many activities, some of which I don't even want to know about. Jody keeps me checked out on messages and news, as much as she can, but it ain't that easy a job.

Across the road and up the hill to the south, my Western town has come back to life again and is full of people. My town is playing the part of Fort Smith in the nine-hour CBS movie of *Lonesome Dove*, from Larry McMurtry's wonderful book.

Today the wind was blowing forty miles an hour from the north, so we only played about thirty holes of golf, all wrapped up in parkas and gloves like a bunch of dogsled racers.

Then I came in here to my office and settled into my wooden armchair behind my mogul-sized desk and put my hands behind my head and leaned back, shifting a little to ease that pain above my right hip, and stared for a long time out the plate-glass window, looking across the pool and the trees and a long blue piece of Lake Travis in the distance. I could see all the way north to where the hills were turning a chilly green-purple color as the norther blew in and smoke started coming out of chimneys of houses on the hills.

I am drawing a picture in my mind of something that is coming. I can hear Mark and Jim and Joel yelling, "Oh, my God—send for more bandages! Willie is dreaming again!"

The fact is, my dreams are still dreaming me.

PHOTO CREDITS

INDEX